T0319805

Organizational Spaces

Organizational Spaces

Rematerializing the Workaday World

Edited by

Alfons van Marrewijk

Professor of Business Anthropology, VU University Amsterdam, the Netherlands

Dvora Yanow

Visiting Professor, Faculty of Social and Behavioral Sciences, Political Science Department, University of Amsterdam, the Netherlands

Edward Elgar
Cheltenham, UK • Northampton, MA, USA

Published by
Edward Elgar Publishing Limited
The Lypiatts
15 Lansdown Road
Cheltenham
Glos GL50 2JA
UK

Edward Elgar Publishing, Inc.
William Pratt House
9 Dewey Court
Northampton
Massachusetts 01060
USA

A catalogue record for this book is available from the British Library

Library of Congress Control Number: 2009941236

ISBN 978 1 84844 650 2

Typeset by Cambrian Typesetters, Camberley, Surrey
Printed and bound by MPG Books Group, UK

Contents

Contributors

Joan M.J. Baaijens is Senior Management Consultant for Ordina (Public Management Consulting) in the Netherlands and Senior Research Fellow at the Department of Organisation Studies, Tilburg University, the Netherlands. His main topics in consultancy are innovation and organizational change, networks and cooperation in public organizations, and policy games for strategic management. His research is focused on innovation in the public sector, in- and outsourcing of ICT functions, and 'evidence-based consultancy'.

Gibson Burrell is Professor of Organisation Theory at the University of Leicester. Previously at the universities of Lancaster, Warwick and Essex, UK, he was Head of the School of Management at Leicester from 2003–2007. His piece with Karen Dale entitled 'Building better worlds? Architecture and critical management studies' in Alvesson and Willmott's *Studying Management Critically* (Sage 2003) is a widely cited article in the field.

Katherine Carroll, a sociologist specializing in the areas of the health professions, the delivery of health services, and transdisciplinary research methodology, is a Post-Doctoral Research Fellow in the School of Sociology and Social Policy at the University of Sydney, Australia. She uses methods such as ethnography, video-ethnography, video-reflexive focus groups, interviews and documentary analysis to examine the complexity of health care delivery at the grass-roots level. Her research approach involves significant collaboration with clinicians throughout the research process, from research design and data collection through to analysis and publication.

Karen Dale has worked at the universities of Warwick, Essex, and Leicester, UK, and is now a member of the School of Management, University of Lancaster. Her most recent book, with Gibson Burrell, *The Spaces of Organisation and the Organisation of Space*, was published in 2008 by Palgrave Macmillan.

Rick Iedema is Professor in Organisational Communication, Faculty of Arts and Social Sciences, and Executive Director, Centre for Health Communication, at the University of Technology, Sydney, Australia. His research focuses on communication in hospitals among clinicians and between clinicians and patients. His most recent publications as editor include *Discourses of Hospital Communication* (Palgrave Macmillan 2007); *Identity*

Trouble, with Carmen Coulthard (Palgrave Macmillan 2008), and *Managing Processes in Health Services*, with Ros Sorensen (Elsevier 2008).

Marja Gastelaars initially trained as a sociologist at the University of Amsterdam. She did her PhD at Leiden University on a history of Dutch sociology and has worked for a number of years in the social studies of science and technology. She has published on the public redefinition of mundane objects such as the water closet and the cigarette. She now works at the Utrecht School of Governance at Utrecht University, the Netherlands. Her most recent publications – among them *The Public Services Under Reconstruction* (Routledge 2009) – concern the societal and organizational embeddedness of the day-to-day performance of a wide range of public and semipublic services. Her current work on buildings is informed by these concerns.

Krini Kafiris is Head of the Research Programme at the Mediterranean Women's Studies Centre (KEGME) in Athens and a visiting faculty member at the University of the Peloponnese, Greece. She holds a DPhil in Media and Cultural Studies from the University of Sussex and has taught at Middlesex University, the University of Cyprus and the University of Athens. Her research interests currently focus on gender, media and cultural politics. She is on the editorial board of *Feminist Media Studies*.

Patrick Kenis is Academic Dean at Antwerp Management School, Belgium. Over the last 15 years he has taught organization sociology, organization theory, network analysis and inter-organizational relations in undergraduate, graduate, and executive programmes. He holds an MPhil from the Free University of Brussels, Belgium, and a PhD from the European University Institute in Florence, Italy, and has published articles in such journals as the *Academy of Management Review*, *International Public Management Journal*, *Journal of Theoretical Politics*, *Journal of Public Administration Research and Theory*, and *Organization Studies*, plus a number of authored and co-authored book chapters and books. His current research interests involve temporary organizations, organizational networks, and Internet communities.

Kristian Kreiner is Professor in the Department of Organization, Copenhagen Business School, Denmark. He is interested in organization, order, efficiency, collaboration, coordination, and so on as effects – as outcomes of historical, social processes. He studies these processes, their circumstances and dynamics, and tries to deduce from them their managerial challenges and issues. He has studied such processes in various contexts, for example, projects, networks and formal organizations. Recently, his empirical research has been focused on the design and management of the building process.

Peter M. Kruyen is a PhD student in the Department of Methodology and Statistics, Tilburg University, the Netherlands. He holds a Research Master's degree in Organisation Studies (*cum laude*) and a Master's degree in Public Administration (*cum laude*), both from Tilburg University. His current research interests concern the reliability of psychological tests and organizational networks.

Debbi Long is a medical anthropologist at the University of Newcastle, Australia. She has undertaken ethnographic research and consultancy in a variety of hospital wards and departments, including maternity, spinal, intensive care and dialysis. She is fascinated by bodily fluids and infection control.

Alfons van Marrewijk is Professor of Business Anthropology in the Department of Culture, Organization and Management at VU University Amsterdam, the Netherlands, where he received his PhD in Organizational Anthropology. He graduated in electronics engineering from the Dutch Technology College and worked in various organizations as telecommunication engineer and project manager. His academic work centres on cultural change and cross-cultural cooperation in technology-driven organizations and megaprojects. He has published on these topics in several key journals, including *Journal of Managerial Psychology*, *International Journal of Project Management, Culture and Organization*, and *Telematics and Informatics*. Van Marrewijk combines his academic interest in business anthropology with international consultancy work.

Mark Mobach is a management and organization scientist, a member of the Faculty of Economics and Business, University of Groningen, the Netherlands, and initiator of www.organizationalspaces.com. His specific interest is in the meeting of organization and architecture. He studies such topics as how organizational spaces affect people in and around organizations, how interdisciplinary spatial configurations can be understood and used for the betterment of organizations, and in what way such an improved understanding and use might foster change in organizational practices. His most recent writing about these topics can be found in his Dutch book *Een organisatie van vlees and steen* [An Organisation of Flesh and Stone], published by Van Gorcum in 2009. In addition, he has published widely in health care and multidisciplinary journals and has also consulted with a variety of organizations in the public and private sectors.

Alexia Panayiotou is Lecturer in the Department of Public and Business Administration at the University of Cyprus, in Nicosia. She completed her undergraduate and graduate studies in economics at Stanford University and has a doctorate in Human Development and Psychology from Harvard

University, USA. Her research interests include the production of discourse in and by organizations; representation of management and organizations in popular culture; feminist analysis of organizations; emotionality of work; and organizational space and symbolism. Her work has appeared in, among others, *Journal of Corporate Citizenship*, *International Journal of Work, Organisation and Emotion* and *Journal of Multilingual and Multicultural Development*. She is also on the board of the Mediterranean Institute of Gender Studies and is an expert for the European Commission's Group on Gender and Employment.

David Weir is Professor of Intercultural Management at Liverpool Hope University, UK and Affiliate Professor of the ESC Rennes School of Business, France. The author of several books, including the best-selling *Modern Britain* series, he has recently co-edited *Critical Management Studies at Work* (Edward Elgar 2009) and is currently completing a book on *Management in the Arab World* (Edward Elgar 2011). Weir's current research interests include intercultural management, with special reference to the Middle East, the Mediterranean and the Arab World; risk and breakdown in complex socio-technical systems; operational management and engineering in society and industry in the UK since 1914, with special reference to the writings and influence of Nevil Shute; and critical management, with a special concern for organizational space, rhythm, poetry and process. His hobbies are cooking – he won first prize for his raspberry jam at the Sedbergh Show in 1974 – supporting Leeds United football club, and playing cricket when selected.

Dvora Yanow is Visiting Professor, the faculty of Social and Behavioral Sciences, Political Science Department, University of Amsterdam. Her research has been shaped by an overall interest in the communication of meaning in organisational and policy settings. Her recent books include *Constructing 'Race' and 'Ethnicity' in America: Category-Making in Public Policy and Administration* (M. E. Sharpe 2003; winner of the 2004 ASPA and 2007 Herbert A. Simon-APSA awards) and the co-edited titles *Interpretation and Method: Empirical Research Methods and the 'Interpretive Turn'* (M. E. Sharpe 2006) and *Organisational Ethnography* (Sage 2009). Her current research explores methodological challenges in organizational and political/policy ethnography, the role of science museums in defining what it means to do 'science', knowing reflective practice when you see it, and race-ethnic categories in Netherlands integration policy and administrative practices.

Introduction
The spatial turn in organizational studies

Alfons van Marrewijk and Dvora Yanow

Organizational Spaces engages various aspects of work-related settings and their relationships to their 'inhabitants', from employees at all levels to clients or customers, and from visitors to onlookers at a greater remove. Spatial settings are coming more and more to figure explicitly in analyses of organizations and organizational practices (Hernes et al. 2006), as seen in recently published works (for example, Gregson et al. 2002, Taylor and Spicer 2007, Dale and Burrell 2008). Studies of organizational spaces have ranged in focus from examining the role of organizations' headquarters and other buildings' spatial design in communicating organizational meanings to onlookers near and far, to the allocation and use of space for communicating organizational meanings internally (Berg and Kreiner 1990, Goodsell 1993, Yanow 1993, Kornberger and Clegg 2004, Van Marrewijk 2009a). Other studies explore more general, theoretical questions concerning the meanings of built spaces and the extent to which these meanings are central to an organization's identity (Goodsell 1988, Lefebre 1991, Preoffitt et al. 2006, Yanow 2006a) or investigate spatial elements that communicate the organization's brands and goals (Bitner 1992, Gregson et al. 2002, Felstead et al. 2005, van Marrewijk 2009b). Still other works seek to articulate how organizational spaces and their meanings might be systematically studied (Yanow 2000, 2006b). These examples demonstrate the growing, explicit attention being given in organizational studies to the importance of engaging spatial settings.

The chapters in this book present new theoretical, empirical and methodological contributions to the field of organizational space studies. The idea for the book began during a gathering of organizational studies scholars in the stream 'Settings and Space' at the December 2005 Asian and Pacific Researchers in Organisational Studies (APROS) conference in Melbourne, Australia, convened by the book's editors. The volume includes a selection of papers from that stream, with added contributions that we first heard in other conferences, capturing a sense of the wide range of topics and approaches of interest to scholars studying the intersections of space and organizations. All contributions, including the more theoretical or conceptual ones, are grounded in empirical research either conducted by the chapter authors or drawn from others' work, based on field studies that used different methods and explored different aspects of the various roles played by built spaces in organizational life.

The book joins the so-called 'spatial turn' that is taking place in a number of fields, from philosophy (the work of phenomenologists such as Casey 1993; see also Goodman and Elgin 1988) to anthropology (as in the re-examination of settings by Low and Lawrence-Zúñiga 2003). In rediscovering 'place' and 'place-ness', this new attention joins a long tradition of spatial studies in such fields as human or social geography (for example, Jackson 1980, Meinig 1979, Rapoport 1982, Tuan 1977; see Hubbard et al. 2004), urban studies and planning (such as the work of Appleyard 1982 and Lynch 1972), and sociology (for example, Soja 1989). The field of study is, in fact, vast. Along with other organizational studies scholars (Hernes 2004, Clegg and Kornberger 2006, Dale and Burrell 2008), we find spatial aspects in organizations of great academic and practical interest and think that they call for greater attention.

THE STUDY OF SPATIAL SETTINGS IN ORGANIZATIONS: A BRIEF TOPICAL OVERVIEW

We note, with some curiosity, the lack of attention to spatial elements in organizational and management studies over the last few decades, given that every employee, student, patient, visitor or researcher entering an office, school, university or hospital experiences the material and concrete dimensions of built spaces. This makes it somewhat premature, we think, to try to present a thorough historical overview of who has made what contributions when, and under what circumstances, to the study of organizational spaces. Although we allude to such a historical account in the next paragraph, to situate the book's chapters we have chosen instead to sketch out some of the key themes that such studies have touched on and to suggest current issues in need of engaging.

Analyses of spatial settings of work actually have a longstanding tradition in organizational and management studies, going back over 30 years in some areas (for example, Steele 1973) and even further if one considers studies employing field research methods of whatever sort (for example, Mayo 1933, Blau 1955, H. Becker et al. 1961), where 'space' often forms part of the backdrop for the action. Although this focus was eclipsed in the 1970s by more behaviouralist work, it enjoyed something of a comeback with the burst of attention to organizational culture(s) in the 1980s and 1990s (for example, Steele 1981, Gagliardi 1990, Hatch 1990, Rosen et al. 1990, Nauta 1991, F.

Becker and Steele 1995, Yanow 1998, Strati 1999). In recent years the material aspects of organizational life have been enjoying a particular resurgence of attention, especially in cultural terms (for example, Hernes 2004, Kornberger and Clegg 2004, Binder and Hellstrom 2005, Rafaeli and Pratt 2006, Dale and Burrell 2008; on material objects specifically, see Orlikowski 2007), with many calling for space and other dimensions of the material world to be brought back into organizational theorizing.

Various explanations have been advanced for this absence, a theme taken up by Dvora Yanow in Chapter 7. Strati (1999, p. 180), for instance, attributes the exclusion of physical space from analytic domains at least in part to scholars' research inexperience: 'Organisational researchers usually see all visual artifacts when doing research in organisations but they do not usually mention these aspects of organisational life in their research reports, both because they deem them to be irrelevant … and because they do not know how to study them.' But why should spatial elements be deemed irrelevant or be a blind spot in research methods? A historical look (albeit brief and truncated) suggests some answers.

During the Enlightenment, as Latour (1993) argues, human and non-human artefacts were established as two irrevocably sundered realms of knowledge and experience. From his perspective, such a separation imposes a binary *on* the world that is not *in* the world. He suggests that the social and the material both need to be studied from a holistic perspective. Theories of socio-technical systems, developed initially by London's Tavistock Institute and articulated in the work of Emery and Trist (for example, Emery and Trist 1965; cf. Vickers 1983), argued, beginning in the 1950s, for their intertwining in studies of work and its settings, on the basis of empirical research, especially among teams of workers in Britain's coal mines (Trist and Bamforth 1951). For some reason, that line of thinking appears to have been forgotten in contemporary organizational studies. Orlikowski (2007), Dale and Burrell (2008, p. 34), and Van Marrewijk (2009b) all call on scholars to stop treating the two domains as distinct and largely independent spheres of organizational life. Organizations – or more precisely, our conceptualization of them in and through our organizational theorizing – need to be re-materialized, so to speak. Moreover, it is less a matter of needing to study the social impacts of material features – a formulation that still treats them as distinct, separable domains – than that organizational life, as with social life more broadly, is a socio-material practice (Orlikowski 2007) in which the two domains are intertwined in mutually constitutive ways and need to be engaged jointly.

One part of the organizational space field does this by exploring management interventions in work settings as a tool for inducing changes in employees' work practices (Kornberger and Clegg 2004). In this view, constructing a new corporate building, (re)designing interior spaces, and renovating existing buildings all can be important ways of transforming organizations (Van Marrewijk 2009a). For instance, an empirical study of two Danish cases shows the interconnectedness of organizational change and architectural design processes (Våland 2010) in the case of open-space (or 'turfless') offices. The socio-spatial relations and aesthetic order of such workplaces are, as Felstead et al. (2005, p. 71) argue, designed specifically to generate intense social inter-actions among employees.

We have ourselves seen this kind of purposive use in two field settings, one in the new National@Docklands office in Melbourne, Australia, which Michael Muetzelfeldt arranged for APROS stream members to tour, the other in the Interpolis building in Tilburg, the Netherlands. National@Docklands, the headquarters of the National Australia Bank, was designed as part of a strategic and cultural change programme following its merger with another bank, one more traditional in organizational cultural terms. The physical plant consists of two low-rise, interconnected, highly transparent glass-walled buildings with sunlight-filled atriums. The National Australia Bank leaders intentionally designed a space that, they felt, would give expression to its more outward-looking, modern culture as a way of promoting that culture among all employees, old and new, and hastening the integration of the new ones.

In a similar vein, the headquarters building of Dutch insurance company Interpolis was intended to support the introduction of a new corporate culture of flexibility, transparency, and employee responsibility (Veldhoen 2005). Twelve floors of workspace were designed as open, 'turfless' offices in which employees take their laptops and rolling file-boxes with them to that day's choice of workplace. The first two floors consist of trendy spaces where employees can work, meet and relax: bars, relaxation rooms, and lounges with music and comfortable sofas were designed to support the new corporate culture.

Both National@Docklands and Interpolis examples have their own vocab-ularies of building materials, size, scale, mass, colour, shape, design, and rela-tionship with their environments, among other things (Nauta 1991, Yanow 2000, 2006a and b, Van Marrewijk 2009a).

Several of the chapters in this book echo these ideas about the use of spatial design to bring about desired behaviour among employees and others. Patrick Kenis, Peter M. Kruyen and Joan Baaijens (Chapter 3), for instance, look at the relationships between the design of a new prison build-ing and the actions of employees and inmates. Such theorizing also needs to extend beyond the design of new buildings and spaces to examine the re-use of existing buildings, designed initially for other purposes. Marja Gastelaars (Chapter 4) explores an old building originally designed and used as a physics laboratory, that was given to a new social science faculty. The chapter looks at how ideas passed along through the earlier design shape present organizational culture.

Not all spatial interventions derive from intentional, conscious design or re-design. Rick Iedema, Debbi Long and Katherine Carroll (Chapter 2) look at the ways in which a seemingly simple, bulging bend in a corridor enabled interactions across professional lines that established professional-culture-based practices might not have allowed. A useful outcome – one that may well have been desired by certain members of the organization – was achieved through spatial media, even though that could hardly be said to have been part of design forethought and planning. We note that the 'back staircase' in the old physics lab described by Gastelaars apparently enables similar encounters among its present occupants.

But let us not be too Pollyannaish in painting an overly, and perhaps unduly, optimistic view of the relationship between organizational spaces and the acts and behaviours of their residents and visitors. For one, in the diachronic processes of organizational and architectural design, outcomes are difficult to predict (Våland 2010). Spatial reorganizations can result in surprising uses of spatial settings, surprising in the extent to which what one finds in the field is different from what one expected to find. A treatment of the intentions of organizational leaders and their architects that assumes that design elements will shape employees' and others' behaviours without according them agency of their own, and without considering the possibilities of voice or exit, along with loyalty (to borrow Hirschman's 1970 title), is, today, theoretically and intellectually untenable. As space commonly embodies relations of power, they, as well as possibilities of resistance to it, must also be engaged and theorized in organizational space studies (see Betts 2006).

Moreover, there is a downside, as Dale and Burrell (Chapter 1) note, in the treatment of organizational workspaces as homes with kitchens and recreation rooms, such as in National@Docklands and Interpolis. This 'aestheticization' of the workplace, they write, 'is combined, almost ironically, with the disappearance of the workplace itself *as a workplace* [emphasis added], … displaced by quasi-constructions of town- or village-scapes … and break-out rooms … using colours, lighting and furnishings which do not evoke a place of labour and employment'. As this kind of 'spatial rhetoric' – invoking the spatial vocabularies of family and community, home and play in the workplace – becomes more and more commonplace, the administrative colonization of private life, supported now even more by non-stop Internet and cell-phone access, reaches ever further into what was once employees' down-time or time off. At the same time, however, its intended meanings become easier to identify and potentially to resist by ignoring and working around (if not outright subverting) them, something that Kunda (1992) noted with respect to employees' responses to the more explicit workings of Digital Equipment Company's (DEC) 'culture chief'.

The darker notes of design elements that communicate fortification, protection and surveillance are at play in the discussion of the prison design, as one might expect: Bentham's and Foucault's panopticon comes readily to mind. But interestingly, Alexia Panayiotou and Krini Kafiris (Chapter 9) found such notes as well in filmic portrayals of organizational spaces, financial corporations and law firms in particular, that do not appear, on the surface, panoptical but which enact certain of its elements. There, the possession of doors and windows, among other things, signals status or its lack, with accompanying degrees of power – or powerlessness. Being able to shut oneself off from the view of one's colleagues by closing one's office door is, however, not enough to establish workplace primacy; one needs at the same time to be able to look out at something beyond the walls of one's building. Power comes not only from denying others' surveillance of you, but in maintaining it on the world outside, even as you are removed from the constant all-seeing overview of those who work for you.

But those theorists who do study organizational spaces (as well as those studying other aspects of organizational life) need to start asking themselves whether their theorizing itself creates a kind of panopticism in controlling the terms of analysis: is spatial use, interpretation, and theorizing as neutral and universal as theories appear to claim? In looking at the spatial design that characterizes business meetings – both the rooms and the behaviours and acts within them – in the Arab Middle East, David Weir (Chapter 6) implicitly raises the question of whether our modes of understanding and researching spaces within organizational studies are highly 'ethnocentric', projecting 'Western' interpretations as universals. The need for awareness of and sensitivity to the non-universal understandings of built space has emerged for us in our respective ethnographic studies. In one, a Dutch multinational in Jakarta was about to move to a newly constructed, spacious office in the business district. The Indonesian staff, however, refused to move there as the new building was situated between Christian and Muslim cemeteries. According to the Indonesian staff, that geographic location would stimulate negative reactions, such as illness, quarrels and jealousy. The Dutch management organized a two-day ritual for all employees – Dutch and Indonesian – performed in the still empty space by an Indonesian shaman, after which the move could begin (Van Marrewijk 1999, p. 265). We think such cross-cultural perspectives are important to consider in theorizing organizational spaces, something we see beginning to emerge in phenomenological and linguistic treatments of space (see for example, the works of Casey 1993, 1997 and of Lakoff and Johnson 1980; but see also Hooper 2001). They serve as an important constraint on universalizing assumptions that are without empirical foundation.

METHODOLOGICAL CHALLENGES

Spatial matters are not only of growing concern to organizational researchers, theoretically and practically. They also pose their own particular methodological challenges. To study organizational spaces, researchers need fuller understandings of the kinds of methods that are best suited to such studies, as well as a greater awareness of their methodological implications. How might researchers assess organizational meanings and their communication through spatial media (including, for instance, the objects used for furnishing and decor)?

The reading of built space and other physical arrangements from the perspective of the arguments in this book requires interpretive methodological questions: those that engage the meanings these spaces and other objects hold for those passing through and/or using them. In some cases, a historical sensibility also informs the analysis: knowing what has come before – earlier prison designs (in Kenis et al.'s Chapter 3), earlier uses of an existing building (Gastelaars' Chapter 4), earlier arrangements and uses of the urban space in which the organization's building is situated or of the characteristics of the work performed there (Van Marrewijk's Chapter 5, as well as Gastelaars) – can usefully inform present-day analyses. Even Panayiotou and Kafiris' analysis of films (Chapter 9) is explicitly aware of their historical and cultural specificity. And, as noted above, spatial designs and the movement and actions they enable can have different meanings in different national cultures (as in Weir's Chapter 6).

Spatial studies draw on one of the central characteristics of interpretive work: the researcher's use of his or her own body as the primary instrument of research (Van Maanen 1996, p. 380). One might even say that this characterizes these studies in the extreme, because studying space rests on the researcher's heightened awareness of that body moving through space as a medium through which to articulate provisional understandings of that space's effects on others' bodies. This is a particularly phenomenological hermeneutics, resting on our own 'knowing bodies' (Casey 1993, p. 52; see also Casey 1997) to generate provisional interpretations of the spaces through which others move, as well, and the material objects and other kinds of artefacts – colour, ambient temperature, the 'feel' of a room (see for example, Turley and Milliman, 2000, on the so-called 'atmospheric effect' on the shopping behaviour of customers) – that they and we experience. These interpretations are, and must be, provisional in that researchers typically follow up on their own bodily based meaning-making by triangulating (Schwartz-Shea 2006), whether on other persons and their experiences (for example, through observations and interviewing, Warren 2008), other times and places (so central to comparative methods), or other sources and methods (for example, organizational documents, architects' and other designers' reports and memos).

Importantly, this checking-in-on follow-up must also include, as its focus, the researcher him- or herself. Reflexivity, as this is called, is increasingly invoked in ethnographic and other interpretive methods; in studies of built spaces and organizational experiences and acts, it is, or should be, *de rigueur*, in light of the phenomenological aspects of spatial study. In order to support arguments or 'truth claims', researchers need to take account of the particular characteristics each of us brings to the field as a researcher and how those personal, intellectual, professional, and other characteristics shape what it is that we may see (or not), whom we might speak or interact with (or not), the events we can experience (or not). A researcher's 'positionality' – all of those things that go into making us the observing and knowing persons we are, with our particular sense-making and meaning-making – also has a spatial-geographic dimension, as Pachirat (2009) so ably demonstrates in discussing how a promotion from the shop floor to the Quality Control catwalk physically enabled other lines of sight and insight.

From here it is not a huge leap to perceive that auto-ethnography (Humphreys 2005) can potentially play a key role in studies of space, as Van Marrewijk's Chapter 5 demonstrates. Note, however, that reflexivity and auto-ethnography are not identical: although the latter rests on the former, it is possible for researchers to be reflexive about their knowledge creation with-out having their research focus primarily on their own experiences. However, being a participant-observer ethnographer and an organizational employee at the same time – the quintessential dual role of the participant-observer – can enable researchers to draw on their own experiences and visceral, emotional and aesthetic responses as they move their bodies through corporate spaces in ways that might have been shut off to other, non-employee ethnographers.

Awareness of the character of spatial design and its impacts can be facili-tated by a comparative perspective, as several chapters demonstrate, whether this entails comparison across place or across time. Van Marrewijk (Chapter 5) shows us how two different spaces within the same organization can evoke radically different experiences among its employees. Kenis, Kruyen and Baaijens (Chapter 3) draw on another kind of spatial comparison, contrasting Prison P's innovativeness, which they know from their field research, with traditional prison designs, which they know from the theoretical literature. By contrast, Gastelaar's comparative analysis (Chapter 4) is historical, looking at earlier and later uses of the same building. Mobach's chapter (8) draws on yet another kind of time-based comparison – that of looking into the future, enabled by 'virtual' computer-based techniques, in order to present a would-be spatial reality that users can contrast with their present organizational spaces.

Researchers who want to engage the spatial dimensions of organizations might pursue any of the foregoing topics, from the more methodological – how *do* people make sense of their surroundings, and how do researchers make sense of that sense-making? – to the more substantive: specific space-act issues raised by or in specific organizations or types of organization; and to the more theoretical – how? The chapters in this book present examples of each of these types, as we outline below. But let us also not forget that spatial study is not only static – it entails more than the identification of stationary spatial vocabularies and their meanings. Spaces are used; they involve movement. And so organizational scholars wishing to study spaces might also shadow executives, managers, employees, clients/customers, and/or visitors (as appropriate to the organization being studied) from the perspective of their movement through its spaces. Such mappings can identify interesting patterns of intersection or avoidance, suggesting in a physical way, for instance, the presence and location of power and powerlessness. The analysis can be gendered or 'raced', or linked with professional, occupational or work practice groupings, and so forth. Such study can draw on GPS and other developing technologies, including their use with old-fashioned walking around (for example, Jones, et al. 2008), or it can rely on 'simple' hand drawings (which rarely turn out to be simple). Analysis can focus on each of the five senses, in sequence, to see what these reveal about organizational members' patterns of grouping and movement. Or it can be more ethnomethodological, exploring how spatial uses are continuously re-patterned, maintained, and/or changed (see for example, Ciolfi 2004, Hall 2009, Stavrides 2001). Adapting these methods for purposes of organizational study is the challenge presently facing scholars of the spatial.

THE CHAPTERS

The chapters are grouped in three parts, reflecting their respective engagement with the key concerns identified in the preceding sections of this introduction. Part I focuses on spatial organizations and reorganizations and their relationship(s) with the behaviour and acts of employees and/or clients of and in those organizations. Having delivered a major theoretical contribution to the study of organizations' spatial settings with their 2008 book, Karen Dale and Gibson Burrell turn their attention in Chapter 1 to the growing popularity of the concept of community within architectural and design practices and rhetoric in the spatial reorganization of workplaces. They argue that changes in workplaces are aimed at the wholesale change of both social and individual motivation and commitment, for the purpose of producing improvements in teamwork and increasing the identification of groups and individuals with the organization and its goals. The community rhetoric emphasizes collective effort within a harmonious context, positioned by Giddens (1998) as 'the third way', in between the state bureaucracy and the free market. Dale and Burrell argue that corporate attention to workplace design represents an attempt to draw the concept of community into the interior of the hierarchic structures of organizational bureaucracies.

Continuing the theme of the spatial 'ordering' of its users' acts, Rick Iedema, Debbi Long, and Katherine Carroll, in their study of professionals working in hospitals (Chapter 2), analyse a space they identified that is surprisingly liminal: a corridor, usually a transit space connecting more formal spaces to each other, whose bulge created 'space' for non-formal negotiations among doctors, nurses, and other medical professionals of complex practice issues. The corridor bulge enabled conjoint reflections on practices in ways that might otherwise not have happened: they provided a 'space out of space' that facilitated cross-specialization consultations that crossed hierarchical power relations which professional practices would otherwise typically militate against. On a methodological note, the identification and use of the spatial surprise – the corridor bulge – to structure enquiry illustrates one of the central methodological aspects of ethnographic and other forms of interpretive research: abductive reasoning (Van Maanen et al. 2007, Locke et al. 2008, Agar 2010).

In Chapter 3, Patrick Kenis, Peter M. Kruyen and Joan Baaijens discuss the relationships between the design features of a new prison facility and officers' and prisoners' behaviours and acts. The original design was intended to influence prisoners' and officers' behaviour through the spatial settings of a panopticon-style design, the absence of a break room for guards, and the use of strict monitoring devices. This, it was thought, would result in a more efficient and safer prison. However, in dealing with design imperfections and other problematic attributes of the resulting setting, officers unintentionally developed solutions to the problems which were surprisingly – to the policy-makers and researchers – creative. In contrast to the bureaucratic behaviour expected, creative behaviours emerged; and these changed the character of tasks, procedures and rules in prison P.

Part II of the book turns its attention to studies that emphasize the historical and cultural specificities of their analyses. In one reading, they might also be said to highlight methodological issues in the study of organizational spaces. These chapters are grounded in their authors' own lived experiences of spatial reorganizations, sometimes as employees, sometimes as researchers, sometimes – as in two of the chapters – both at once. Marja Gastelaars (Chapter 4) looks at the institute in Utrecht in which she has taught since its inception. Using the 'six S's' Stewart Brand (1994) proposed to conceptualize the durability of buildings, she explores the building's Site, Skin (or *façade*),

Structure, Space plan, Stuff (furnishings and artefacts), and Service. We learn that the institute building, a former physics laboratory, provides its employees with an 'inner sanctuary', separating their teaching and research life from the goings-on of the busy Utrecht street outside in much the same way Utrecht's medieval sanctuaries – *hofjes* – once protected their own inhabitants from the inner city. This is in contrast to the main Utrecht University campus, called the '*Uithof*' – the *outer court*, which is at some distance from the bustling downtown. Her lived experience gives her a familiarity with the many 'cultural' and historical echoes that appear in the present re-design.

Whereas Gastelaars writes as a participant who happens also to be observing (Gans 1976), Alfons van Marrewijk (Chapter 5) writes from an explicitly established dual role as both employee and active ethnographer. His ringside seat in Dutch telecom operator KPN enabled him to engage the aesthetic experience of two organizational buildings, something that other non-employee researchers might have a more difficult time accessing. The chapter reflects upon these experiences and the methodological advantages of auto-ethnography for the study of spatial settings. Van Marrewijk's work also adds to the literature on aesthetics in organizational life, as his insider's seat enabled an intimate appreciation of the symbolic richness of physical and other artefacts, and their aesthetic dimensions.

In Chapter 6, David Weir, drawing on his own first-hand participatory experiences, explores the patterns of decision-making in a specific spatial design, the *diwan*. Commonly found in public and private settings in the Middle East and North Africa regions, *diwan* is most characteristically associated with a room with low seats lining the walls. Weir argues that the concept of *diwan*, perforce, intertwines spatial settings with management and employee behaviours and acts which are shaped by its design. His reflections on the *diwan* setting show the importance not only of a cross-cultural perspective for studying spatial settings but also for not assuming that interpretations of spatial experiences are universal: meanings attributed to spatial settings have to be located within their cultural contexts.

Moving away from empirical realities, the chapters in Part III look at representational aspects that arise in studying organizational spaces. In Chapter 7, Dvora Yanow asks what is lost in the silencing of space and other aspects of the organization's material world when organizational analysis, especially that informed by many discourse analytic theories, privileges words over objects. This practice, she argues, can be explained by looking at the professional practices of academics, socialized to a world of words and the production of texts. Consequently, their bodily experiences of spatial settings and objects receive little attention, and are even excluded, from organizational analysis. This affects interpretive researchers as much as it does those taking more realist-objectivist approaches to their studies. Yanow argues that this results in the loss not only of physical objects in the study of organizational realities, but of particular kinds of research questions and processes of study, as well.

Having recently published a book on organizational space (2009), Mark Mobach here turns his attention (Chapter 8) to an elaboration of the use of virtual technologies in the processes of design and construction. He argues that architects and managers, in cooperation, want to intervene in organizational space settings in order to influence the behaviours of their users: organizational members, customers and visitors. But end-users are hardly incorporated in this collaboration, resulting often in dissatisfaction with the design and even in resistance once the building is occupied. He argues that virtual reality could be used in a participatory design process in ways that give the end-user the opportunity to experience the new spatial settings before they are set in cement. They could then communicate any undesired attributes to the architects, who might then modify the design in ways that would make the overall process, and its outcomes, more successful.

Virtual reality is not the only medium for the visualization of organizational spaces. In the final chapter of the book, Alexia Panayiotou and Krini Kafiris turn to commercial films as a powerful medium for presenting visual images of organizational spaces. They analyse six well-known Hollywood films about financial corporations and law firms in which organizational spaces were a central 'actant', to use the term from actor network theory (see Latour 1993, Orlikowski 2007). Studying the geographic location, the size, scale and material of the buildings, the use of doors and windows, and the décor and furnishings of the organizations presented in these films, they found that stories of gender and power relations were expressed, symbolically, through spatial designs and uses. The films do not treat organizational spaces as neutral stages for the setting of action, but instead draw on a range of spatial vocabularies to actively construct or solidify existing gender relations and asymmetrical relationships of power.

Finally, in the afterword, Kristian Kreiner, co-author of one of the earliest critical assessments of organizational spaces (Berg and Kreiner 1990), reflects on the chapters and their contributions to the ongoing discussion of space, meanings and organizations in the organizational studies field.

REFERENCES

Agar, Michael (2010), 'On the ethnographic part of the mix', *Organizational Research Methods*, **13**, 286–303.
Appleyard, Donald (1982), *Liveable Streets*, Berkeley, CA: University of California Press.
Becker, Frank and Fritz Steele (1995), *Workplace by Design,* San Francisco, CA: Jossey-Bass.

Becker, Howard S., Blanche Geer, Everett C. Hughes and Anselm Strauss (1961), *Boys in White,* Chicago, IL: University of Chicago Press.

Berg, Per-Olof and Kristian Kreiner (1990), 'Corporate architecture: turning physical settings into symbolic resources', in Pasquale Gagliardi (ed.), *Symbols and Artifacts: Views of the Corporate Landscape*, New York: Aldine de Gruyter, pp. 41–67.

Betts, Jan (2006), 'Framing power: the case of the boardroom', *Consumption, Markets & Culture*, **9** (2), 157–67.

Binder, Thomas and Maria Hellstrom (eds) (2005), *Design Spaces*, Helsinki: IT Press.

Bitner, Mary Jo (1992), 'Servicescapes: the impact of physical surroundings on customers and employees', *Journal of Marketing*, **56** (2), 57–71.

Blau, Peter M. (1955), *The Dynamics of Bureaucracy: A Study of Interpersonal Relations in Two Government Agencies*, Chicago, IL: University of Chicago Press.

Brand, Stuart (1994), *How Buildings Learn: What Happens After They're Built*, revised 2nd edn. London: Phoenix Illustrated.

Casey, Edward S. (1993), *Getting Back into Place*, Bloomington, IN: Indiana University Press.

Casey, Edward S. (1997), 'By way of body', in *The Fate of Place,* Berkeley, CA: University of California Press, pp. 202–42.

Ciolfi, Luigina (2004), 'Understanding spaces as places: extending interaction design paradigms', *Cognition, Technology and Work*, **6** (1), 37–40.

Clegg, Stewart R. and Martin Kornberger (eds) (2006), *Space, Organizations, and Management Theory*, Oslo and Copenhagen: Liber and Copenhagen Business School Press.

Dale, Karen and Gibson Burrell (2008), *The Spaces of Organization and the Organization of Space: Power, Identity and Materiality at Work*, Basingstoke: Palgrave Macmillan.

Emery, Frederick E. and Eric Trist (1965), 'The causal texture of organizational environments', *Human Relations* **18**, 21–32.

Felstead, Alan, Nick Jewson and Sally Walters (2005), *Changing Places of Work*, New York: Palgrave Macmillan.

Gagliardi, Pasquale (ed.) (1990), *Symbols and Artifacts: Views of the Corporate Landscape*, New York: Walter de Gruyter.

Gans, Herbert (1976), 'Personal journal: B. On the methods used in this study', in M. Patricia Golden (ed.), *The Research Experience*, Itasca, IL: F.E. Peacock, pp. 49–59.

Giddens, Anthony (1998),*The Third Way: the Renewal of Social Democracy*, Oxford: Blackwell.

Goodman, Nelson and Catherine Z. Elgin (1988), 'How buildings mean', in *Reconceptions in Philosophy*, Indianapolis, IN: Hackett, pp. 31–48.

Goodsell, Charles T.. (1988), *The Social Meanings of Civic Space*, Lawrence, KS: University Press of Kansas.

Goodsell, Charles T. (ed.) (1993), 'Architecture as a setting for governance', *Journal of Architectural and Planning Research*, themed issue, **10** (4) (Winter).

Gregson, Nicky, Louise Crewe and Kate Brooks (2002), 'Shopping, space, and practice', *Environment and Planning D: Society and Space*, **20**, 597–617.

Hall, Tom (2009), 'Footwork: moving and knowing in local space(s)', *Qualitative Research*, **9** (5), 571–85.

Hatch, Mary Jo (1990), 'The symbolics of office design', in Pasquale Gagliardi (ed.), *Symbols and Artifacts*, New York: Aldine de Gruyter.

Hernes, Tor *(2004), The Spatial Construction of Organizations,* Amsterdam: John Benjamins.

Hernes, Tor, Tore Bakken and Per Ingvar Olsen (2006), 'Spaces as process: developing a recursive perspective on organizational space', in Stewart R. Clegg and Martin Kornberger (eds), *Space, Organizations and Management Theory,* Copenhagen: Liber and Copenhagen Business School Press, pp. 33–63.

Hirschman, Albert O. (1970), *Exit, Voice, and Loyalty: Responses to Decline in Firms, Organizations, and States,* Cambridge, MA: Harvard University Press.

Hooper, Barbara (2001), 'Desiring presence, romancing the real', *Annals of the Association of American Geographers,* **91** (4), 703–15.

Hubbard, Phil, Rob Kitchin and Gill Valentine (2004), *Key Thinkers on Space and Place,* London: Sage Publications.

Humphreys, Michael (2005), 'Getting personal: reflexivity and auto ethnographic vignettes', *Qualitative Inquiry,* **11** (6), 840–60.

Jackson, John B. (1980), *The Necessity for Ruins, and Other Topics,* Amherst, MA: University of Massachusetts Press.

Jones, Phil Ian, Griff Bunce, James Evans, Hannah Gibbs, and Jane Ricketts Hein (2008), 'Exploring space and place with walking interviews', *Journal of Research Practice,* **4** (2), Article D2, accessed 22 February 2010, at http://jrp.icaap.org/index.php/jrp/article/view/150/161.

Kornberger, Martin and Stewart R. Clegg (2004), 'Bringing space back in: organizing the generative building', *Organization Studies,* **25** (7), 1095–114.

Kunda, Gideon (1992), *Engineering Culture,* Philadelphia, PA: Temple University Press.

Lakoff, George and Mark Johnson (1980), *Metaphors We Live By,* Chicago, IL: University of Chicago Press.

Latour, Bruno (1993), *We Have Never Been Modern,* London: Harvester Wheatsheaf.

Lefebvre, Henri (1991), *The Production of Space,* Oxford: Blackwell.

Locke, Karen, Karen Golden-Biddle and Martha S. Feldman (2008), 'Making doubt generative: rethinking the role of doubt in the research process', *Organization Science,* **19** (6), 907–18.

Low, Setha and Denise Lawrence-Zúñiga (eds) (2003), *The Anthropology of Space and Place: Locating Culture,* Oxford: Blackwell.

Lynch, Kevin (1972), *What Time Is This Place?,* Cambridge, MA: MIT Press.

Mayo, Elton (1933), *The Human Problems of an Industrial Civilization,* New York: Macmillan.

Meinig, D.W. (ed.) (1979), *The Interpretation of Ordinary Landscapes,* New York, NY: Oxford University Press.

Mobach, Mark P. (2009), *Een organizatie van vlees en steen* [*An Organization of Flesh and Stone*], Assen, Netherlands: Van Gorcum.

Nauta, Rein (1991), 'Symboliek in organizaties' ['Symbols in organizations'], in Jasper van Grumbkow (ed.), *Cultuur in organizaties* [*Culture in Organizations*], Assen, Netherlands: van Gorcum, pp. 55–80.

Orlikowski, Wanda J. (2007), 'Sociomaterial practices: exploring technology at work', *Organization Studies,* **28** (9), 1435–48.

Pachirat, Timothy (2009), 'The *political* in political ethnography: reflections from an industrialized slaughterhouse on perspective, power, and sight', in Edward Schatz (ed.), *Political Ethnography: What Immersion Contributes to the Study of Power,* Chicago, IL: University of Chicago Press, pp. 143–61.

Preoffitt, W. Trexler Jr, and G. Lawrence Zahn (2006), 'Design, but align: the role of organizational physical space, architecture and design in communicating organizational legitimacy', in Stewart R. Clegg and Martin Kornberger (eds), *Space, Organizations and Management Theory*, Copenhagen: Copenhagen Business School Press, pp. 204–20.

Rafaeli, Anat and Michael Pratt (eds) (2006), *Artifacts and Organizations: Beyond Mere Symbolism,* Mahwah, NJ: Lawrence Erlbaum Associates.

Rapoport, Amos (1982), *The Meaning of the Built Environment*, Beverly Hills, CA: Sage.

Rosen, Michael, Wanda J. Orlikowski and Kim S. Schmahmann (1990), 'Building buildings and living lives', in Pasquale Gagliardi (ed.), *Symbols and Artifacts*, New York, NY: Aldine de Gruyter, pp. 69-84.

Schwartz-Shea, Peregrine (2006), 'Judging quality: evaluative criteria and epistemic communities', in Dvora Yanow and Peregrine Schwartz-Shea (eds), *Interpretation and Method: Empirical Research Methods and the Interpretive Turn*, Armonk, NY: M E Sharpe, pp. 89-113.

Soja, Edward W. (1989), *Postmodern Geographies: The Reassertion of Space in Critical Social Theory*, New York: Verso.

Stavrides, Stavros (2001), 'Navigating the metropolitan space: walking as a form of negotiation with otherness', *Journal of Psychogeography and Urban Research*, **1** (1), accessed 3 December 2009 at http://courses.arch.ntua.gr/stavrides.html.

Steele, Fritz I. (1973), *Physical Settings and Organization Development*, Menlo Park, CA: Addison-Wesley.

Steele, Fritz I. (1981), *The Sense of Place*, Boston, MA: CBI Publishing Co.

Strati, Antonio (1999), *Organization and Aesthetics*, London: Sage.

Taylor, Scott and Andre Spicer (2007), 'Time for space: a narrative review of research on organizational spaces', *International Journal of Management Reviews,* **9** (4), 325–46.

Trist, Eric and Ken Bamforth (1951), 'Some social and psychological consequences of the longwall method of coal getting', *Human Relations,* **4** (3), 3–38.

Tuan, Yi-Fu (1977), *Space and Place: The Perspective of Experience*, Minneapolis, MN: University of Minnesota Press.

Turley, Lou W. and Ronald E. Milliman (2000), 'Atmospheric effects on shopping behaviour: a review of the experimental evidence', *Journal of Business Research,* **49** (2), 193–211.

Våland, Marianne Stang (2010), 'What we talk about when we talk about space: end user participation between processes of organizational and architectural design', PhD dissertation, Department of Organization: Copenhagen Business School.

Van Maanen, John (1996), 'Commentary: on the matter of voice', *Journal of Management Inquiry,* **5** (4), 375–81.

Van Maanen, John, Jesper B. Sørensen and Terence R. Mitchell (2007), 'The interplay between theory and method', *Academy of Management Review*, **32** (4), 1145–54.

Van Marrewijk, Alfons (1999), *Internationalisation, Cooperation and Ethnicity in the Telecom Sector: An Ethnographic Study of the Cross-cultural Cooperation of KPN in Unisource, The Netherlands Antilles and Indonesia*, Delft, Netherlands: Eburon.

Van Marrewijk, Alfons (2009a), 'Corporate headquarters as physical embodiments of organizational change', *Journal of Organizational Change Management,* **22** (3), 290–306.

Van Marrewijk, Alfons (2009b), 'Retail stores as aesthetic experiences of brands. The case of fashion house Oger', paper presented in sub-theme 15, 'Making brands come alive: how organizations, stakeholders and customers mobilize their identity', at the 25th European Group on Organizational Studies annual conference collo-quium, 2–4 July, Barcelona.

Veldhoen, Erik (2005), *The Art of Working,* Den Haag: Academic Services.

Vickers, Sir Geoffrey (1983), *Human Systems are Different,* New York: Harper & Row.

Warren, Samantha (2008), 'Empirical challenges in organizational aesthetics research: towards a sensual methodology', *Organization Studies, 29* (4), 559–80.

Yanow, Dvora (1993), 'Reading policy meanings in organization-scapes', *Journal of Architectural and Planning Research,* **10**, 308–27.

Yanow, Dvora (1998), 'Space stories; or, studying museum buildings as organizational spaces, while reflecting on interpretive methods and their narration', *Journal of Management Inquiry,* **7** (3), 215–39.

Yanow, Dvora (2000), 'Symbolic objects – built spaces and their "props"', in *Conducting Interpretive Policy Analysis*, Newbury Park, CA: Sage, chapter 4.

Yanow, Dvora (2006a), 'Studying physical artifacts: an interpretive approach', in Anat Rafaeli and Michael Pratt (eds), *Artifacts and Organizations*, Mahwah, NJ: Lawrence Erlbaum Associates, pp. 41–60.

Yanow, Dvora (2006b), 'How built spaces mean: a semiotics of space', in Dvora Yanow and Peregrine Schwartz-Shea (eds), *Interpretation and Method: Empirical Research Methods and the Interpretive Turn,* Armonk, NY: M E Sharpe, pp. 349–66.

PART I

Seeing organizational spaces

1. 'All together, altogether better': the ideal of 'community' in the spatial reorganization of the workplace

Karen Dale and Gibson Burrell

In recent years many companies, frequently aided by consultancies, designers and architects, have sought to reshape their workplaces in order to achieve organizational goals directly through their spatial arrangements. These goals naturally include economic ones of maximizing the use of expensive built assets, but what particularly distinguishes this trend is an approach to spatial manipulation that goes much further than the economic. The move to reorganize these workplaces is aimed at the wholesale change of both social and individual motivation and commitment to the organization. The objective is to break down barriers to cooperation and communication perceived to be a result of current spatial arrangements, and in so doing to produce improvements in team-working and increase the identification of groups and individuals with the organization and its goals.

This approach is perhaps best expressed by one of the foremost architects involved in promoting it, Frank Duffy, one of the founding members of DEGW (a major international consultancy involved in workplace design) and past president of the British architectural community's professional body, the Royal Institute of British Architects (RIBA). Duffy argues that buildings are 'agents of change. Buildings have a catalytic effect. They can express new ideas and push new possibilities forward' (Duffy 1996).

One of the most startling organizational changes involves the removal of over seven miles of internal walls at the UK Treasury Department – literally dismantling the original 'corridors of power' to establish open-plan working spaces. Here the rationale was to open up the British government's most important organ of state to more communication, less hierarchy, more openness to new ideas and to a 'transparency' in government with respect to the outside world. This project clearly illustrates the application of Duffy's beliefs in the power of space to change organizational relations. Commenting on the effects of a similar project at Scottish Enterprise (a quasi-governmental body whose objective is to stimulate the Scottish economy), employee Michelle

Hynd argues: 'We moved minds, as well as offices – accelerating our business and cultural change by years. You realize just how much the old working environment held us back' (Allen et al. 2004, p. 81).

We believe that a number of overlapping themes can be discerned in the presentation of workplace spatial reorganizations as explained by companies and consultancies in their corporate publications and websites (Dale and Burrell 2008). The main themes include play or fun at work (see also Alferoff and Knights 2003, Costea et al. 2005, Warren 2002), the employee as consumer, the workplace as home, and the workplace as community. These themes incorporate an aestheticization of the workspaces, consciously designing them to produce pleasurable and sometimes sensuous effects. This is combined, almost ironically, with the disappearance of the workplace itself as a workplace. Traditional organizational workspaces are displaced by quasi-constructions of town- or village-scapes, 'neighbourhoods', game rooms, 'domesticated' spaces of kitchens, and break-out rooms with soft sofas, decorated with commercial or even work-team produced art, using colours, lighting and furnishings which do not evoke a place of labour and employment.

The redesigned workplaces, then, seem to be appealing to different aspects of individuals' experiences and identities than those of the traditional employee. The themes that are evoked within spatial reorganizations can be seen as 'narratives' that are given physical, material shape alongside the traditional discursive form of organizational stories that are conveyed through the written and spoken words of policy documents and corporate newsletters and passed via management teams to employees face to face. The significance of this fashion for the reconstruction of organizational space lies in the way that organizational members have to 'live through' the spaces – or at least to 'work through' them on a daily basis. In other words, organizational culture initiatives and changes have often relied on rhetoric, symbol, and semiotics, but here the whole workscape is constructed as the embodiment of the desired culture. Employees move through the spaces, interacting with each other and with the designed environment, and as they do so they 'perform' the organizational culture thus constructed; they enact, and then repeatedly re-enact, these spatial narratives with their whole embodied persons. Grey (2009, p. 70) argues that 'the manipulation of symbols provides some of the deepest techniques of culture management', but what if the reshaping of the workplace means that employees actually have to step into these symbols, that they become an embodied part of that symbolic structure?

In these ways, organizational spaces are lived and experienced in a holistic, ongoing and dynamic manner which potentially produces immersion and reproduction of cultural norms and expectations that are not, and cannot be, matched by a textual representation of that culture. Although this of course does not preclude resistance and the possibilities of living through these spaces in multiple and different ways, it still goes 'beyond' words, making the narrative that much more powerful because it is simultaneously more taken for granted and embedded, because it is 'inserted' into spatial elements that are themselves not explicitly 'narrated'. Therefore, the narrative of lived-in space is more difficult to perceive as a set of rhetorical devices, compared to, for example, mission statements and corporate advertising.

In this chapter we want to explore further the reshaping of the modern workplace in relation to one particular theme which is commonly found, explicitly or implicitly, within these physical reconfigurations: the use of 'community' as an organizing motif. We focus on its use as a managerial device in two ways, internally within an organization and externally, within society. We draw on parts of Lefebvre's work (1991) which enable us to highlight some of the contradictions within, and the connections between, these levels of analysis.

THE IDEA OF COMMUNITY

Workplace redesign is replete with images and language that evoke community. For example, within the work of design consultancy DEGW, one can find organizations being portrayed as 'neighbourhood spaces' (Google HQ, Boots), 'streets' (British Airways HQ), a media 'village' (the BBC), a 'townscape' (Capital One bank's HQ in Nottingham), a vertical 'village' or 'street' (MLC Sydney), and an 'office-village' (Apicorp, Saudi Arabia) (DEGW n.d.). At an electricity generating company which we have studied (Dale 2005) and discuss below, areas called 'village pumps' were designed to facilitate the greatest degree of interaction possible.

An example of the change process and the managerial investment in this narrative can be seen in a case study given by Area Sq, another design company, on its website (Area Sq 2008). This is of a design brief for the relocation of Galileo International (an electronic solutions provider to the travel industry) that brings together five different offices into one purpose-built 55,000 sq ft headquarters office in Axis Park, Langley (near Heathrow Airport). The brief was specifically to redesign the space so as to produce more effective teamwork and communication. Elizabeth Harraway, Galileo's Director of Marketing Communications, claims that the redesign of their workplace has meant that: 'Internal communication has definitely improved. It was very important to create an environment which encouraged and enabled everyone to work much closer together' (Area Sq n.d.). She goes on to talk about the removal from one location to the new one and the processes involved here. 'Moving is difficult for employees, even if it's just next door, so keeping our employees informed at every opportunity was key to success. We had a special area on our intranet called "Project Home" to convey that we were moving home together.' A maxim of 'all together, altogether better' was used to convey to employees a key image of the objective of the move. For us, this slogan captures the key theme of community in companies' spatial reorganizations.

The diversity of the ideas and forms of 'community' drawn upon by consultants and managers, as well as their ubiquity, alerts us to particular ways in which 'community' is being utilized as a modern managerial technique. In this chapter, we argue that 'community' can be seen as a managerial device at two levels. The first operates within the organization, attempting to reshape the relationship between the organization and its members, as an extension of corporate culture initiatives designed to 'capture hearts and minds', uniting all employees in a form of 'unitarist' collectivity (Burrell and Morgan 1979, p. 204). There are connections here with a longer context of attempts to produce organizational community as a substitute for more traditional community forms, a process described evocatively by Bauman (2001) as 'rerooting the uprooted'. The second way in which the 'community' device is drawn upon is in the legitimation of the position and activities of the organization within society, through emphasizing the common goals and shared meanings between companies and civil society. This simultaneously obscures the competitive, conflictual and exploitative aspects of the relationship between the capitalist corporation and wider society. In the rest of the chapter we will provide some analysis of the use of 'community' in these two ways, but before we turn to that it will be useful to outline some aspects of Lefebvre's conceptualization of the social production of space which we find helpful in our analysis.

Lefebvre (1991) starts from the argument that space is not an empty vacuum, waiting for something social to happen within it, but that space is itself socially produced. In his discussions of this, he connects two aspects of space: its physical materiality and its simultaneous 'imaginary', cultural, symbolic and historical meanings. As we will see, from the point of view of the use of 'community' in workplace redesign, both the material aspects of the design of spaces that generate interaction and particular sorts of sociability, and the imaginary evocations of the idea of 'community' are involved. Lefebvre develops a variety of concepts to try to capture the multiplicity of ways that space is socially produced. Two of these are especially useful for exploring the use of 'community' in workplace design. The first is that of 'representations of space', or 'conceived space' (Lefebvre 1991, p. 39). This is the element of social space which is planned and designed to embody certain conceptualizations in materialized form. These are spaces which we would additionally characterize as 'organized' and 'managed', as they particularly capture the explicit intentions of designers and managers in the remodelling of workspaces.

Lefebvre (1991) explicitly connects such spaces with the 'dominant spaces in any society (or mode of production)' and thus with another conceptualization that forms a key theme throughout his *Social Production of Space*: that of 'abstract space'. This is the social space produced by capitalism, characterized by 'accumulation and growth, calculation, planning, programming' (Lefebvre 1991, p. 307). It is an instrumental space, dominated by exchange relations, political in the sense of being produced through power, and institutional. Lefebvre sees its key elements as being 'geometric', in that it is a representation of space which is 'isotropic' or homogeneous, 'which guarantees its social and political utility' (Lefebvre 1991, p. 285); 'visual', in that the representation is conveyed through image and symbol with an aggressive ocular-centrism that subordinates other senses; and 'phallic', in that however it appears on the surface, it is a space dominated by the force and violence of having been dominated by particular relations of power and knowledge. One of the most significant aspects of Lefebvre's discussion of abstract space is that it embodies contradiction, so that whilst it frequently appears to have surface characteristics such as homogeneity or transparency, these in fact obscure the appropriation of the space through particular power relations.

With these ideas in hand, we turn to exploring the relationship between the organizing motif of 'community' and the formation of modern workplaces, endeavouring to unpack some of these contradictions.

THE MANAGEMENT OF 'COMMUNITY'

Day (2006) argues that community is a slippery concept, yet it is one which still grips the imaginations of people. 'Community' is practically impossible to pin down and define, such that for Abercrombie et al. (1984, p. 44) it has become a term that is 'one of the most elusive and vague in sociology and is now largely without meaning'. However, as we will discuss, in this elusiveness lies much of its power of evocation in the workplace. The last thing that is required for maximizing its great potential as a managerial tool is for it to be given some sort of fixed, neutral and objective definition, such as referring to a particular set of people in a specific locale. Its very ambiguity enables it to perform work of a particular sort. It plays out in a multiplicity of ways to provoke resonances and associations.

'Community' works as a spatial organizing principle, and it does so in a diffuse way. Regardless of the experience one might have of any particular community, the idea in itself provokes almost Garden of Eden images of harmony, belonging and cohesion. In this way, the use of 'community' in the reshaping of organizations has much to do with cultural and emotional management. Bauman puts this succinctly when he says (2001, p. 1): 'Words

have meanings: some words, however, also have "a feel". The word "community" is one of them. It feels good: whatever the word "community" may
mean, it is good "to have a community", "to be in a community".' We see
parallels between the idea of 'community' as used in modern organizational
life and Anthony Cohen's formulation of the 'social construction of community' (1985). This is a view of 'community' as essentially a sense-making
aspect of social life, predominantly existing through symbolic meanings:

> Community plays a key role in how people think about themselves, their personal
> and social identities, and their subjectivity. It has value as an analytical concept,
> because it focuses attention on how individuals, groups and places become tied
> together through the sense of belonging.   (Day 2006, p. 157)

In this way, it often has distinct overtones of 'nostalgic and romantic notions
of a mythical past' (Pahl 1996, p. 89).

Day comments on Cohen's perspective to the effect that:

> It is not structures and institutions that define a community, but the feelings and
> experiences of its members, and the manner in which they express them. Most
> centrally, they do this by drawing boundaries, between themselves and others, stip-
> ulating who 'belongs', and who falls outside the limits of 'their' community.   (Day
> 2006, p. 159)

As Cohen goes on to explain:

> The symbolic nature of the opposition means that people can 'think themselves into
> difference'. The boundaries consist essentially in the contrivance of distinctive
> meanings within the community's social discourse. They provide people with a
> referent for their personal identities. Having done so, they are then expressed and
> reinforced through the presentation of those identities in social life.   (Cohen 1985,
> p. 117)

In these symbolic terms, a key image which is drawn upon by organizational
designers is that of the 'village'. Day (2006, p. 39) claims that 'of all the familiar settings for traditional community, it is the village which provides the most
archetypal, to the extent that, at times, the two become almost synonymous'.
The village is predominantly small and self-contained spatially; often built
around the common purpose of small-scale agricultural subsistence, where the
populace have shared pre-occupations, as well as the shared occupation of
being agricultural labourers. For Day (2006, p. 40), the village 'epitomizes the
social wholeness which many expect from community'. In a similar vein,
Fisher and Kling (1993, p. xi) opine that

> village signifies a place where there are few disruptions of the routines of living,
> few surprises and few threats. In the village, strangers are rare, and if everyone does

not quite know everyone else, people at least recognize most of the faces they pass in the street. It is a metaphor for the closeness of people and the reassuring familiarity and durability of the day to day.

Day argues that this is a mythic village, a village of the imagination. But it could be argued that this notion of 'community as village' exercises such a powerful draw over management and their consultants precisely because it is able to attract strong local loyalties and create a clear sense of identity, place and order, in a way that appears to be natural and unchanging (Newby 1987, p. 79). Pahl (1970) suggests that people can inhabit a 'village in the mind' even whilst physically living within an urban environment. This is the type of 'imagined community' (Anderson 1983) which is being evoked within many modern workspaces.

However, the symbolic and communicative properties of 'community' in workplace reorganization are combined with and achieved through a physical reshaping of organizational spaces. It is to these material changes that we now turn.

RESHAPING SPATIAL MATERIALITY: COMMUNITY, CIVILITY AND CONTROL

Traditionally, organizational status and hierarchy have been associated with spaces that are separate and bounded. Conventionally, greater enclosure in private offices has signified higher degrees of power and eminence, with the largest offices of the most senior organizational members being located literally on the highest levels of buildings. However, contemporary approaches to organizational redesign have centred on a much more open use of space, with very few private offices. Even where there are enclosed spaces, these are not allocated to individual employees as their marked 'territory' but rather are to be used for particular purposes, such as meetings or tasks which require confidentiality or quiet and lack of interruption, and can be used by any employees as appropriate to the needs of their jobs. The material reshaping of the workplace places an emphasis on openness, 'transparency' and a greater homogeneity of space, such that although there are different sorts of spaces (from the open 'street' or office-scape to the almost domesticated kitchens or lounges and break-out zones), these are generally accessible to the whole range of employees. These practices and places very much mirror the characteristics that Lefebvre associates with 'abstract space' (1991, p. 287). Modern workplaces appear to be offering homogeneity in the sense of 'horizontal' access to all levels and occupational groups of staff along with a dismantling of 'vertical', hierarchical segregations. But this homogeneity is illusory in that the spatial arrangements are linked with other forms of control, and, as Lefebvre argues, they are designed to 'render homogeneous' (1991, p. 287) a certain sort of common subject and subjectivity which they, in fact, have a hand in producing.

Within this material reshaping, we can distinguish two broad types of spatial formation, operationalized through the organizing device of 'community'. These are socio-petal and socio-fugal movements (Hall 1966). Socio-petal or centripetal arrangements produce spaces where people are encouraged to gather together. This is where teamworking is seen as the primary benefit and where stasis is more encouraged in the sense that organizational members actively engage with each other within these spaces, rather than merely passing through them. Socio-petal spaces include break-out rooms and such social spaces as cafes, kitchens, lounges and games rooms (table football and pool being perhaps the most organizationally sanctioned activities). They also include areas where a number of services or facilities are deliberately gathered together, drawing people together in their use. It is often here, where community is understood in its sense of proximity and gathering together, that the image of the 'village' or 'neighbourhood' is evoked.

In contrast, socio-fugal or centrifugal spaces encourage people to move on and through. Socio-fugal spaces include the 'streets' which have become prevalent in many state-of-the-art organizational buildings. Van Marrewijk (2009) discusses an example from Kotter and Cohen (2002, pp. 155–7) of a company which redesigned its space to produce a mingling of factory and office workers through a zone called 'the street', which included a range of common areas such as washrooms and coffee facilities. These encourage a different sort of sharing of space, one where people are in constant contact with each other, but with a different sort of interaction in mind. This has been described as 'street-sociability' and is often associated with the more impersonal interaction of the shopping mall (Lehtonen and Maenpaa 1997, p. 156).

However, even though this may appear to be quite different from the evocation of the cohesive community that much of the rhetoric seems to be aimed at, it potentially produces two other social and power effects which may actually integrate very well with the overall managerial thrust of spatial reorganizations. First, the internalization of the 'cityscape' *within* the organization draws upon some positive facets frequently associated with city life: the appearance of freedom of movement to follow one's own 'desiring paths', often combined with consumption which tends to resonate with ideas of autonomy, choice and the fulfilment of desire.[1] If these potentially positive aspects of modern identity can be incorporated *within* organizational identity, then this strengthens affirmative associations between the individual and the organizational 'community'.

The second social effect of linking 'community' with socio-fugal spaces in the organization is that it maintains a stabilizing cohesive 'feel' whilst people are moving through corporate spaces. Even as organizational members simply share common facilities, the organizing device of 'community' gives a meaning to these movements and spaces. Felstead et al. (2005, p. 71) have argued that 'the socio-spatial relations and aesthetic order of collective offices are specifically designed to generate intense social interactions among employees by virtue of high levels of movement'. Studies of the changing employment relations of the manufacturing sector have often described attempts to break down barriers between different categories of employees through the 'harmonization' of terms and conditions, including getting rid of divisive staff and blue collar facilities. This would include the example from Kotter and Cohen, mentioned above, along with Zaha Hadid's design for the BMW plant in Leipzig which features a centralized node bringing together production and office workers, management and visitors, and which was shortlisted for the RIBA Stirling Prize in 2005 (Channel 4 2005).

In order to see why 'community' is such a powerful notion within contemporary managerial devices, it is useful to compare it with the helpful discussion of the spatial production of 'civility' by Muetzelfeldt (2006). He defines civility as 'the unacknowledged but still crucial lubricant' (2006, p. 113) for interpersonal interactions based upon market or power relations, that is, those which tend to be centred around instrumentality or authority. Civility eases these relations, mediating the potential contradictory and conflictual aspects of them by producing 'rules of interaction' that provoke 'constraint and interpersonal attunement' (2006, p. 113). Civility is akin to community, then, in as far as it is 'predicated on and emerges through trust, mutuality and a sense of interdependence among its members' (Muetzelfeldt 2006, p. 117). However, it is a more limited concept than 'community' in its production of a collective sense of identity as a form of managerial and cultural control strategy. As Muetzelfeldt demonstrates through his examples, civility maintains a sense of distance, both social and physical, despite proximity. For instance, in the arrangement of a lecture theatre to promote individual attention of the learners to the teacher, the instructor's 'standing' [sic] is facilitated through the placement of a central and elevated position, compared to the linear seating of the students. The traditional arrangement of private office spaces within organizations could be said to produce civility rather than community. There is more of an element of 'emplacement' (Dale and Burrell 2008, p. 53) in the spatial production of civility, even where people are mobile, in that it keeps people in their social (and sometimes physical) places. It maintains boundaries of a particular sort.

'Community' as evoked within recent organizational spatial reordering produces social space in different ways from that of civility. As we have already mentioned, 'community' is a way of organizing and producing certain aspects of identity and identification with the institution. Hatch suggests, following Steele (1983), that open design 'leads to greater team working, interpersonal familiarity and spontaneous interaction amongst those who are mutually accessible' (Hatch 1990, p. 131). Hofbauer comments that 'The underlying assumption of this design type is that affective bonds rather than management hold organization together' (Hofbauer 2000, p. 174). However, we would suggest that it is not a mutually exclusive choice between management *or* affective bonds, but rather that it is management taking place *through* the attempted manipulation of those affective bonds.

In some ways, the use of 'community' as an organizing device has a long history within managerial control strategies; but in other ways it partakes of more recent developments. It is helpful to see the spatial redesign of workplaces, then, both in the light of a continuity of a particular trend in organizational relations and in relation to broader changes in organizational contexts and managerial control. Bauman (2001) argues that in the development of capitalism, in both agrarian and industrial forms, communal bonds had to be decisively broken. Enclosure threw people off the land, breaking the ties of localism, and the factory system (whether by design or not is still debated, but certainly in consequence) further separated workers from themselves, their history and their common bonds of labour. Bauman (2001, pp. 34–5) describes two tendencies within capitalism: one to replace the 'natural understanding' of community with an 'artificially designed and coercively imposed and maintained routine' (2001, p. 34), and a second (predominantly subordinate) tendency to create a new 'community feeling' within the framework of the new power structures. This second impulse was seen initially in company 'model villages' where, contained and constrained, the individual could face work as a whole life pursuit (Lefebvre 1991, pp. 318–19). The design of Saltaire in England or Pullman in the US (outside of Chicago), would be examples. This preoccupation with social harmony, not only within industrial organization but between business and civil society, was to be further developed and refined within the Human Relations School (for example, Roethlisberger and Dickson 1939, Mayo 1949), in which it was theorized as an important element or device in what might be described as a valorization of a 'sociology of order', as we discuss more extensively below.

By acting as a device in this way, the use of the notion of community is a contrivance for creating understandings within the workforce, understandings that would have been assumed to occur naturally in more 'traditional' communities. Bauman (2001, p. 11) comments:

> Of course, a contrived, an achieved understanding may also be tacit, or turn into a sort of contrived and internalized intuition. Protracted negotiation may result in an agreement which, if obeyed daily, may in its turn become a habit which no longer needs to be thought about, let alone monitored and policed.

By embedding these community narratives spatially and materially and having them being repeatedly performed by organizational members, organizational cultural initiatives may effectively bypass at least some of the need for 'protracted negotiations' in achieving this internalization.

However, the 'community' narrative device within the contemporary reshaping of organizational workplaces also reflects new organizational forms and managerial control practices which have emerged over the last 30 years or so, in articulation with changing economic conditions: international competition and deregulation, trends towards an accelerated new international division of labour and associated uncertainties, changes in structures of western economies towards greater reliance on the service sector and financial markets, and technological innovations (especially electronic information and communication technologies). Of course, there are continuities alongside these changes, but overall there is a greater degree of heterogeneity and unpredictability in organizational life. Zanoni and Janssens (2006, p. 96) follow Harvey (1989) in recognizing that economic space is simultaneously 'more fragmented, due to decentralizing practices, and more integrated, due to the internationalizing practices strengthening interdependencies'. In this dynamic world, the use of 'community' as an organizing device can be a particularly powerful tool. In many ways it can act as a 'comfort blanket', downplaying and obscuring the potentially threatening and individualizing forces of new organizational contexts and practices. Where there are uncertainties in both the external labour markets (circuits of recession and economic restructuring, the new international division of labour) and internal labour markets (circuits of downsizing, organizational restructuring, flexibility including peripheralization of some employees, individualization of contracts and the weakening of traditional forms of collective representation), then 'community' can work to mask and counter, representationally, this fragmentation, replacing it with the narrative of a unitarist, interdependent, cohesive form of organizational collectivity. This is the case even where the economic rationalities of the firm belie the harmony implied by 'community', as in the example of an electricity generating company discussed below.

Such changing economic and organizational situations and forms are played out through changing managerial control strategies. A major aspect of modern organizational control arises from the conflicting pressures between the uncertainties of organizational life and the need for greater *employee* commitment to the organization and involvement in their work practices, and in this it is important to stress that managers are not external agents, but are also very much subject to the same changing forms of control as their employees. Thus, much of the production of the modern organization is not simply of products and services to be sold, but entails the production of the employees themselves, as Zanoni and Janssens (2006, p. 93) say: 'By providing constructions of the working subject that are in line with organizational interests and from which workers can draw for self-definition.'

Many of the managerial practices which have aimed at this reconstitution of identity and meaning in the workplace have concentrated on the employee as an individual. For example, performance management and performance-related pay schemes have focused on individual rewards, provided for individual self-fulfilment and achievement. The individual is seen as an autonomous agent in control of his or her own career, which becomes part of a wider 'project of self' (Grey 1994; Rose 1990). However, the spatial construction of 'community' attempts to recombine these individualized identities into a new form of collectivism: one which is centred on identification with organizational goals and, indeed, on the organization itself as a source of collective identity. In this, it can be seen as parallel to the re-appropriation of identity through diversity management, discussed by Zanoni and Janssens, which they see as 'promoting multiple, less antagonistic group identities in the organization' (2006, p. 103).

It also works in another way, namely to aid the extension of the employee identification with a company beyond the physical and temporal bounds of the organization itself. Since much modern work tends itself not to be physically limited to within the organizational walls, facilitated by information and communication technologies, employees need to be connected to the organization in ways which are not dependent on actually being present within its precincts. If employees have internalized the culture and goals of the organization through enactment, they will also 'carry' these internalized meanings with them as they work for the organization in extra-organizational settings (cf. Felstead et al. 2005). The community rhetoric emphasizes in particular that the individual organizational member is part of a larger social group, that they are an 'insider' in this group (wherever they may physically be located), and that they share common goals and norms with this group even when they are not with them in person.

The 'community' device within organizational design and rhetoric about that design, then, can be seen as part of the corporate culture movement, one of the central instruments in trying to achieve organizational effectiveness through the management of identity and meaning. Willmott (1993, pp. 515–16) says that: 'Improvements in productivity and quality, it is argued, flow from corporate cultures that systematically recognize and reward individuals, symbolically and materially, for identifying their sense of purpose with the values that are designed into the organization.' Although in an important sense, culture is necessarily collective, since it depends upon shared understanding and goals, yet it does not necessarily promote collectivism, and indeed it may even reward very opposite anti-collective, highly individualist tendencies. As Miller and Rose (1990, p. 26) have observed: 'The "autonomous" subjectivity of the productive individual has become a central economic resource: such programmes promise to turn autonomy into an ally of economic success and not an obstacle to be controlled and disciplined.' Willmott (1993) has powerfully argued how corporate culture initiatives constitute a 'seductive double-think' in relation to this individual autonomy. At the same time as they appear to affirm the value of each employee as self-defining, what they enforce is a necessary conformity and consensus through an underlying logic of authoritarianism: those who do not internalize the culture will be weeded out. Drawing upon 'community' is in some ways a new facet of corporate culture initiatives. The material embodiment of these cultural norms within the very physical structure of the organization and the employees' daily routes and routines is a powerful and hidden extension of corporate culture, and the appeal to the nostalgic imaginary 'community' may serve to further obscure their underlying contradictions and totalitarian impulses.

Thus, in a number of ways we can see the use of the organizing device of 'community' as an appropriation of social space in the sense that Bauman (2001) described it, as a substitute for 'natural' community in order to inure employees to capitalist relations of production. This conceptualization leads us back to Lefebvre and the development of the 'abstract space' of capitalism. It also embodies the contradictory aspects of abstract space that demonstrate Willmott's 'seductive double-think' in material form. To illustrate what we have been theorizing as the psycho-social appropriation of organizational space, we will draw out some of the salient aspects of a newly built headquarters for a UK electricity generating company, opened in 1994, and reflecting the change of the organization from a nationalized utility to a private business.

An Illustration of the Spatial Organization of Community: Generating Electricity in the UK

The building was specifically designed to maximize interaction, using the principles of SpaceSyntax, a consultancy operating out of the Bartlett School of Architecture in London and based upon the work of Bill Hillier (Hillier 1997, Hillier and Hanson 1984). Three floors, arranged around a central atrium, provided an almost completely open plan, with homogeneous, horizontally organized space. The idea was to dismantle both spatial and social barriers within the organization, emphasizing and facilitating through mobility and visibility a holistic understanding of the business unimpeded by traditional bureaucratic departments and loyalties.

Within these open expanses, central socio-petal gathering areas were located, known as the 'village pumps'. These were intended to be the nodes where employees from all different teams met together to share knowledge and experience, reinforcing the idea of the organization as community rather than as hierarchy or bureaucracy. The spatial narrative of community was also reiterated within a new integrated human resource strategy, which was designed around flexibility, teamworking, networking, and the integration of disparate parts of the business. Successful progress within the company, through opportunities for promotion, was to be achieved through the individual's demonstration of integration within these community values. Thus, the like-mindedness and belonging associated with community was contrived through the pressure to conform. Loyalty and integration in the 'community' were required.

The contradictory nature of the relationship was further emphasized when we considered the rationalizing logic of the organization at this time. In its transformation from national to private company, a considerable number of employees were made redundant. Indeed, the aggregate employee figures masked the total number of redundancies since long-standing employees from its nationalized days were being replaced with the recruitment of new, young business graduates. This marked a more fundamental restructuring and change in culture, since those who might have had a longer relationship with an organizational 'community' that had its basis in the provision of a public utility as a collective social good were forcibly ejected from it, whilst new employees without such ties were selected for their profit-based business orientation.

In a further spatial instantiation of this, another major socio-petal space of the organization was the restaurant, where employees were encouraged to gather together, including the use of the space for informal teamworking. The apparent autonomy of the use of this space throughout the day was belied by the constant display of the company's share-price flashing around its walls. This became part of the everyday experiential background, but inevitably reminded employees that even while ostensibly autonomous subjects, gathering together over coffee, they were part of a 'community' whose rationale was profit-making for shareholders. Indeed, employees were even further integrated into this organizational community through employee share-ownership schemes, thus further blurring the boundaries of insiders and outsiders, emphasizing a commonality of interests between 'owners' and 'employees'.

Here, then, we observed some of the contradictions within organized 'abstract space' ordered around the material and symbolic device of 'community'. It can be used as a means to attempt to construct employee identity around a unitarist collective ideal. Indeed, through the company's spatial arrangements individuals had to enact this 'community' in their day-to-day working lives whilst appearing to be following autonomous 'desiring paths'.

Although it evokes a warm harmonious glow, 'community' has its dark sides: it separates people into 'insiders' and 'outsiders'. In relation to modern organizations, organizational community is about a re-formed collectivity which is not organized around traditional us/them distinctions such as worker/manager and owner/employee, or between different occupational groups or departmental demarcations created through division of labour. Instead, the spaces are designed to be inclusive of these groups within the community of the organization. This can obscure power differentials and relations, excluding those who do not 'fit in' in prescribed ways. Thus, potentially one unintended consequence of the construction of organization as community may be to produce the reproduction of 'sameness' and the exclusion of diversity and difference (cf. Kanter 1977). In these ways the 'abstract spaces' of capital are reinforced within organizational life, but they can also be utilized to extend these 'abstract spaces' into wider areas of social life more generally.

SOME IMPLICATIONS OF THE ORGANIZATIONAL APPROPRIATION OF 'COMMUNITY'

In this final section, we consider some of the implications of the use of 'community' as a spatial ordering device for the wider relations between organizations and society: the meeting of organizational and societal 'communities'. As we have described above, Bauman (2001, p. 34) sees the use of 'community' as one historical 'tendency' to incorporate individuals within the new power structures of capitalism. So far we have examined this in relation to the idea of the community device *within* the organizational context itself. Here, we turn to reflect on how the idea of organization as community may be drawn upon in its spatial manifestations to legitimate the position and activities of capitalist organizations within society, potentially obscuring their more conflictual and exploitative effects within that wider society. The more that it seems to be 'normal' for every individual within society to be part of an organizational 'community' as an expression of belonging in that wider society, the more the commonality of interests between organizations and society is stressed and becomes taken for granted and unquestioned. Capitalist societies have a long history of normalizing the selling of labour power and pathologizing any individual or group who stands outside this, from the criminal to the gypsy, the 'unemployed' to the member of a commune.

It is in light of this that we note that from the nineteenth century onward, social theorists have been wrestling with the ideal of community within rapidly changing forms of capitalist society: what does 'community' consist of when related to capitalist relations of contract, the sale of labour power, and the organization of industrial production? Central to this shift are the changing spatial relations between community and organization: how does the concept of community fare in the new spatial concentrations of people within factories and offices, when compared to pre-industrial patterns of place-making? Nisbet

(1967, p. 47), the great commentator on much of this period, says that community is one of sociology's most fundamental and far-reaching ideas, at the same time that he cautions us against approaches that are too diffuse and ill defined.

Nisbet owes much to the prodding of Durkheim, for whom community held the key to French social problems. It was 'social solidarity' and not 'anomic individualism' which contained the solution, in his view, to French social upheaval. One form of solidarity, which Durkheim (1972) termed mechanical, was based upon common sentiments and beliefs, such as within an undifferentiated population typical of the rural hamlet. This is a 'conscience collective'. What he called organic solidarity, on the other hand, comes from contractual relationships based upon differentiation and concomitant interdependence within a metropolitan-based, high level of the division of labour. Both forms of solidarity reflect an ideological community of shared ideas and a shared moral order. For Durkheim, the community based on shared ideas integrates the social fabric through identity, whilst the community based on a shared moral order unites classes and occupational groups within a unified objective – the maintenance of order through a communality of interests. This was to be governed by the professionals, who were to be the guardians of the new 'conscience collective'. In some senses, we might argue that in the context of the modern organization, we are seeing managers and the design professionals who serve their interests as attempting to fulfil this role.

In ways similar to Durkheim, Ferdinand Tonnies (1963), too, had distinguished between bygone community, *Gemeinschaft*, and modern community, *Gesellschaft*, with the former marked out by a common understanding, a natural one-mindedness shared by all members based on consanguinity and face-to-face relations. In many ways, this is exactly what the spatial narrative of community in the modern organization aims to achieve: the generation of like-mindedness through all its members. However, the underlying contradiction will always be that this is not a natural, self-evident like-mindedness, as in Tonnies' sense, but a contrived thing, achieved through artifice, by mechanisms designed from outside and engineered for bringing employees into face-to-face contact with their co-workers. The abstract spaces of modern capitalist organizations are involved in the social production of this form of *Gesellschaft*.

Whilst Durkheim and Tonnies wrote at the turn of the nineteenth century, Elton Mayo returned to these issues of societal breakdown half way through the twentieth century. In a chapter entitled 'The seamy side of progress', he writes (Mayo 1949, p. 12; [italics in original]): '*We have in fact passed beyond that stage of human organization in which effective communication and collaboration were secured by established routines of relationship.*' Rather than blaming the extreme division of labour or the rise of the city for societal breakdown, it seemed to Mayo that 'technical advance was provocative of social chaos and anarchy' (Mayo 1949, p. 30). For him (Mayo 1949, p. 9), modern society had paid attention to the satisfaction of material and economic needs but neglected the maintenance of cooperation and communitarian values. In the Human Relations approach within organizational studies, of which Mayo, along with George Homans, Fritz Roethlisberger, and Chester Barnard, was a founder, the concept of community was very real in several senses. For one thing, in adopting an anti-Marxist position in the 1930s, they were all concerned with providing elements of a conservative response to the high levels of industrial unrest then apparent across the USA. They came to focus on shared value systems within society. So when Mayo writes of the Hawthorne experiments at the Western Electric Company, it is not with an interest in industrial efficiency per se – the original starting point of these studies. Nor is he writing with a philanthropic interest in workers' experiences and needs. What he is concerned to do is illustrate the need for the convergence of social relations within the organization for the greater good of a harmony of interests between industry and society. Indeed, even further than this, he believed that order within society as a whole is predicated upon the production of industry as a community of harmonious social relations.

Today, Mayo's view is certainly prevalent again within the contemporary project and presentation of 'organization as community', especially as enacted through organizational spaces. As an extension of Lefebvre's abstract space, and looking outwards, the modern organization today emphasizes the commonality of goals and interests between corporation and society through the presentation of 'organization as community'. This is because in this anomic society, with fast-changing economic conditions and the prospect of depression, any appeal to community resonates with the nostalgic imaginary of collective forms of social action from a 'long-lost' time, and inevitably the concept appears as positive. Corporate social responsibility, stakeholder theory, environmental issues, and 'wellness' initiatives all work to give the impression of community involvement and interest. These in combination form a unitarist approach (aided by the legal assumption, originating from the development of corporations over the centuries) that they are 'individuals', that the organization is a unified and unifying entity.

However, the spatial treatment of organizations symbolically as 'communities' obscures this individuated unification of the corporation as a legal body. Whilst they *are* corporations, they are not structured nor do they function like communities – despite the rhetoric. And whilst they rest on individualism, the chance of a moral or 'conscience collective', such as theorized by Durkheim, developing remains a chimera. Although they facilitate collective effort, the economic and power relations that organizations rest upon are fundamentally divisive. Organizations and society do not necessarily share a common functionality. They are in a relationship of *contradiction*, one that is embedded within the notion of 'organization as community'. On the one hand 'organization' is a collectivity designed for a common purpose, but on the other it is an overarching entity whose *raison d'être* is to extract individual effort in the pursuit of surplus ultimately for individual, not collective gain. All notions of wholeness, in other words, including those enacted in and through organizational spaces, obscure the power relations of capitalism vis-à-vis society as a totality. This is why it is important to recognize forms of 'abstract space' throughout society, not solely 'within' the organization. The former may also be seen in the construction of semi-privatized, semi-public spaces of consumption, such as shopping malls with their security presence; the appropriation of space by corporations through pollution or branding; and even the construction of the home through the management of organized products and services (Dale 2009).

The recent attempts in architecture and spatial design to build upon the rhetoric of 'community' draw upon a long history in social sciences which emphasizes collective effort within a harmonious context. This is unsurprising, given the renewed desire of some organizations to re-engineer their social and economic arrangements to provide working conditions and workspaces more conducive for employee commitment and productivity. However, the history of the concept of community also contains a very different strand of social theory which emphasizes that social relationships within a collectivity are subject to conflict, contestation and contradiction (for example, Campbell 1993, Crow and Maclean 2000, Farrar 2001). These concerns, which revolve around power, may be perceived in a *parallel* architecture of organization, where elements of fortification, protection, surveillance and exclusion can also be seen in built form. Within the organization, the building of 'security' rather than 'sociability' can be seen in the regulatory regimes associated with entry, exit and movement within many corporate headquarters. The dual nature of the 'transparency' and 'openness' associated with 'community' can be seen in surveillance architecture, from the original overseers' walkways perched above factory production lines, such as that at Rowntree's chocolate factory, to the modern ubiquity of camera technologies videotaping movements in entrances, hallways, and elsewhere. In the relations between the organization and its 'outside', too, architecture expresses the limits of 'community' and the contradictions of 'abstract space'. From the construction of the skyscrapers around the new Twin Towers site in New York, which express a paranoia based around fear of attack, to the Maryland Science Center, also in the US, which contrasts an openness to commerce at its front with a total closure to the local African American community at its back, where it looks like a fortress (Harvey 2000, p. 145, plate 8.9), 'organizational community' is a contradictory and ambivalent device.

In conclusion, the rise of the concept of community within architectural and design practice and rhetoric has to be seen as part of the development of communitarian idea(l)s in the last decade. In the discussions of the 'third way', which lies, according to Giddens (1998) and its other proponents, between models of 'state bureaucracy' on the one hand and 'the free market' on the other, great play is made of the necessary role of civil society and communities. Three regimes are proposed as possibilities for organizing human life: bureaucracy, market, community. Architects perhaps have not been immune to a burgeoning rhetoric of the 'third way' in which the value of 'community' to building projects becomes re-recognized. As the problems of the unfettered market became blatant, Fukuyama (1999), for example, encouraged the notion of community and the trust one finds there, arguing for its cultural benefits (see also Etzioni 1995), but placed these within the context of economic success. Shared values, experiences and norms allegedly allow capitalist enterprise to flourish. The relationship between community and economy is seen as positive, with benefits flowing in one direction – from community to economy.

However, others such as Sennett (1999) and Gorz (1999) see that relationship as a negative, corrosive one, with harmful effects flowing in the other direction. Thus, the economy within capitalist societies destroys communities and civil society. Flexibility in the workplace undermines social cohesion; it destroys trust. As Putnam (2001) argues, changes in the workplace and in the community mean that the employee goes 'bowling alone'. We should note, of course, that Fukuyama and Giddens, as well as Sennett and Gorz, see 'community' as a macro-level entity, separable from hierarchy and market. Anderson (1983) writes of the notion of 'nation' as a form of imagined community: a community not in the localized sense of people who interact with each other, but of ties among large numbers of people who do not personally know each other but are still held imaginatively as a 'deep, horizontal comradeship' (1983, p. 16).

But 'community' has become used as a meso-level notion within the corporation itself. As organizations become cast as 'imagined communities', this reaffirms the congruence of interests – the similarities of the 'insiders' – of all organizational members with the organization itself, and in comparison, the 'outside' of organizational life seems more different (Day 2006, p. 159). But it can also be argued that this move is even more powerful because it is materially as well as imaginatively constructed: it appeals to the whole embodied individual, not just relying on imaginative participation.

It is our argument, then, that the recent corporate focus upon workplace design and upon architectural 'fixes' represents an attempt to bring community into the bureaucratic hierarchy. If the communitarianism of the 'third way' sees trust and the sharing of values as important to economic activity, and if the 'corrosion of character' and 'bowling alone' theses emphasize the rediscovery of community in the face of corporate demands for flexibility, what better than for the corporation to offer 'community' from within, through its cafes, games rooms, and open office-scapes? At a stroke, that corporate architecture based on the rhetoric of community appears to offer improved productivity of the firm on one hand and a shared cooperative value system on the other. It offers, but can never entirely produce, 'all together, altogether better'.

ACKNOWLEDGEMENTS

A large number of people have shaped and shared our preoccupation with space over the years, and although we can't name them all here, we are very grateful. In this paper, we are hugely indebted to Dvora and Alfons, whom we want to thank for their work on the APROS stream for which this paper originated, their patience and concern for us when illness interrupted writing, and for the professional and painstaking care they have taken as editors, which has contributed to and improved the paper enormously.

NOTES

1. Theorists such as de Certeau (1984) and at time Lefevbre seem to hold up the city as the epitome of freedom, whilst other critics have pointed out that it is only apparent freedom, underlying which are potent inclusions and exclusions, no-go zones and prohibitions.

REFERENCES

Abercrombie, N., S. Hill and B. Turner (1984), *The Dominant Ideology Thesis,* London: HarperCollins.
Alferoff, C. and D. Knights (2003), 'We're all partying here: targets and games, or targets as games in call centre management', in A. Carr and P. Hancock (eds), *Art and Aesthetics at Work,* Basingstoke: Palgrave Macmillan, pp. 70–92.
Allen, T., A. Bell, R. Graham, B. Hardy and F. Swaffer (2004), *Working Without Walls: An Insight into the Transforming Government Workplace*, Norwich: HMSO.
Anderson, B. (1983), *Imagined Communities*, London: Verso.
Area Sq (n.d.). accessed 15 October 2008 at www.areasq.co.uk/casestudies/galileo.php.
Bauman, Z. (2001), *Community,* Cambridge: Polity.
Burrell, G. and G. Morgan (1979), *Sociological Paradigms and Organisational Analysis,* Aldershot: Ashgate.
Campbell, B. (1993), *Goliath: Britain's Dangerous Places*, London: Methuen.
Channel 4 (2005), accessed 14 June 2009, at www.channel4.com/4homes/architecture/riba-stirling-prize/riba-stirling-prize-2005/riba-stirling-prize-2005-08-06-26p1.html, page no longer available.
Clegg, S. and D. Dunkerley (1980), *Organization, Class and Control*, London: Routledge and Kegan Paul.

Cohen, A. (1985), *The Social Construction of Community*, London: Tavistock.

Costea, B., N. Crump and J. Holm (2005), 'Dionysius at work? The ethos of play and the ethos of management', *Culture and Organisation*, **11** (2), 139–51.

Crow, G. and C. Maclean (2000), 'Community', in G. Payne (ed.), *Social Divisions*, Basingstoke: Macmillan.

Dale, K. and G. Burrell (2008), *The Spaces of Organisation and the Organisation of Space: Power, Identity and Materiality at Work*, Basingstoke: Palgrave Macmillan.

Dale, K. (2005), 'Building a social materiality', *Organization*, **12** (5), 649–78.

Dale, K. (2009), 'Ideal homes? Managing the domestic dream', in P. Hancock and M. Tyler (eds), *The Management of Everyday Life*, Basingstoke: Palgrave Macmillan, pp. 127–46.

Day, G. (2006), *Community and Everyday Life,* London: Routledge.

De Certeau, M. (1984), *The Practice of Everyday Life,* Berkeley, CA: University of California Press.

DEGW (n.d.), accessed 6 June 2004 at www.degw.com.

Duffy, F. (1996), 'Architectural group to merge with consultancy', *Management Consultancy*, 13 November, accessed 30 July 2009 at www.v3.co.uk/articles/print/2076131.

Durkheim, E. (1972), *The Division of Labour*, London: Routledge and Kegan Paul.

Etzioni, A. (1995), *The Spirit of Community: Rights, Responsibilities and the Communitarian Agenda*, London: HarperCollins.

Farrar, M. (2001), *The Struggle for 'Community' in a British Multi-ethnic Inner City Area: Paradise in the Making*, Lampeter: Edwin Mellor Press.

Felstead, A., N. Jewson and S. Walters (2005), *Changing Places of Work,* Basingstoke: Palgrave Macmillan.

Fisher, R. and J. Kling (1993), *Mobilising the Community*, London: Sage.

Fukuyama, F. (1999), *The Great Disruption*, London: Profile.

Giddens, A. (1998), *The Third Way: The Renewal of Democracy*, Cambridge: Polity and Blackwell.

Gorz, A. (1999), *Reclaiming Work*, Cambridge: Polity.

Grey, C. (1994), 'Career as a project of self', *Sociology*, **28** (2), 479–97.

Grey, C. (2009), *A Very Short, Fairly Interesting and Reasonably Cheap Book About Studying Organization*, 2nd edn, London: Sage.

Hall, E. (1966), *The Hidden Dimension*, Garden City, NY: Doubleday.

Harvey, D. (1989), *The Condition of Postmodernity,* Oxford: Blackwell.

Harvey, D. (2000), *Spaces of Hope*, Edinburgh: Edinburgh University Press.

Hatch, Mary Jo (1990), 'The symbolics of office design', in Pasqual Gaglardi (ed.), *Symbols and Artifacts*, Berlin: De Gruyter, pp. 129–35.

Hillier, B. (1997), *Space is the Machine: A Configurational Theory of Architecture*, Cambridge: Cambridge University Press.

Hillier, B. and J. Hanson (1984), *The Social Logic of Space*, Cambridge: Cambridge University Press.

Hofbauer, J. (2000), 'Bodies in a landscape', in J. Hassard, R. Holliday and H. Willmott (eds), *Body and Organization*, London: Sage, pp. 166–91.

Kanter, R. M. (1977), *Men and Women of the Corporation*, New York: Basic Books.

Kotter, J. and D. Cohen (2002), *The Heart of Change: Real-life Stories of How People Change Their Organizations*, Boston, MA: Harvard Business School Press.

Lefebvre, H. [1974] (1991), *The Production of Space,* translated by D. Nicholson-Smith, Oxford: Blackwell.

Lehtonen, T-K. and P. Maenpaa (1997), 'Shopping in East Centre Mall', in P. Falk and C. Campbell (eds), *The Shopping Experience,* London: Sage.

Mayo, E. (1949), *The Social Problems of an Industrial Civilisation*, London: Routledge and Kegan Paul.

Miller, P. and N. Rose (1990), 'Governing economic life', *Economy and Society*, **19** (1), 1–31.

Muetzelfeldt, M. (2006), 'Organizational space, place and civility', in S. Clegg and M. Kornberger (eds), *Space, Organizations and Management Theory*, Oslo and Copenhagen: Liber and Copenhagen Business School Press, pp. 113–28.

Newby, H. (1987), *Country Life*, London: Sphere Books.

Nisbet, R. (1967), *The Sociological Tradition*, London: Heinemann.

Pahl, R. (1970), *Patterns of Urban Life*, London: Longman.

Pahl, R. (1996), 'Friendly society?' in S. Kraemer and J. Roberts (eds), *The Politics of Attachment*, London: Free Association Books.

Putnam, R. (2001), *Bowling Alone: The Collapse and Revival of American Community*, New York: Simon and Schuster.

Roethlisberger, F. and W. Dickson (1939), *Management and the Worker*, Cambridge, MA: Harvard University Press.

Rose, N. (1990), *Governing the Self*, London: Routledge.

Sennett, R. (1999), *The Corrosion of Character*, London: W. W. Norton.

Steele, Fritz (1983), 'The ecology of executive teams', *Organizational Dynamics*, **11** (4), 65–78.

Tonnies, F. (1963), *Community and Association*, London: Routledge.

Van Marrewijk, A. (2009), 'Corporate headquarters as physical embodiments of organizational change', *Journal of Organizational Change Management,* **22** (3), 290–306.

Warren, S. (2002), 'Creating creativity: the organizational manipulation of aesthetics in a web design department', *The Pink Machine Papers*, **9** (2), Department of Industrial Economics and Management, Royal Institute of Technology, Stockholm, accessed 24 July 2003 at http://pink-machine.com/PMP/nr9.pdf.

Willmott, H. (1993), 'Strength is ignorance; slavery is freedom: managing culture in modern organizations', *Journal of Management Studies,* **30** (4), 515–52.

Zanoni, P. and M. Janssens (2006), 'Diversity management as identity regulation in the post-Fordist productive space', in S. Clegg and M. Kornberger (eds), *Space, Organizations and Management Theory*, Oslo and Copenhagen: Liber and Copenhagen Business School Press, pp. 92–112.

2. Corridor communication, spatial design and patient safety: enacting and managing complexities

Rick Iedema, Debbi Long and Katherine Carroll

Spatial arrangement has long been seen as key to marking and structuring social interaction (Low and Lawrence-Zuñiga 2003). Central to early efforts to map practices onto spaces was the study of how and to what extent spaces were institutionally inscribed and of how boundaries between social spaces were marked and maintained (Douglas 1966). These socio-cultural descriptions of social space have since converged with political analyses of space (Lefebvre 1991), engendering interest in how 'techniques of the body' and habitus can be related to socio-political space (Bourdieu 1977). Another strand of spatial enquiry has turned to the complex relationship between space as structure and place as phenomenology (Bachelard 1964). This nexus between social space and experiential place was further pursued in the work of Hall (1966) and Goffman (1959), both of whom underscored the importance of identifying the *interactive* affordances of spatiality.

In analysing the micro-geographies of social life, Goffman proposed that spaces are experienced as being either public 'frontstages' or more private 'backstages', with both favouring different performances and different selves. Subsequent anthropological work has suggested that backstage spaces may be seen as being less inscribed with conduct regulations and institutional prerequisites than are frontstage spaces (Irvine 1979). In the case of hospitals, backstage spaces would include transit spaces such as stairwells and corridors that create connections among frontstage spaces such as consultation rooms, wards, meeting rooms, operating theatres, entrances, offices, and so forth. But connecting spaces, such as stairwells and corridors, are to some extent 'in between' or 'liminal' spaces (Turner 1957). Definitionally, liminal spaces are not inscribed with specific activities, rules of conduct or dress codes. They are 'fill-in' or 'add-on' spaces that fall outside of the geographic grid of identifiable social and organizational events, conducts and functions.

As a non-frontstage space, corridors enjoy a degree of liminality, depending on their shape and placement. Some corridors are very public spaces, of course (think of those in shopping malls), while others take on very private functions (for example, back alleys). Given their omnipresence, it is curious that social scientific scholarship has so far been rather silent with regard to corridors and their potential liminality (see for example Lefebvre 1991, Harvey 1996, Baldry 1999, Low and Lawrence-Zuñiga 2003). This scholarly silence becomes all the more intriguing when we find that the corridor plays a critical role in the life of organizations, generally, and of hospitals, specifically. It is the hospital corridor and the conducts that it affords that are the focus of the present chapter.

LIMINAL SPACE: THE CORRIDOR BULGE AS A SPATIAL RESOURCE

Corridors play an important pragmatic role in hospital life for a number of reasons. First, corridors are frequently the place where senior doctors engage in educational sessions with juniors. According to Hicks (1999, pp. 10–11), it 'could be argued that by far the greatest amount of instructional consultation takes the form of quite incidental and informal advice sought and received by colleagues in the faculty common room or the corridor'. Heard et al. note that corridor conversations are 'part of the daily discourse of hospital medicine' (Heard et al. 2003, p. 43). Noting the lack of attention paid to corridor interaction, Pearce is so convinced of the centrality of corridor communication to medical instruction that he advocates for corridor teaching to be taken into account in medical education (Pearce 2003). Arguing that 'teaching during corridor consultations is an important and integral part of general practice training' (2003, p. 47), Pearce highlights the importance of the corridor allowing discussions to target emerging issues:

> This ad hoc teaching usually occurs in response to a specific problem – a patient with a condition the registrar doesn't recognize or doesn't know how to treat. The response needs to be timely and appropriate... 'corridor teaching' [provides] an important area of learning that was underappreciated by policy setters... (Pearce 2003, p. 747)

Pearce's point about the corridor being a space where emergent issues can be dealt with anticipates, in part, our argument below.

Aside from the opportunities it offers clinicians to engage in ad hoc kinds of teaching, the corridor is regarded in the clinical literature as a space that elicits unscheduled and therefore potentially inappropriate communication. Due to a lack of formal meeting spaces in contemporary hospitals, corridors are not infrequently the sites where doctors negotiate with families over end-of-life and palliative care decisions; that is, where emotional and difficult discussions take place (Bliton 1999, pp. 11–12, Johnson et al. 2000, p. 282). Much existing research is critical of clinicians using the corridor for these important discussions. For example, Hanley (2003, p. 156) comments on the ethical and medico-legal implications of conversations being overheard in corridor space. Corridor consultations are particularly called into question because of the potential for 'documentation shortfall' (Heard et al. 2003, p. 46, Swan and Spigelman 2003, p. 580); that is, the likelihood that the informality of corridor talk will fail to translate into the formal documentation necessary for decision-making by others down the track.

In addition, corridors are a site where clinical colleagues consult with one another. In a survey of over 100 practitioners, Peleg et al. (1999, p. 241) reported that 82 per cent of their respondents 'had been asked by their colleagues to provide hallway medicine'. Shadbolt (2002) reports that '"corridor consultations" are common, with 22 per cent of respondents admitting to requesting a prescription from a work colleague' when encountering him or her in a hallway. Anderson (1999) recommends that doctor-to-doctor consultations should take place in 'optimal circumstances' – which 'is not the corridor'.

As seen, some commentators report on the corridor as a site where the complexities of contemporary care are profitably dealt with, while others regard clinicians' use of the corridor as inappropriate. And yet, in spite of being 'an integral part of physicians' medical culture', 'little is known' about corridor communication (Peleg et al. 1999, p. 241). So while there is agreement that the corridor plays a central role in clinical life, this phenomenon has not received the empirical attention it deserves from social scientists, health facility designers, or from those interested in clinical efficacy and safety.

This chapter describes how a multi-disciplinary clinical team occupies its clinical space and, in particular, its corridor. When we started to observe the practices of this clinical team in a metropolitan teaching hospital in Sydney in 2004,[1] the character of the work conversations that clinicians enacted there signalled to us that the corridor performed an important role. These conversations became possible in this corridor space, we suggest, because the team capitalized on what they probably perceived to be a 'liminal' space; that is, a space that does not embody strong indications for staff about what is to take place within it. What appears to underscore the liminal character of this clinic's corridor is its 'bulge' – a widening of the walls in part of the corridor. This bulge drew people into it, not because it harboured a pre-defined functionality, but precisely because it lacked functional definition. In it, staff were able temporarily to step away from the linearity inscribed into their clinical practice, organizational purpose and professional procedure. The 'bulging' of the usually linear corridor walls created a niche that facilitated a kind of work-related 'hanging out'. The corner space that this 'bulge' created may also have engendered a feeling of being protected, affording kinds of conversations and exchanges that otherwise would not customarily take place. The 'corridor bulge' as liminal space helped members of the spinal rehabilitation team suspend the formalities of their respective clinical status and expert professional roles.

Commonly, clinical interaction is determined by quite strictly defined professional boundaries and rules (Degeling et al. 1998), and these are rehearsed and reinforced during ward rounds, handovers, patient consults, case conferences, etc. Generally, medical clinicians limit their interactions with nursing clinicians, and both these groups limit their interactions with allied health staff (Degeling et al. 2001). In suspending these pre-determined professional boundaries and rules that would normally be enacted in more traditional and central kinds of clinical work and space, the corridor bulge elicited conversations that ignored, or actively negated and denied, these interactive norms. Staff were enabled to step outside of their normal roles and busywork trajectories and engage with work issues in a way that only an interruption to behavioural flow makes possible. This interruption, we suggest, was made possible by the excess space – the bulge – that was built into the corridor.

As a space whose social logic did not align with that of surrounding clinical spaces, the corridor bulge provided practitioners with reflective and creative or *diffractive* (Haraway 1998) opportunities. Specifically, the corridor bulge served as a conduit for the discussion of issues that could not be raised in the presence of the patient in the consult room and that did not get raised during the case conferences that occurred away from the consult rooms on different days. The niche that the bulge created provided a space at a slight remove from the ordinary flow of traffic – a kind of harbour outside of patient and staff earshot, at once private and public. In that sense, the corridor bulge provided a spatial resource for the enactment, the negotiation, and thereby the *management* of complexity. This meant, paradoxically, that the excess and seemingly *wasted* space of the corridor bulge in fact played a critical role in ensuring the safety and effectiveness of clinical practice.

To describe the interactions that took place in the corridor bulge, this chapter presents an analysis of selected corridor conversations. The data were collected as part of a video ethnography project exploring clinician identity in multidisciplinary health care teams (Iedema et al. 2006). We spent ten months observing and videoing a variety of interactions between and among team members. We started focusing on the corridor space in the clinic when it became apparent that interactions there were taken very seriously by staff. We videoed these corridor conversations to enable us as researchers to capture and replay the cross-professional dynamics that took place in this liminal space. The excerpts presented are transcripts of video footage of one particular clinic, a two-hour multidisciplinary session that occurred in 2005.

We present our study as follows. First, we provide some background about the clinical service that is under focus here. Then we turn to consider some transcript extracts obtained from the visual data that we collected in the clinic's corridor. When presenting in empirical terms how it is that the corridor bulge affords informal, dialogical and dynamic interactions, we emphasize how important these conducts are to realizing workplace and patient safety. We conclude the chapter by returning to consider the paradoxical role of liminal spaces in contemporary organizations that harbour high levels of complexity.

CASE STUDY

Background: The Outpatient Clinic

The clinical team described in this case study includes a doctor (staff specialist), nurse (clinical nurse consultant), occupational therapist, physiotherapist, dietician, social worker and peer support worker. Other specialists are on call as required: an orthopedic surgeon, a plastic surgeon, infectious diseases staff specialists, as well as junior doctors from each of these specialties (that is, doctors recently graduated from university and with one or two years of full-time in-hospital work experience).

The team members come together in an outpatient clinic in a hospital setting every fortnight. They normally see three or four patients during any one of these clinics. Due to the type of care offered in the clinic (often involving multiple clinicians) and the special needs of the clinic's patient population (special transport; the protracted and complex nature of their chronic care), all patient appointments are booked for the same time, 10.00 a.m. The clinic is scheduled to finish at 12.00 noon; however, it rarely does, and it is not unusual for clinicians still to be consulting with patients well after 1.00 p.m.

Also present during the clinic are at least one, but often two nurses who are based in the outpatient clinic and who assist the multidisciplinary team with patient organization, follow-up appointment scheduling, specialist appointment booking, test ordering and wound dressing. There are other outpatient clinics running in the hospital simultaneously, and nurses from those other clinics come through the corridor of this clinic to get equipment for their own clinics or to help out if this clinic is busy and theirs is slow. The clinic's outpatient nurses most normally liaise with the team's clinical nurse consultant;

however, they occasionally also liaise directly with other team members. Similarly, the on-call specialists (surgeons and infectious diseases specialists) most normally liaise with the team's staff specialist; however, they also occasionally liaise directly with other team members.

Apart from their bi-monthly meeting in the actual outpatient clinic, clinicians meet as a team once a month for a case management and team meeting and at other times, as required, for teleconferences with community and/or rural general practitioners (GPs), specialists or social workers. The core members of the team– the doctor, physiotherapist and occupational therapist – have been working together in various capacities for a number of years. The other clinicians had joined the team within the year prior to our study. Most team members work with other members of the team in other capacities as well: seeing inpatients on the ward, working in rehabilitation or working in other multidisciplinary clinics.

The doctor and nurse have their offices in the same place, in the offices of the unit specialty. Allied health team members have offices in their professional units (that is, the dietician in the dietetics department, the physiotherapist in the physiotherapy department, etc.). Two implications follow from this: structurally, the only times all team members are together are during the fortnightly clinics and the monthly team meetings; and spatially, some people have more access to others in the daily course of their work. For example, the physiotherapy and occupational therapy departments are next to each other, as are the social work and dietetics departments. But all four of these departments are on different floors from the unit specialty's offices, where the spinal rehabilitation staff specialist and clinical nurse consultant (a senior nurse) are based. This means that some members of the team are more likely than others to encounter one another without having to schedule formal appointments, something conducive to case-oriented problem solving.

Figure 2.1 shows the layout of the clinic space. The totality of this space is comprised of three patient consultation rooms, a small office, a storeroom (for storing medical supplies) and a pan room (for storing bed pans), all of them off a corridor which links this area to the rest of the hospital. Lacking in furnishings, the space further has two mobile trolleys that carry files and medical supplies. Conversations most frequently take place in the corridor bulge between the procedures room and the office, where the otherwise straight lines of the corridor widen somewhat in an irregular pattern.

In the next section we analyse selected transcripts of corridor talk, chosen because they highlight different aspects of what becomes possible in liminal spaces such as the corridor bulge.

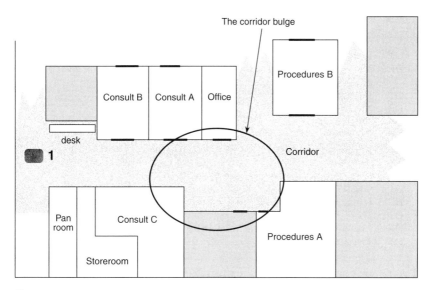

Source: Long, Iedema et al (2007).

Figure 2.1   The clinic's rooms, corridor, and the corridor bulge (solid grey spaces are rooms that do not belong to the clinic). Number 1 marks the desk at the end of the corridor

The Complexity of Corridor Work

The first extract shows how the clinicians are sharing information that has just come to hand. One of their patients, E, is sick again. He was admitted to the Intensive Care Unit (ICU), and has had a number of tests. Being on a particular treatment regimen, he has to stay in the ICU. In the discussion that follows, the doctor remarks that it might be worth checking whether patient E is on an appropriate mattress, one that changes shape to avoid patients getting bedsores. Most critically, the doctor hints at the difficulty the Occupational Therapist (OT) may experience trying to make sure the patient is on an appropriate mattress. Implicitly touching on inter-specialty tensions, the doctor prepares the OT for the possibility that ICU staff may object to the OT telling them to use a special-purpose mattress.

Excerpt 1
(OT = occupational therapist; DR = doctor)

> DR   [Patient E] is back in intensive care ... [*explains tests that he has ordered*]
> OT   Great.

DR   He's still on ionotropes and still in intensive care, but the only other thing I could think of is it might be worth swinging by there and just checking what mattress he's on.

OT   In intensive care?

DR   Yeah. [*Makes comment about how important it is to provide good pressure relief in intensive care, to avoid pressure sores*]

OT   I heard he was coming back up to the ward today?

DR   No way.

OT   That's not true?

DR   [*Shaking his head – makes comment that patient can't come to ward while still needing ionotropes: he needs to stay in the intensive care unit for that*]

OT   What's ionotropes?

DR   It's something to keep your heart going.

OT   OK, so we need to swap the mattress again …

DR   I think we should get him on to one of ours, if we can, [name OT].

OT   That's fine.

DR   I know that's an easy thing to say but a hard thing to do ...

OT   That's fine.

Two issues stand out in this first extract. First, the doctor is able to communicate an instruction to the occupational therapist: 'Go check on patient E's mattress in ICU and get it changed if it is not appropriate.' Patient E is not currently in the clinic, and so not only is this discussion additional to the work currently going on in the clinic, there is nothing in that work to precipitate that particular conversation. We cannot be certain, of course, about what prompted this exchange, but it is possible that finding himself with the OT in the spatial margins of the existing workflow created the opportunity for the doctor to think of patient E in the first place.

Secondly, the allied health professional (the OT) asks the doctor a technical question – 'What's ionotropes?' In asking this question, the OT signals that she is not afraid to be heard as being ignorant or as unduly taking up the doctor's time. In a more ordinary setting, such interdisciplinary exchange would not be common. Professional hierarchies and struggles that define the contemporary hospital (Strauss et al. 1963) would typically make such an admission of ignorance risky and therefore unlikely. Again, their spatial location in the corridor bulge may play a role in making this exchange possible, as it places the clinicians in liminal space – space that is at a remove from more customary interactive space where traditional norms and conducts would prevail. Figure 2.2, taken from the videotape of this exchange, shows the doctor speaking with the OT, with the junior doctor and nurse listening in.

The second extract offers further insight into the interactive affordances of the corridor bulge. Here, besides admitting he does not know what is the matter with a patient, the doctor acknowledges that he should not have made a particular comment in front of the patient and the clinical team.

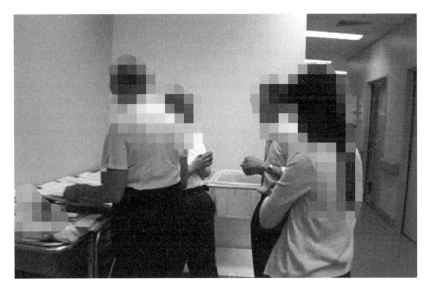

Source: Long, Iedema et al. (2007). Footage shot by Debbi Long.

Figure 2.2   Doctor talking to the clinical nurse consultant in the corridor bulge, with another nurse and junior doctor standing by

Excerpt 2
(DR = doctor; CNC = clinical nurse consultant)

DR   Once [name OT] gets out we need to pow-wow about [patient F], I'm not convinced we have a full [picture] ... And he's had a year of [treatment], and it's still in this situation ... so I think we need to look at ... if there's another way we can break that ... there's something going on here that's not allowing him to move forward. It may be cognitive as well.

CNC   I know, it may be related to the depression.

DR   Yeah, well, did you see what he did, what his behaviour was when I mentioned that? [*CNC grimaces and covers eyes with hand*] I was thinking, 'I shouldn't have said this'.

CNC   No. Maybe it would have been different if it was just you there... [*The procedures room had a large number of clinicians with the patient at the time*]

DR   Let's have a talk about it, and then we can decide whether I go back in and talk to him again. If we feel strongly that it's worth pushing for an antidepressant, then I'll sit down in there with him for as long as it takes and see if I can convince him, because there's something that's stopping this man moving forward and I just don't know what it is.

This extract highlights two important issues. When the doctor says, 'I was thinking "I shouldn't have said this" ', he is admitting to the nurse that his behaviour in the patient consult room may have been inappropriate. Thanks to his 'reflection-in-action' when addressing the patient (Yanow and Tsoukas 2009), he was able to recognize his error when the patient responded negatively to his mentioning the issue of depression in front of the whole team. At a remove from that consult situation, the corridor bulge allows the doctor to connect this moment of 'reflection-in-action' to a publicly-shared moment of post hoc 'reflection-on-action' (Schön 1983). Likewise, the doctor and the nurse can debrief about issues and reflect on their practice in ways that more formal engagements would not readily permit because those spaces inscribe expected conducts and customary hierarchical relationships on the parties involved. Again, we propose that these moments of non-traditional exchange became possible because the clinicians were able to step away from the ongoing workflow into the reflexive space of the corridor bulge.

In our third and final transcript, another aspect of how interaction is enabled by taking place in a liminal space becomes apparent. Here, we witness the clinicians being 'heedful' (Weick and Roberts 1993) to one another's gown-tying while discussing a clinical case.

Excerpt 3
(DR = doctor; OT = occupational therapist; CNC = clinical nurse consultant):

DR	[He has to not] sit up so much. He's sitting up for six to eight hours.
OT	How is the pressure area?
DR	It's a grade one area [*Indicating size with fingers*], but he's got no fat over his IT [ischial tuberosity] area, so he's going to have to be another couple of weeks off it, just to finish it off.
OT	But he hasn't ... [*Tying apron around front*]
CNC	[*Reaching hand in OT's direction*] Don't tie it around the front
DR	Yeah [*Reaching hand out, smiling*], I can't do the back tie.
OT	[*Ties apron around her back on her own*] He hasn't agreed to ... um … any equipment or anything. He's not on a mattress, or anything. [*Looking at CNC*] He's just on his own bed.
DR	I'm not sure what's happening.
CNC	I can't remember.

Critical issues in this third extract include the following. First, the clinicians are discussing a clinical case while at the same time being attentive to how they tie their protective gowns. The nurse warns the occupational therapist that her gown should not be tied round the front (the tie ends may dangle into infected areas and thereby pick up and spread infections). The doctor sees this and remembers that he, too, was recently warned against tying his gown at the front: 'Yeah, I can't do the back tie.' In this exchange, then, different things happen simultaneously. They are discussing a patient's pressure sore and mattress, and they pay attention to each other's infection-control behaviour.

Infection control is critical in this spinal clinic due to the infection-prone pressure wounds that patients get from lying still for too long. If clinicians have the opportunity to remind each other about infection-control measures, the complexity of how the clinical work and infection control intersect may be alleviated (Iedema and Rhodes 2010).

Another important feature of this exchange is that the clinicians express uncertainty about a patient's condition. More than this, they admit to having forgotten some critical issues (CNC: 'I can't remember'). While these conducts are, of course, not unthinkable in other kinds of clinical meetings and interactions, their co-occurrence in the corridor bulge leads us to suggest that this spatial arrangement plays a role in facilitating such insights, reflections and confessions. An earlier study that we carried out across an entire hospital suggested that clinicians' modes of talk are generally quite routinized and restricted to professional and specialty concerns (Iedema et al. 1999). In the present case, stepping out of the flow of the work into neighbouring space may enable clinicians to be more open to or mindful of what is going on. Indeed, in what follows we suggest that this stepping out into the corridor bulge short-circuits the team's post hoc 'reflection-on-action' and their in situ 'reflection-in-action' (Yanow and Tsoukas 2009).

The Role of Liminal Space in Clinical Work: Discussion and Implications

What we see in analysing the interactions captured in this clinic's corridor bulge is that it has a special affordance. The corridor bulge provides a space where, for this team at least, professional boundaries and organizational rules can be suspended. The corridor bulge allows the occupational therapist to interrupt the doctor; the CNC to advise the doctor, her professional superior, according to medical custom, on appropriate infection control; the doctor to express regret about something he said in front of a patient and the team; and everyone to express uncertainty and ignorance without needing to fear scrutiny or rejection. In that regard, the corridor bulge allows competing definitions of particular medical situations to co-exist. We see this in Excerpt 3 for example, where clinicians display different understandings about what has happened to the patient in the ICU. It also affords explanations that can be contingent, contradictory, or both. This is apparent in Excerpt 2, where the doctor and the nurse are exploring explanations for why the patient is not responding well to treatment.

The corridor bulge makes these complex discussions possible, we suggest, because it is a 'liminal' space. It frees clinicians from the expectations inscribed into the rest of the clinic, where the spatial interpellation of conduct is stronger and more focused: the patient consult room where the team consults with patients and family members; the office where clinicians make work-related phone calls and file their paperwork; the front desk where visitors are received and directed to their destinations. The corridor bulge, in contrast, lacks functional specification. It enables the clinicians to position themselves momentarily as 'outsiders' to their own workflows. This creates the possibility for clinicians to confront and reflect on their work from a perspective that has 'room', literally and figuratively, for the various uncertainties and contradictions that form integral and inescapable parts of clinical work, but that usually remain unexpressed in such cross-specialization exchanges. In that regard, the corridor bulge offers a spatial resource for dealing with workplace complexity.

These conclusions have critical implications for patient safety as well as for health facility design. Patient safety research tends to target 'gaps in knowledge' and articulate 'best practice' guidelines (Runciman et al. 2007). The central aim of this research is to prescribe what has been proven to work and proscribe everything else, on the view that practice can be wholly and comprehensively pre-determined. No space (pun intended) is left for those dimensions of practice that come into play when clinicians need to connect formal knowledge to the complexity of in situ work, or even when they have insufficient or no knowledge about what is happening and need to work out what to do. The data presented above, in contrast, show clinicians negotiating the complexities of practice when withdrawing from its flow and initiating ad hoc, unplanned, informal and creative behaviours. The analysis of their exchanges in the corridor bulge makes clear that, rather than using the space to carry on about matters that are immaterial to patient care, thereby wasting time (NHS Institute for Innovation and Improvement 2007), clinicians are enabled by that very space to address clinical complexities in important and creative ways by placing themselves at a minimal remove from the flow of care as facilitated by the bulge.

With regard to existing health facility design and the guidelines that govern it, the trend has been to move away from allowing excess or 'unnecessary' space in health facilities (New South Wales Health Department 1993). In contrast, general architectural thinking has begun to explore the potential of spaces to nurture complex interactions in the form of 'heterogeneous communication' (Rosen et al. 1990). Contemporary architecture encourages heterogeneous communication through an 'absence of building' (in architect Rem Koolhaas' words, quoted in Kornberger and Clegg 2004, p. 1106). Such thinking recognizes that heterogeneous communication offers enterprises important creative potential, something that spatial design can enable. In using such 'interaction-promoting design' (Allen 1977), architectural thinkers and designers have begun to move beyond focusing on the 'objective' dimensions of space (shapes, sizes, heights) to also take into account the interactive affordances of space (Kornberger and Clegg 2004). But while new ways of reasoning about space and process are emerging (Thrift 2004), clear connections between spatial design and in situ interactive processes remain elusive, beyond the idea that spatial openness allows for unplanned interactions that may engage workers in achieving creative solutions for complex problems.

While the connection between generative space and heterogeneous communication has now found strong support in the commercial sphere, it remains under-researched in the context of technological and clinical complexity such as is typical of hospital work. This may be because contemporary hospital design is in the first instance oriented towards accommodating the demands of high-technology medicine (Verderber and Fine 2000), bypassing the implications of spatial design for how clinicians operate in an environment of constantly changing patients, technologies, team configurations and information – that is, situations fraught with ambiguities and uncertainties, as the three excerpts illustrate. It is in the interest of patient safety, however, that health facility design should take account of clinical complexity and of how clinicians confront and negotiate that complexity. The spatial principle presented here may well offer an important clue to how design can accommodate that which clinicians find most challenging: understanding and resolving the complexities that are inherent in their everyday work.

Acting in the 'margins of formal spaces' provides relief from the ongoing flow of work and at least some of the power dynamics that go with it. By allowing people to mingle and linger, spaces such as the corridor bulge make possible a convergence of dynamic physical movements created by spatial design and ad hoc, reflective negotiation of complex practice issues. Such space in effect engenders a kind of attention that differs from in situ 'reflection-in-action' that accompanies and contextualizes proceduralized work, and from post hoc 'reflection-on-action' that is retrospective and cerebral. The special affordance of the bulge, we contend, emerges from how it enables clinicians to straddle being at once outside and inside of what they are doing. This 'being-in-and-out' traverses the past, the present, *and* the future of clinical decision-making and treatment trajectories, producing a meta-perspective on the weave of clinicians' own and their colleagues' actions, and on the trajectories that these actions potentially inhabit (Iedema et al. 2009). The bulge's lack of functional definition, its spatial excess, and therefore its liminality, then, position clinicians in different places at the same time, both outside and inside the flow of action. It is here, in this 'reflection-on/in-action', that we locate the essence of practiced safety (Gherardi and Nicolini 2002).

Finally, this point harbours another important implication. The argument that excess space affords 'reflection-on/in-action' is particularly relevant for complex organizations. 'Reflection-on/in-action' closely intertwines with how work processes unfold, and this renders the special affordance of excess space critical to how clinicians handle and manage complexity. Given that complexity in health care is not going to go away, and given that training clinical professionals in how to negotiate complexity is challenging, such a spatial solution may come at a critical time.

While excess complexity is certainly detrimental to effective practice and to clinical safety, our analysis suggests that we do not need to regard all aspects of complexity as per definition disabling (as argued by Vincent and Wears 2002) or as needing to be tamed (Woods et al. 2007). If 'excess' – unusual, design-wise, even 'inefficient' – space can encourage 'reflection-on/in-action', spatial design may strategically be able to affect clinicians' negotiations, understandings and insights regarding the safety and effectiveness of their own practices.

CONCLUSION

Due to growing patient numbers, static hospital budgets, multiplex chronic disease and medical technologization, the twenty-first century will witness a rapid rise in the complexity of clinical care. Hospital work can no longer be regarded as reducible to or as simply encompassing set procedures and pre-planned routines facilitated by IT and other technologies. Instead, hospital work now encompasses intricate and emergent networks of clinicians, drawing on an astonishing range of doctors, nurses, allied health staff, pathology scientists and experts controlling constantly diversifying specialties and technologies. These clinicians deal with cohorts of patients whom they share (not always happily) with their colleagues across a range of medical disciplines and knowledge, and who, therefore, transition through intricate and dynamically organized service arrangements. The design of existing hospitals and hospital procedures has begun to move on from being based purely on static, hierarchical and discipline-independent definitions of medical-clinical work. However, these intricacies of contemporary clinical practice inform the design of future hospitals only in limited ways (Verderber and Fine 2000).

The increasing complexity of care, we suggest, renders liminal spaces central to enabling clinicians to engage in meta-perspectival kinds of clinical communication and dialogue (Iedema et al. 2009). As we have shown in this chapter, this safety work appears to be engendered in liminal space. Liminal space affords complex, emergent kinds of decision-making that effectively also nurture teams' collective competence (Boreham et al. 2000). For too long now, health facility designers, patient safety scientists and health organizational theorists have taken a mechanistic view of how design contributes to making clinical work safe. Instead, we need to acknowledge that clinical complexity requires interactive complexity to be harnessed rather than designed out of clinical care. We contend that if clinicians are provided with spatial configurations that enable them to do their work *and* put themselves at one or more removes from it, their dependence on mechanistic work process solutions will recede, their attentiveness to safety challenges will increase, their ability to handle complexity will be enhanced, and their capacity for enacting safety into being in the present will strengthen.

NOTES

1. This research is part of an Australian Research Council Discovery grant (DP0450773; 2004–06) with Rick Iedema as Principal Chief Investigator. Debbi Long was the project's Senior Research Fellow and Dr Katherine Carroll the PhD candidate.

REFERENCES

Allen, Thomas (1977), *Managing the Flow of Technology*, Cambridge, MA: MIT Press.

Anderson, Walter (1999), 'Doctoring doctors', *British Medical Journal*, **319** (July 31).

Bachelard, Gaston (1964), *The Poetics of Space*, translated by Maria Jolas, Boston, MA: Beacon Press.

Baldry, Chris (1999), 'Space – the final frontier', *Sociology*, **33** (3), 535–53.

Bliton, Mark (1999), 'Ethics talk, talking ethics: an example of clinical ethics consultation', *Human Studies*, **22** (1), 7–24.

Boreham, Nick, C.E. Shea and Kevin Mackway-Jones (2000), 'Clinical risk and collective competence in the hospital emergency department in the UK', *Social Science & Medicine*, **51**, 83–91.

Bourdieu, Pierre (1977), *Outline of a Theory of Practice,* Cambridge: University of Cambridge Press.

Degeling, Pieter, Michael Hill and John Kennedy (2001), 'Mediating the cultural boundaries between medicine, nursing and management – the central challenge in hospital reform', *Health Services Management Research*, **14** (1), 36–48.

Degeling, Pieter, John Kennedy and Michael Hill (1998), 'Do professional sub-cultures set the limits of hospital reform?', *Clinician in Management*, **7** (2), 89–98.

Douglas, Mary (1966), *Purity and Danger: An Analysis of Concepts of Pollution and Taboo*, London: Routledge & Kegan Paul.

Gherardi, Silvia and Davide Nicolini (2002), 'Learning the trade: a culture of safety in practice', *Organization*, **9** (2), 191–223.

Goffman, Erving (1959), *The Presentation of Self in Everyday Life*, Harmondsworth: Pelican.

Hall, Edward T. (1966), *The Hidden Dimension*, New York: Doubleday.

Hanley, John (2003), 'Ignorance of the law excuses no man', *Directions in Psychiatry*, **23**, 151–58.

Haraway, Donna (1998), 'The persistence of vision', in Nicholas Mirzoeff (ed.), *The Visual Culture Reader*, London: Routledge, pp. 191–8.

Harvey, David (1996), *Justice, Nature and the Geography of Difference*, Oxford: Blackwell.

Heard, S.R., C. Roberts, S.J. Furrows, M. Kelsey and L. Southgate (2003), 'Corridor consultations and the medical microbiological record: is patient safety at risk?', *Journal of Clinical Pathology*, **56**, 43–7.

Hicks, Owen (1999), 'A conceptual framework for instructional consultation', *New Directions for Teaching and Learning*, **79**, 9–18.

Iedema, Rick, Pieter Degeling and Les White (1999), 'Professionalism and organizational change', in Ruth Wodak and Christoph Ludwig (eds), *Challenges in a Changing World: Issues in Critical Discourse Analysis*, Vienna: Passagen Verlag, pp. 127–55.

Iedema, Rick, Debbi Long, Rowena Forsyth and Bonne Lee (2006), 'Visibilizing clinical work: video ethnography in the contemporary hospital', *Health Sociology Review*, **15** (2), 156–68.

Iedema, Rick, Eamon Merrick, Dorrilyn Rajbhandari, Alan Gardo, Ann Stirling and Robert Herkes (2009), 'Viewing the taken-for-granted from under a different aspect: a video-based method in pursuit of patient safety', *International Journal for Multiple Research Approaches*, **3** (3), 290–301.

Iedema, Rick, and Carl Rhodes (2010), 'An ethics of mutual care in organizational surveillance', *Organization Studies*, **31** (2), 199–217.

Irvine, Judith (1979), 'Formality and informality in communicative events', *American Anthropologist*, **81** (4), 773–90.

Johnson, Nancy, Deborah Cook, Mitta Giacomini and Dennis Williams (2000), 'Towards a "good" death: end-of-life narratives constructed in an intensive care unit', *Culture, Medicine & Psychiatry*, **24**, 275–95.

Kornberger, Martin and Stewart Clegg (2004), 'Bringing space back in: organizing the generative building', *Organization Studies*, **25** (7), 1095–115.

Lefebvre, Henri (1991), *The Production of Space*, translated by D. Nicholson-Smith, London: Blackwell.

Long, Debbi, Rick Iedema et al. (2007), 'Corridor conversations: clinical communication in casual spaces', in Rick Iedema (ed.), *Discourses of Hospital Communication: Tracing Complexities in Contemporary Health Organizations*, Basingstoke, Palgrave Macmillan, pp. 182–200.

Low, Setha M. and Denise Lawrence-Zuñiga (2003), *The Anthropology of Space and Place: Locating Culture*, Oxford: Blackwell.

New South Wales Health Department (1993), *Process of Facility Planning Manual,* prepared by Capital Works Branch, Sydney, VIC: Government Printing Service.

NHS Institute for Innovation and Improvement (2007), *Going Lean in the NHS*, Warwick: NHS Institute for Innovation and Improvement.

Pearce, Chris (2003), 'Corridor teaching: "Have you got a minute ...?"', *Australian Family Physician*, **32** (9), 745–7.

Peleg, Aya, Roni Peleg, Avi Porath and Yael Horowitz (1999), 'Hallway medicine: prevalence, characteristics and attitudes of hospital physicicans', *Israeli Medical Association Journal*, **1** (4), 241–4.

Rosen, Michael, Wanda Orlikowski and Kay Schmahmann (1990), 'Building buildings and saving lives: a critique of bureaucracy, ideology and concrete artifacts', in P. Gagliardi (ed.), *Symbols and Artifacts*, Berlin: de Gruyter, pp. 69–84.

Runciman, William, Allan Merry and Merrilyn Walton (2007), *Safety and Ethics in Health Care*, Aldershot: Ashgate.

Schön, Donald (1983), *The Reflective Practitioner: How Professionals Think in Action,* New York: Basic Books.

Shadbolt, Narelle (2002), 'Attitudes to healthcare and self-care among junior medical officers: a preliminary report', *Medical Journal of Australia*, **177**, S19–20.

Strauss, Anselm, L. Schatzman, D. Ehrlich, R. Bucher and M. Sabshin (1963), 'The hospital and its negotiated order', in E. Freidson (ed.), *The Hospital in Modern Society*, New York: Free Press of Glencoe, pp. 147–69.

Swan, Judith and Allan Spigelman (2003), 'Audit of surgeon awareness of readmissions with venous thrombo-embolism', *Internal Medicine Journal*, **33** (12), 578–80.

Thrift, Nigel (2004), 'Movement-space: the changing domain of thinking resulting from the development of new kinds of spatial awareness', *Economy and Society*, **33** (4), 582–604.

Turner, Victor W. (1957), *Schism and Continuity in African Society*, Manchester: Manchester University Press.

Verderber, Stephen and David J. Fine (2000), *Healthcare Architecture in an Era of Radical Transformation,* New Haven, CT: Yale University Press.

Vincent, Charles and Robert L. Wears (2002), 'Communication in the emergency department: separating the signal from the noise', *Medical Journal of Australia*, **176** (May), 409–10.

Weick, Karl and Karlene H. Roberts (1993), 'Collective mind in organizations: heedful interrelating on flight decks', *Administrative Science Quarterly*, **38**, 357–381.

Woods, David D., Emily S. Patterson and Richard I. Cook (2007), 'Behind human error: taming complexity to improve patient safety', in Pascale Carayon (ed.), *Handbook of Human Factors and Ergonomics in Health Care and Patient Safety*, Mahwah, NJ: Lawrence Erlbaum, pp. 459–76.

Yanow, Dvora and Haridimos Tsoukas (2009), 'What is reflection-in-action? A phenomenological account', *Journal of Management Studies*, **46** (8), 1339–64.

3. Bendable bars in a Dutch prison: a creative place in a non-creative space

Patrick Kenis, Peter M. Kruyen and Joan M.J. Baaijens

Traditionally, prisons are unbendable, non-creative places. Because security is their primary function, they are designed to be predictable, and both prisoners' and officers' behaviour is standardized (Kommer 1991). In a pilot project, policy-makers and engineers of the Dutch Ministry of Justice designed both the physical space and social structure of the prison with these priorities in mind. As the chapter concerns a politically sensitive project, we have chosen to keep the name of the prison anonymous. In what follows we will call the prison 'P'. It was the purpose of this pilot to standardize the work processes of the officers even more than they typically are in existing Dutch prisons. However, the officers and supervisor in Prison P reconstructed the social structure and physical space in a way that encouraged considerable team creativity for the officers. This chapter chronicles this evolution.

In the first section we introduce Prison P as it was originally conceived and designed by policy-makers and engineers. Next, we introduce the methods we used to study the prison. Then, based on the data we collected and analysed, we demonstrate how the new design enabled the development of creativity in this setting. We conclude by discussing the implications of our findings for understanding creativity in organizations, while also presenting some limitations of our study and directions for future research.

SPACE AND BEHAVIOURAL CONTROL: THE RESEARCH SETTING

The idea that a dialectical relationship exists between a type of space and the behaviour of individuals within that space is generally accepted (for example, Hernes et al. 2006). Prison spaces are, generally speaking, designed in such a way that the control of inmates' behaviours and the security of the officers are maximized. The design principle that most clearly reflects this idea is that of the panopticon, which dates back to 1787. At that time Jeremy Bentham (1787

[1995]) introduced the panopticon as his plan for a centrally located semi-circular prison, designed to keep each prisoner under constant surveillance from a central location.

Foucault (1975) discusses the idea of the panopticon extensively in his work about punishment and discipline. According to Foucault, the rationale underlying the physical form of prison space is, in the first place, to enable social discipline. The creativity literature (for example, Anderson 1989, Amabile 1996, Amabile et al. 2002, Anderson and Gasteiger 2007) suggests that it is unlikely to expect creative behaviour in such settings. Creativity is linked to degrees of freedom that enable people to connect freely to others in non-axiomatic and non-constrained ways. In a prison this type of behaviour is as unlikely to take place among officers as it is among inmates. The conditions present in a prison are expected to be non-conducive to creativity.

This is in contrast with a Professional Service Organization (PSO) which is generally characterized on six dimensions (Mills et al. 1983): a client-organization interface, colleague consultancy, colleague authority,[1] coordinating and facilitating management, structural decomposition, and flexible and creative-focused employees capable of intellectual analysis. The term PSO is often applied to work systems in which the work of professionals – doctors, lawyers and accountants – is coordinated (Mills et al. 1983), and it is these kinds of work systems which generally are more conducive to creative behaviour. We mention PSOs here because, as we will see later, Prison P developed, much to our surprise, into a setting similar to a PSO. This is all the more surprising as prison officers are not considered professionals in the classical sense, because they do not possess the institutional and behavioural characteristics that usually define professionals (see Hall 1968, Mills et al. 1983, Fogarty and Dirsmith 2001). For example, they do not follow a long-term educational programme, they are given little autonomy, and they do not hold a unique body of knowledge and skills that have to be applied in flexible and creative ways. How and why Prison P nevertheless developed as a creative space is part of the focus of this paper.

Like all prisons, Dutch prison organizations are commonly built on an internal coercive principle. Prisoners are kept under control through the use of physical power, which is legitimized by the state and the implied legal order. The unique consequence of this phenomenon, as compared to other organizations, is that the majority of organizational 'clients' – the inmates – have a very negative attitude towards the organization (the prison) and its formal members (officers and managers). This attitude and the coercive principal that brings it about are fundamental characteristics of this type of organization. Therefore, organizational designers and planners have to take steps to make the organization inhabitable for its employees – staff and management – as much as for the prisoners.

Based on this fundamental coercive principle, the common structural form of the conventional prison is a kind of mechanistic bureaucracy (Burns and Stalker 1961). This means, among other things, a strong accent on hierarchical authority, hierarchical supervision, task specialization (technocratic division of labour), and the elaboration of procedures for work. In the case of prisons, the need for this bureaucratic structural design originates from its coercive control requirements and the balance of power that is permanently at stake. In addition to this structural design feature, prisons place a strong accent on safety for all their inhabitants, employees as well as prisoners. What seems, however, somewhat specific to Dutch prisons compared to other prison systems is the attention to individual interactions between prisoners and officers (Kommer 1991). This includes, for example, officers helping prisoners with practical problems, making small talk with them, and pacifying them when aggressive behaviours arise. These interactions can be interpreted as a form of social service provided to the prisoner. In a more ideological sense this third set of practices stems from two considerations: first, the desire for resocialization of the prisoner to everyday life; and second, a desire for the social re-integration of the prisoner into society.

In 2005, policy-makers from the Dutch Ministry of Justice, in close collaboration with an ICT consultancy firm (Geijn Partners BV 2006), developed Prison P, which was intended to be a pilot prison embedded within a traditional Dutch prison facility (what later will be referred to as the 'mother organization'). The design of Prison P was initiated by a coalition within the Ministry of Justice, which could be called a mechanical-judicial coalition. P was scheduled to open by 2006 (Dutch House of Parliament 2005–06) as a short-term facility (for up to four months' sentencing) for male prisoners. The intention was for P to be a customary prison space for 150 inmates, staffed with one team of 15 officers and one supervisor.

The space was designed so that the behaviours of both inmates and officers could be closely monitored (Dutch House of Parliament 2006–07). The architectural design innovation of Prison P was to have the officers' core duty be to monitor prisoners and their activities (like work, eating, rest and exercise) from afar, through the use of electronic information technology devices which had been developed by the ICT consultancy firm. This meant that the officers would be required to give up their customary social role. In P, officers were directed to remain aloof from the prisoners and avoid direct contact. Due to this different task structure and officers' restricted responsibilities, it was theorized that fewer officers would be needed to run the prison system. Efficient treatment and focused control would now be the main elements of the new prison organization, along with the monitoring of and concentration on groups of prisoners, rather than on individuals, as discussed below.

This new arrangement was implemented via design principles that had an impact on four features of the prison: the physical building, the technical reporting and monitoring system, a behaviourist approach to the prisoners, and standardized work processes.

Physical Building

In the physical building of Prison P, three design elements were implemented to facilitate monitoring: the panopticon, group cells, and the absence of a team room for the officers' use.

Prison P was designed as a panopticon, 'the all-seeing place', a physical form constructed to enable social discipline (see Foucault 1975). Officers in Prison P were instructed to sit in a control post separated from the inmates by a glass wall. From this central post, officers could observe the entire building: the common areas (central hall, sports room, education room and library); all cell doors; the airing yard; the outdoor sports field; and, via a camera system, the blind spots in the building. The glass wall worked in two directions, however: in addition to contributing to central monitoring of prisoners' behaviours, it also controlled officers' acts, preventing them, for instance, from reverting to their familiar person-oriented approach, such as making small talk with prisoners and circulating freely among the prisoners. In these ways, the panopticon governed the behaviour of the prisoners as well as that of the officers. The panoptic principle fit the control regime very well, especially when combined with electronic monitoring devices, such as the electronic wrist band that each inmate in P received to track his exact position at all times.

A second prison building design feature, intended to facilitate monitoring, was to put six prisoners together in one cell instead of the more common Dutch prison practice of having one prisoner per cell. The designers and policy-makers gave three reasons for this choice. First, group cells would lower the average cost per prisoner per square metre. Next, fewer officers would be needed because of a social 'economies of scale' effect, in which prisoners would enact more self-regulating (or self-help) behaviour. Instead of the traditional practice of prisoners asking officers questions all the time (for example, about visitor regulations, doctor requests, the functioning of the bonus system, etc.; Kommer 1991), prisoners would now consult each other. Third, if they were in a group cell, inmates could be expected to socialize within the group and, given group social pressures, behave appropriately and hygienically. Under such circumstances no officer would be needed to stimulate proper behaviour.

The third new design choice for the physical building was to eliminate the separate employee team room. This is in strong contrast to other Dutch prisons. Designers and policy-makers reasoned that the standardization of processes would eliminate the need for prison officers to sit together and consult with one another. Moreover, policy-makers wanted to optimize work schedules by eliminating time for drinking coffee, playing cards and reading newspapers in the team room, common behaviours in other prisons.

Technical Reporting and Monitoring

In addition to physical design elements, the second design pillar put in place in Prison P was a technical reporting and monitoring system. As noted above, prisoners wore electronic wristbands for tracking and tracing. Moreover, some cells and common rooms were equipped with aggression detectors. These electronic devices were activated by excessive noise from the human voice, such as screaming and yelling. When the devices detected excessive noise, officers were alerted. Furthermore, officers had their own handheld computers containing personal information about every inmate in P. These technical arrangements were intended to make monitoring prisoners easier for the officers. As a consequence, policy-makers and designers assumed that fewer officers would be needed, without this staffing decrease posing any threat to both prisoner and officer safety.

Behaviourist Approach

Increasing prisoner self-responsibility was the goal of the third design pillar – a behaviourist approach to treating prisoners. First, each inmate had a touch screen affixed to his bed. This screen allowed inmates to watch television, make phone calls and order goods from the shop (such as food, magazines and tobacco). This is in contrast to regular prisons, where prisoners have to consult an officer in order to buy goods. Furthermore, by touching this screen, prisoners had to plan their own daily activities in advance. Some activities, like cleaning their cells and educational pursuits, were mandatory. Others, such as sports and spiritual aid, were voluntary. Making the prisoners accountable for their own daily schedule was expected not only to increase prisoners' self-responsibility but also to save officers' time.

Inmates who obeyed the rules were rewarded with a weekly bonus of 5, which they could put in their individual bank accounts and use to buy goods from the shop or to make phone calls. Prisoners who broke the rules were denied this bonus. The Ministry of Justice discouraged the discretionary approach hitherto in place for awarding bonuses, and during the pilot phase of the Prison P project, it produced a detailed, standardized checklist to instruct officers under which circumstances prisoners would or would not merit a bonus. However, in implementing the new design, officers in P continued to use their discretionary power in order to decide whether a prisoner was to be awarded or denied a bonus.

Standardized Work Processes

The fourth design pillar of Prison P was the standardization of officers' work processes. Their work day was largely predetermined and their tasks routinized. Officers worked in pairs. Every day, three two-person teams had duty in P from 8.00 a.m. to 5.00 p.m. During the day these teams alternated among the following three tasks: overseeing prisoners' chores, inspecting and coordinating prisoners' activities (such as sports and education), and monitoring P from the central post. Officers were expected to follow specific protocols in executing each of these tasks.

What is interesting is that despite these highly restrictive intentions and plans developed by the Ministry of Justice, we observed that the officers at Prison P developed a high degree of creativity in their treatment of the prisoners and their management of the prison. This observation struck us in particular since Prison P was initially strongly conceptualized as creating a situation with a high degree of formalization and routinization. The question therefore arose as to why this creativity developed.

METHODOLOGY

Following the exploratory research aim of this study, we developed an inductive research design, collecting mainly qualitative data. These data were gathered from the time the first inmates arrived at the new prison in January 2006 until the end of the first pilot phase in April 2007. We had the opportunity to study the development of Prison P because we were asked by the Dutch Ministry of Justice to investigate which competences prison officers needed to have in order to fulfil their job adequately. We were asked because of our scientific background and our independent position with regard to Prison P. The Ministry's question was very appropriate given the fact that their own staff had no experience with the competence and functioning of officers in the new prison they had designed. It was in the course of studying the fit between necessary competences and the functioning of Prison P that we observed that the officers had developed competences which were quite different form those which the Ministry had expected to be generally necessary for that prison situation.

Data were primarily collected through direct observation. We were frequent visitors to and participants in organizational life at P, accompanying officers during their shifts and taking part in their meetings and breaks. We accompanied the officers in their daily work and were present when they walked through the building, talked to and instructed prisoners, had discussions with each other, smoked their cigarettes, filled out their paperwork and held meetings. We felt that they did not mind our being present. In fact, the officers seemed to like the attention, as will be further elaborated on below. Moreover, they treated us in a very friendly manner. We engaged in small talk with them and reflected with them on the life of a prison officer. However, we only had distant contact with the prisoners. We could see them moving and being active in the prison, but we had no direct contact: the Ministry of Justice did not allow us to talk to them.

By observing the officers and their supervisor in their work setting, we were able to witness the impact of prison design on behaviour firsthand. In addition, to get a fuller understanding of how the officers perceived their work in P, we conducted face-to-face, semi-structured individual interviews with a number of officers and with the supervisor. Out of the 15 officers working in P, we interviewed eight individually, without the supervisor being present. In addition to these individual interviews, we held two focus groups with the team, both of which included the supervisor. This enabled us to gain a general impression of the team, as well as of possible and actual work-related problems. We do not believe that the presence of the supervisor biased the focus group data since we found no conflict between those data and the data acquired from the individual interviews and our observations.

We then analysed the 70 pages of field notes we had from our participation in the prison routine, checking and cross-checking those data with our interview and focus group data. Finally, the officers, the team supervisor, and several policy-makers from the Ministry of Justice gave us policy and internal documents, such as memos, meeting minutes and house rules. We used these documents for fact checking (for example, to confirm such things as the capacity of the prison, the amount of bonus provided to the prisoners, and so forth).

Our qualitative research approach was consistent with what Barley and Kunda (2001) reported. They argued that situated field studies of work practices are likely to produce the most insightful theoretical lens for seeing how post-bureaucratic forms of organizing take shape. Such a practice-oriented approach focuses on work activity (Orr 1996, Orlikowski 2002) and, more specifically, on the repertoire of actions that reflect people's understandings of 'how to get things done' within complex settings (Orlikowski 2002, p. 249). It also focuses on 'what people actually do and think' (Dougherty 2002, p. 851) as opposed to 'what one hopes for' or 'the rationality myth' (Czarniawska 2003, pp. 361, 355). This fit our aim because we were interested in the development of an outcome in Prison P that is usually unexpected in a prison context: a place characterized by a considerable and consistent amount of creativity. We wanted to understand why team creativity developed in this context.

To do so we analysed our data using the methodology of process-tracing (George and Bennett 2005). Process-tracing offers an alternative solution for making causal inferences when it is not possible to do so through controlled comparison and when there is no theoretical model available to explain a certain outcome. The process-tracing method 'can identify single or different paths to an outcome, point out variables that were otherwise left out in the initial comparison of cases, check for spuriousness, and [therefore] permit causal interference on the basis of a few cases or even a single case' (George and Bennett 2005, p. 215).

FINDINGS

The theoretical literature, discussed above, would lead one to expect prison settings not to develop creativity. In our study we found the contrary: we observed a remarkable level of team creativity among officers, evidence of which will be provided below. Furthermore, the creativity-oriented literature would suggest that the reason team creativity did develop in this setting is due to the fact that the original conditions had changed. What our findings suggest, however, is that change can emerge not only from revisions. Here, for a number of reasons, new conditions evolved, enabling creative activities to emerge.

Numerous instances of creative team behaviour became apparent during our visits to P. These included officers inventing a bonus system for prisoners as compensation for technical malfunctions (such as broken telephones or televisions), and officers using group dynamics to structure prison behaviour in the newly designed group cells. Officers also experimented with placing certain prisoners in particular group cells. For instance, an aggressive prisoner was put into a 'calm' cell in the hope that the quiet prisoners in that cell would have a pacifying effect on his aggression. Furthermore, officers invented the function of 'prison concierge' and assigned to that position responsibilities for cleaning corridors, weeding the courtyard, and distributing lunches. Prisoners who behaved in exemplary ways were rewarded with this function. They liked to become the concierge because of the monetary reward and the status associated with it. The officers noted that the concierges started to reprove fellow prisoners who misbehaved. Prisoners respected the concierges because of their privileged position and therefore were willing to listen to them and to correct their behaviour, without any intervention by the officers.

In addition, officers took the initiative to develop and improve their own computer system, on which they maintained the inmate work schedule and stored information about the prisoners and the distribution of bonuses.

Other examples of team creativity with respect to the officers' work arrangements were based on changing procedures. Although formal procedures dictated, for instance, that the officers should stay very close to each other when inspecting cells, the team decided that keeping an eye on each other from a greater distance was sufficient. Also, whereas the original plans stipulated that prisoners had to bring their mail to the central office, officers placed mail boxes on each cell corridor in order to decrease prisoners' movements and thus increase security.

Initially, we thought that the instances of creative behaviour were idiosyncratic and entirely pragmatic. However, upon further analysis of our data, we concluded that these behaviours were similar to those of the generic professional service organizations (PSO) discussed above, in which creative behaviour is common. The six-person cells, the technical functionalities, and, most of all, the increased autonomy of the prisoners put in place a de facto client-organization interface. Without the cooperation of the prisoners, the 'clients' in this organization, it is unlikely the Prison P regime would have functioned as it does.

The creative behaviour of officers did not arise automatically but was stimulated in numerous ways. To start with, the supervisor used various group-dynamic techniques, such as rotating the function of team chair among the officers attending the team meetings and organizing team-building activities. Moreover, the team had wide-ranging responsibilities, and members were expected to help each other with a variety of tasks, like constructing the work schedule and maintaining the self-built database. Besides this, they were required by the supervisor to address each other regarding their conduct, for instance, when colleagues did not fulfil their duties or did not treat prisoners in a proper way.

In addition, the typical lack of pre-established procedures for running this kind of a prison meant that the officers needed to be creative, sometimes even modifying existing procedures for the prisoners as well as for themselves. Besides the creation of the prison concierge, for example, the officers rescheduled sports activities to motivate inmate participation. The type of help prisoners asked for varied greatly and could not be dealt with in standardized ways, as expected by the Ministry. Some prisoners had physical problems and therefore needed special attention, others had specific questions about the legal system, and still others wanted to do something about the forbidden drug use in their cells, without becoming victims because they snitched and told tales 'out of school'. In all these circumstances, officers had to develop tailored solutions to deal with the questions and problems effectively.

As there was no team room, officers spent their breaks in the central office. Since this was also a workroom, those officers who were monitoring prisoner movements and coordinating the activity schedule were often distracted by the small talk of those on break. At the same time, the officers who were working were often helped by those on break in solving difficult situations and getting advice. The upshot of this was that the absence of a team room stimulated the development of colleague consultancy.

The policy-makers of the Ministry believed that the technical reporting and monitoring facilities would make life for both officers and prisoners easier. In practice, however, there were substantial problems with several of these technologies. For instance, the tracking and tracing system and the prisoners' touch screens often malfunctioned. But these kinds of problems stimulated the development of team creativity. For example, when the prisoner telephone system was down for more than a day, prisoners became annoyed, and officers had to come up with solutions to prevent the escalation of unrest. Some solutions included the distribution of extra bonus cards and the rescheduling of activity programmes. Furthermore, technical problems motivated the officers to design their own information system.

Moreover, the establishment of a self-regulating team, the role of the supervisor, and a possible Hawthorne effect (discussed further below) stimulated creative team behaviour with the characteristics of a PSO. Just prior to the implementation of the Prison P pilot, a new dominant coalition within the Ministry of Justice emerged, creating a lateral intervention (Cyert and March 1963) within the prison system that proposed a self-regulating team model for the pilot. This coalition, referred to below as the 'team-coalition', consisted of the initiators of the idea for Prison P, a project leader from another prison who had been experimenting with a self-regulating team, consultants from a private consultancy company, and members of the Human Resources Department of the Ministry of Justice. The coalition bypassed the existing mechanical-juridical-coalition within the Ministry of Justice which had originally designed the technologically oriented and standardized Prison P. Instead of implementing the structure proposed by that coalition, the team-coalition advocated the use of a self-regulating team concept. They designed Prison P to have considerable discretionary power vis-à-vis the mother organization, the traditional prison in which P was embedded. In addition, they appointed a supervisor whom they knew would support the self-regulating team idea.

Rather than taking an autocratic, directive lead, however, the supervisor acted as a coordinator and facilitator within P. From the onset of the project, the supervisor signalled that it was up to P officers to make most of the decisions. The supervisor instilled in them confidence in their own decision-making abilities and gave each officer appropriate feedback, both positive and negative. When conflict arose among the officers, the supervisor encouraged them to find their own solutions. Furthermore, the supervisor stimulated the officers to hold each other to account, as stated above, and to consult with one another about the best way to deal with specific situations, such as conflicting procedures and prisoners who misbehaved.

Furthermore, the supervisor acted as a buffer between P and the mother organization. For instance, at the onset of the pilot project he talked to department heads in the mother organization to make sure they accepted that the officers in

P could act without a supervisor's signature. In line with this buffer function, the supervisor communicated clearly to the officers that problems might indeed be caused by the mother organization or by technical malfunctioning, but that it was, nevertheless, up to them to find solutions. In encouraging this problem-solving behaviour, he created the circumstances in which the officers could become creative. Thus, when presented with a problem, they learned to identify it, its cause(s), potential solutions, implementation of solutions, and potential results.

Another reason that creative PSO-style behaviour might have emerged can be explained by a possible Hawthorne effect. First noticed in the Hawthorne plant of Western Electric (Mayo 1933), this effect is defined as changes in a production process caused by the obtrusive observation of that process by outsiders. In the Hawthorne case, productivity increased not as a consequence of actual changes in working conditions introduced by the plant's management, but because management, represented through on-site researchers, was perceived as demonstrating positive interest in the workers and their activities. In the case of Prison P, officers were selected based on their willingness to work in this prison, their enthusiasm to be part of a new project, and their ability to cope with setbacks. Moreover, driven by the enthusiasm of their supervisor, officers strongly believed that P would work out well and, consequently, wanted to demonstrate that P was indeed a success. They also appeared to appreciate the attention they received from researchers, national and international visitors, and the media, all of whom were very much interested in this new prison concept. This attention seemed to energize them, to encourage them to come up with alternative solutions when current practices failed, and, generally, to work hard to make the project a success.

DISCUSSION

Underlying the spatial design of the new prison was the policy-makers' intention to change the behaviour of both prisoners and officers in specific ways. Our observations in Prison P show that this was achieved only to a limited extent. Instead, we observed the development of creative behaviours which were diametrically opposed to the desired behaviours. Creativity should have been constrained by two factors: the design of the space itself should have prevented the development of creative behaviour, and those responsible for the design's implementation should have frustrated any initiative that might have led to creativity. For example, the supervisor spent a year lobbying the policy-makers and designers for a team room in an effort to decrease the turmoil created at the central office by its absence. As the size of building P was fixed, the financial and political costs for this addition would have been substantial.

But the change could nonetheless have been made, for example, by erecting an extra wall in P's library. However, because the policy-makers and designers did not want to enable the officers to shirk responsibility – something they thought having a separate, designated team room space would do – they deliberately never considered adding it. For this reason and because negotiation processes – budget approval, safety checks, fire risk assessments, and discussions with the policy-makers and designers – were time-consuming, the team room was never built.

Other factors that might have blocked the development of team creativity in P were related to behavioural elements. At the start of the pilot, the officers were mainly concerned for their safety, not for the development of a place in which they could interact with inmates in comfort. It was equally hard in the beginning to establish colleague consultancy and collegial authority because the officers found it difficult to accept criticism from others (which they perceived as a personal attack) or to provide constructive feedback.

However, because the supervisor constantly encouraged the officers to communicate their critiques clearly, cooperation in the search for improvements was enhanced. One typical example of this evolution concerns procedure. Initially, officers wanted to obey procedure even if disregarding the official rules led to better solutions. Over time, deviating from procedure became generally accepted, as long as the officers who did so could justify their choices. Officers even started to thank their colleagues for suggesting 'deviating' improvements.

In addition to these spatial design and behavioural elements, there were other basic rules and procedures that limited the development of creativity, such as prisoner concerns. For instance, officers could not formally permit any of the prisoners to work, even if they thought that it would be good for the prisoners' well-being, because one of Prison P's explicitly stated rules was that prisoners were not allowed to work. In other situations, the team itself dismissed new officer-initiated proposals. For example, for the sake of efficiency, an officer proposed having the prisoners' mail delivered by the prisoner concierge. However, the team vetoed this creative idea because of privacy concerns.

In most of the innovation and creativity literature, team creativity is explained by scorekeeping – the number of critical or explanatory reasons for creativity. From another perspective, however, it is not so much the score that helps to explain creativity in a place, but the meaning attached to it (De Certeau 1984). Prison P's creativity developed in reaction to unplanned and unanticipated dysfunctionalities of the design and the unintended introduction of a self-regulating team. The original design was intended to influence prisoners' and officers' behaviour through the use of strict monitoring devices. Most of the monitoring devices turned out to some extent to be ineffective in practice. This situation resulted in the development of a prison which was quite different from its design. Originally intended for behavioural control of the prisoners and for security of the officers, Prison P developed into a place where problems were solved in a creative way.

This case challenges the functional perspective that is common in the literature concerning the deterministic relationship between spatial design and human behaviour. The behaviour observed in Prison P is far from a direct and straightforward result of the designed space. Rather, it is the result of the processes and social interactions described in this study. This research originated in a study of the ways in which organizational design shapes or even determines behaviour. But its findings make a strong case for considering the potential of organizational space to be interpreted in various ways. It provides evidence for the argument (for example, Hernes et al. 2006, Van Marrewijk 2009) that organizational space not only shapes action and interaction in organizations but can also be, and is, reshaped by these interactions. The processes which we observed unfolding in Prison P seem to be a clear confirmation of this theoretical position.

DOES CREATIVITY CONTINUE? CONCLUDING THOUGHTS

We completed our study of Prison P at the beginning of April 2007. During a short visit one month later, the supervisor said that the officers missed the researchers' attention and that they had become less motivated. This suggests that the Hawthorne effect mentioned above was very real, but was also fading. If so, it would imply a decline in further creativity on the part of the officers. We did not have the opportunity to follow up on this idea.

There is much potential for future research into creative behaviour in a non-creative space like the panopticon, Prison P. First, it would be interesting to do a longitudinal study of this facility and follow the officers' behaviour into the near future, now that the pilot study has ended. Because the supervisor left P in June 2007, soon after the conclusion of the pilot, the consequences of his leaving and the impact of his successor on the prison would be worth observing.

Furthermore, it would be valuable to study the development of a creative space from a variety of perspectives, for instance, from the perspective of the inmates. Developing a 'client's' perspective is key to understanding the relation between spatial settings in prisons and the behaviour of its users. While the six-person cell design stimulated the officers' self-responsibility, it also had the unintended and undesirable result of stimulating 'creative behaviour' among prisoners. When prisoners uncovered loopholes in the prison regime, they were able to spread this knowledge through P more quickly because of the group cells. In one instance, when a prisoner ordered goods from the shop, the money was added to his bank account instead of being subtracted. As soon as that prisoner discovered this, other inmates started buying large amounts of goods from the shop. One of the prisoners spent 800 and, after that sum turned up in his account as a credit, was able to pay his outstanding fines, thereby becoming eligible to be released from the prison. Officers discovered this technical error just before his release went into effect.

New spatial interventions in P might also affect creativity, and not necessarily in a planned way. For instance, were a team room built for officers to sit together and consult with each other, the central office would no longer be a place for small talk on operational issues, leading perhaps to increased shirking of responsibilities during work time. Constructing a team room specifically designed to generate intense social interaction among employees might thus have negative outcomes.

Finally, the struggle between the team-coalition and the mechanical-juridical-coalition within the Ministry is ongoing. It would be interesting to see what happens to P if the mechanical-juridical coalition regains its dominance and converts P to a more traditional form of prison.

What would happen in another prison like P, built somewhere else? Would the creative place that was established unintentionally in P also arise? What would be the consequences for the performance of the prison if such creativity were designed into it? Due to the recursive process of the production and reproduction of the prison space we observed in P, it is impossible to formulate answers to these questions now. Clearly, the spatial settings in Prison P do not exhibit a deterministic influence over the social world of officers and prisoners. Further research on the establishment of a creative place in a characteristically non-creative context like a prison might build upon the foundation we have laid here.

NOTES

1. Mills et al. (1983) use 'self-supervision' instead of 'colleague consultancy' and 'self-management and entrepreneurial-type responsibilities' in lieu of 'colleague authority'. We deviate from these terms because we found our own to be better descriptors.

REFERENCES

Amabile, Teresa M. (1996), *Creativity in Context*, Boulder, CO: Westview Press.
Amabile, Teresa M., J.S. Mueller, W.B. Simpson, C.N. Hadley, S.J. Kramer and L. Fleming (2002), 'Time pressure and creativity in organizations: a longitudinal field

study', accessed 5 June 2007 at www.hbs.edu/research/facpubs/workingpapers/papers2/0102/02-073.pdf.

Anderson, N.R. (1989), 'Management team innovation and effectiveness', paper presented at the 4th West European Congress on the Psychology of Work and Organization, April, Cambridge.

Anderson, N.R. and R.M. Gasteiger (2007), 'Helping creativity and innovation thrive in organizations: functional and dysfunctional perspectives', in J. Langan-Fox, C.L. Cooper and R.J. Klimoski (eds), *Research Companion to the Dysfunctional Workplace: Management Challenges and Symptoms*, Cheltenham, UK and Northampton, MA, USA: Edward Elgar, pp. 422–41.

Barley, Steven R. and Gideon Kunda (2001), 'Bringing work back in', *Organization Science*, **12** (1), 76–95.

Bentham, J. [1787] (1995), *The Panopticon Writings*, M. Bozovic (ed.), London: Verso.

Burns, Tom and Gerald M. Stalker (1961), *The Management of Innovation,* London: Tavistock.

Cyert, Richard M. and James G. March (1963), *A Behavioral Theory of the Firm,* Englewood Cliffs, NJ: Prentice-Hall.

Czarniawska, Barbara (2003), 'Forbidden knowledge', *Management Learning*, **34** (3), 353–65.

De Certeau, Michel (1984), *The Practice of Everyday Life,* Berkeley, CA: University of California Press.

Dougherty, D. (2002), 'Grounded theory research methods', in J.A.C. Baum (ed.), *Companion to Organizations*, Oxford: Blackwell.

Dutch House of Parliament (2005–06), 28 979 and 24 587, nr. 10, 's-Gravenhage: Sdu Uitgevers.

Dutch House of Parliament (2006–07), 28 979 and 24 587, nr. 225, 's-Gravenhage: Sdu Uitgevers.

Fogarty, T.J. and M.W. Dirsmith (2001), 'Organizational socialization as instrument and symbol: an extended institutional theory perspective', *Human Resource Development Quarterly*, **12** (3), 247–66.

Foucault, Michel (1975), *Surveiller et Punir: Naissance de la Prison* [*Discipline and Punish: The Birth of the Prison*], Paris: Gallimard.

Geijn Partners BV (2006), *Gevangen in Ketens, Modernste Gevangenis: Opvallend Resultaat van Gedurfde Visie* [*Imprisoned in Chains, Most Modern Prison: Notable Result of a Daring Vision*], Houten, the Netherlands: Report.

George, Alexander L. and Andrew Bennett (2005), *Case Studies and Theory Development in the Social Sciences,* London: MIT Press.

Hall, R.H. (1968), 'Professionalization and bureaucratization', *American Sociological Review*, **33** (1), 92–104.

Hernes, Tor T., P. Bakken and O. Olsen (2006), 'Spaces as process: developing a recursive perspective on organizational space', in Stewart Clegg and Martin Kornberger (eds), *Space, Organizations and Management Theory*, Oslo and Copenhagen: Liber and Copenhagen Business School Press, pp. 33–63.

Kommer, M.M. (1991), *De gevangenis als werkplek* [*The Prison as Workplace*], Arnhem, the Netherlands: Gouda Quint.

Mayo, Elton (1933), *The Human Problems of an Industrial Civilization*, New York: Macmillan.

Mills, P.K., J.L. Hall, J.K. Leidecker and N. Margulies (1983), 'Flexiform: a model for professional service organizations', *Academy of Management Review*, **8** (1), 118–31.

Orr, Julian E. (1996), *Talking about Machines: An Ethnography of a Modern Job*, Ithaca, NY and London: Cornell University Press.

Orlikowski, Wanda J. (2002), 'Knowing in practice: enacting a collective capability in distributed organizing', *Organization Science*, **13** (3) 249–73.

Van Marrewijk, Alfons H. (2009), 'Corporate headquarters as physical embodiments of organizational change', *Journal of Organizational Change Management*, **22** (3), 290–306.

PART II

Living organizational spaces

4. What do buildings do? How buildings-in-use affect organizations

Marja Gastelaars

This chapter focuses on the organizational impact of buildings-in-use – that is, what happens when an existing building is reused for purposes of a new organization, rather than being designed and constructed *ab origine* for the occupying organization [as in the case of Prison P, Chapter 3. Eds.]. I draw on illustrative data from a respected nineteenth-century physics lab that was reoccupied by a newly founded School for Public Governance – from now on called the School – that is part of Utrecht University, in the Netherlands. To explore the impact of this quite venerable building on this new School's activities, I make use of the six Ss Stewart Brand once proposed to conceptualize the durability of buildings (Brand 1994, pp. 12–13).

Following Brand, I focus on a number of material aspects that any building might have and that are summarized in terms of six concepts beginning with the letter S. Drawing on Latour's (2005) conceptualization of material actors (and *actants*), I show how this old building's Site, Skin (or *façade*), Structure, Space plan (creating its hallways, rooms, etc.), Stuff (its furnishings and other mobile accoutrements), and Service (its infrastructure, which, for Brand, denotes various facilities, from plumbing to coffee machines and IT) take part in the new School's activities. These material aspects are not only there to 'keep randomness from invading [our] minds' (Csikszentmihalyi 1993, p. 22), nor should an understanding of their impact be limited to symbolic functions such as 'revealing the continuity of the self through time', for instance by 'providing one with signposts for the future' (Csikszentmihalyi 1993, p. 23). Instead, these material aspects are presented here as non-human actors. To use one of Lefebvre's phrases, they take part as material things, in the 'multitude of intersections' (Lefebvre [1974] 1991, p. 33) that constitute the (re)production of space.

Latour insists that 'anything that does modify a state of affairs by making a difference is an actor – or, if it has no figuration yet, an *actant*' (Latour 2005, p. 71). By 'figuration' he means a network consisting of both human and non-human actors that contextualizes the actions observed. In other words, the various physical elements of the building presented here can not only be seen as *actants* in their own right, but also as active participants in such social networks. In following Brand (1994), who invites us to walk towards a building, literally, circle it, and then go inside, I shall also make sense of the organizational impact of these physical characteristics in terms of the social networks of which they are a part.

The chapter is structured as follows. After some methodological remarks in the next section, I shall follow Brand's invitation and, in the subsequent section, focus on the School building's Site – its geographical setting, in its own historical context – and Skin. I discuss how these external characteristics take part in the new School's connection with the outside world (Lefebvre [1974] 1991, p. 33; see also Yanow 2006). After this, I follow Brand's instruction to go inside and observe the impact of this former laboratory's Structure and Space plan – how its various floors and quite high-ceilinged halls and staircases, not to mention its various rooms, contribute to the daily work that constitutes this academic establishment: its teaching and research, in particular. The local impact of the building's Stuff, or the loose objects that can freely move around it, will also be discussed.

In the fourth section, I shall pay attention to Brand's final concept, the Services which, in his view, can be considered as a building's 'working guts' (Brand 1994, p. 13). As Bowker and Star ([1999] 2000) have pointed out, these Services now also include such non-human actors as computers and IT-supported formats. They also produce organizing effects.

METHODOLOGICAL NOTES

The fieldwork data presented here are primarily based on observations conducted by the author between 2000 and 2008 as a participant in the School's teaching and research. In this sense I have been collecting data ever since the School occupied the building. In addition to this, my data also rely on a number of public sources, among them a public tour performed by one of the interior architects, some public presentations performed by the School's managers, and written and electronic documents related to its university's building efforts. As it is the researcher him- or herself who is the primary research 'tool' in such a study (Van Maanen 1995; see also Yanow 2006), I have to reflect upon the possible impact of my personal involvement in the School on the observations I report here.

The building will be presented here as a physical thing, so for my observations I rely on physical experiences of my own. When I move through the building and take the School's public presentations into account, for the sake of this research, I am primarily interested in what the various aspects of the building, presented by Brand, can physically disclose about the work processes of the School, as well as about its managerial activities; but I am quite aware that the selection of my data must have been informed, at least to an extent, by my insider knowledge as a participant. The day-to-day physical practices of the people who are present in the School have not been observed in detail; neither have I conducted interviews with them about their personal experiences or concerns in relation to this building, although, as a participant, I might be quite aware of who these various human actors are and what they are up to. Had I focused on their actions and experiences, I might have discovered as many buildings-cum-organizations as there are people.

My interpretations are personally informed. On the one hand, and like any social researcher tackling a subject related to university life, I have the advantage of knowing what an academic establishment is about because I naturally try to make sense of a world I relate to on a day-to-day basis (Latour and Woolgar 1986, p. 43). On the other hand, the fact, for example, that I single out the School's teaching and research, rather than its consultancy and coaching efforts, may also have been a product of my personal involvement and perspective. And, of course, my personal preoccupations may not be confined to my experiences with the School itself. Being a regular visitor of Utrecht and a convinced city dweller, myself, I am perhaps more 'in the know' about the city locations I am discussing than another observer might be.

My data analysis is primarily informed by a long-term scientific interest in the everyday practices performing the work processes of (semi-)public service organizations, such as the School (Gastelaars 2009). This is why the managerial activities that I observed are treated, here, as more or less subservient to these everyday work processes. Moreover, my insistence on taking networks as a starting point for part of my analysis is consistent with a (neo-)institutionalist approach to the study of such organizations. As a historical sociologist I am very much inclined, in addition, not only to contextualize my data in local terms but also to put them into a socio-historical perspective. This approach may be very much in tune with that of Dale and Burrell (2008) [see also Chapter 1, this volume. Eds.] who present a similar historical concern.

THE BUILDING'S SITE AND SKIN: THE SCHOOL'S PHYSICAL CONNECTIONS WITH THE OUTSIDE WORLD

According to Brand the building's Site amounts to 'the geographical setting, the urban location, and the legally defined lot, whose boundaries and context outlast generations of ephemeral buildings' (Brand 1994, p. 13). This setting is simply there and will keep being so, even after the buildings on it have gone to ruin. In this specific case, this permanence of the building's site can also inform us about the connectedness of the School to a number of networks. These include the local university environment and the local city. The city is, for instance, represented by a park that leads us towards the School building.

The City Park

There are many ways to approach this building's site, but the School's brochure advises visitors who arrive on foot from the central railway station to take the footpath that follows the Outer City Canal (*Stadsbuitengracht*). When one is underway along this route, one crosses through a park – the so-called Zocher Park – which borders the canal on one's right-hand side and is bordered, on one's left-hand side, by some beautiful houses and gardens that were constructed at the end of the nineteenth and the beginning of the twentieth centuries (De Jonge and Visser 2008).

J.D. Zocher, a famous Dutch landscape architect, had been commissioned as early as 1829 to transform the former city fortifications into a promenade, as part of an expansion of the city beyond its old fortifications. The idea was to create shaded paths, winding freely through a landscape, in accordance with the English style of landscaping that was considered exemplary at the time (Van der Woud 1987, p. 331; see also De Jonge and Visser 2008). In this respect this city is not unique. Richard Sennett (1991, p. 56) described similar ambitions for other cities.

To arrive at the building, one must take a turn to the left and leave the park to enter a rather narrow street which presents one with the front of the building, while the park, itself, continues around its back side, where it is bordered by a turning loop in the canal. This is why, to an outside observer, the building may seem to be directly connected with this distinctive city park and, through this specific physical location, with the city's history as well.

The City and University Through Time

The city of Utrecht is essentially medieval in its origins, and the university's origins are also located in its city's medieval centre. Some of the current university buildings – including the Academy building that now usually houses the university's formal events – still present green and leafy inner courts that were quite characteristic of the spatial enclaves that used to be very prominent in this city. They were called 'immunities' at the time and housed relatively autonomous religious communities that were granted some local administrative independence from the city government. The term 'immunity' relates to such essentially legal claims. The city planner currently involved in the redevelopment of the inner city university may simply be drawing on the attractions provided by these immunities' inner courts, but he may be inadvertently relating to their semi-autonomous status, as well, when he points out, 'Utrecht used to be a city consisting of walled-in convents and of communities within the community' (Roelevink 2008).

The building we discuss does not contain such an enclave. It is positioned near the edge of the medieval part of this city, near the so-called Empty Place (*Ledig Erf*), which derives its name from the 'fields of fire' that needed to be kept open for the cannons of the city's former fortifications (De Jonge and Visser 2008, p. 77). This area now provides a lively ambience with a lot of street-side cafés. And, although this attractive city square has no apparent connection with the building, it reinforces the attractiveness of its site.

The building is particularly related to a nineteenth-century city expansion which took place in the area and was intended to attract more well-to-do people to the newly built residential neighbourhoods that were situated there (De Jonge and Visser 2008). No wonder that several museums and other cultural establishments have also been founded there. A large number of office buildings was erected in this area, as well, due to the fact that, given its geographic location in the middle of the country, Utrecht had become the administrative centre for a number of organizations relating to the then-expanding national state. A university expansion coincided with this nineteenth-century city development plan. It involved, apart from some labs, elaborate complexes built to house the university's academic hospital and its veterinary school. The building that is the contemporary home of the School was erected in 1875 as a physics lab for the famous Dutch meteorologist, Buys Ballot, who founded the Royal Dutch Meteorological Institute.

Most of these office buildings can be classified as institutional buildings, to use Brand's vocabulary, but the term applies to the new cultural establishments and university buildings as well. According to Brand, such buildings were not only meant to make an enduring impression on the outside world, they were also expected to 'act as if they were designed specifically to prevent change for the organization inside and to convey timeless reliability to everyone outside' (Brand 1994, p. 7). As a consequence, they seem to confirm Richard Sennett's observation, as well, that, physically speaking, they do not seem to relate to their urban environment. These institutional buildings are often 'sited as though [they] could be anywhere' (Sennett 1974, p. 13) and present themselves as standing apart. The outward appearance of the School building seems to confirm this point, as we shall see later on.

The University Moving Outwards

The importance to Utrecht University of its nineteenth-century institutional buildings changed over time. In the late 1960s and beginning of the 1970s, most of the university's departments – among them its veterinary school, its science departments, and most of its social sciences, but not its humanities and law faculties – moved out of these venerable buildings at the city centre's edge to a so-called campus situated on a former polder at the outer edge of the city (Reinink 1984). The university's administrative centre moved there, as well. This campus was to be called the university's outer court (*Uithof*), possibly in reference, once again, to the traditional legitimacy of such outer spaces to Utrecht's medieval institutions. The label may also have helped to support the city's expansion (Reinink 1984, p. 21). In a way, the university's inner city buildings were left behind, but they have remained intact to this day.

Another evaluation of these older buildings was produced when the academic hospital left the city centre and moved to the *Uithof* campus, as well. The physical rejuvenation of the *Uithof* area that was involved with this move did not take place until the 1990s. It included some spectacular buildings, produced by the internationally renowned Dutch architect Rem Koolhaas and others (Ibelings 2009). This meant, once again, that the relevance to the university of its inner city locations was reconsidered. But the intended 'finalization' of the university's relocation to the outskirts of the city was averted, and an 'inner city campus project' was to accompany this rejuvenation of the *Uithof*. The renovation of the School building became a part. Apparently, the attractions of the inner city prevailed.

The Physical Production of Autonomy

As a consequence of the university's move to the *Uithof*, the School building is located at a fair distance from the university's administrative centre. When seen from the *Uithof*, the building can be perceived as being 'out there', in the city centre. From the perspective of the founders of the new School, however, this distancing may, in fact, have been quite intentional. According to a presentation made by one of them, a managing professor, the new organization itself aimed at some physical distance from its university context, as well.

In order to be able to further its principal intellectual and academic aims, its leadership not only argued that it should have its 'own staff; own budget; administrative autonomy'; it also asked for 'no bi-location [meaning a location split between central and outer campuses]; one (and only one) building; preferably in an old part of town' (Bovens 2006). All of these demands were honoured by the university administration, and the School was allowed to house most of its activities, its teaching in particular, in a single building – and the nineteenth-century physics lab just happened to be available at the time. That the School was also allowed to apply a *numerus fixus* to the yearly admission of its first year students – an exceptional privilege among Dutch universities, which commonly have to enrol all who register – enabled it to physically contain most of its student population in this single location, as well.

A Nineteenth-Century Materialization Providing Immunity in the Twenty-First Century

In a way, the School's ambition to found a physically independent academic community was materialized in the physical appearance of its nineteenth-century institutional building. In Sennett's words, such institutional buildings may very well be able to provide an inner sanctuary to their occupants, 'separating their "inner life" from the busy street life outside' (Sennett 1991, p. 32). As the notion of immunity that was introduced above suggests some degree of administrative autonomy and some institutional 'inner-directedness' as well, leaving aside the 'sacred' core that is quite essential to the notion of a sanctuary, it might even provide a more preferable term.

But we should be careful, once again, not to rely too much on this term's specific medieval connotations. For its present purposes, the School itself may even have relied much more on the nineteenth-century tradition of institutionalization from which these institutional buildings derive their name. This institutional tradition is particularly relevant to the field of education. It usually frames 'institutions' – and their associated buildings – in terms of specific, mostly state-regulated forms, that may even become 'self-evident', precisely because of the institutional traditions that govern their behaviour. The degrees of autonomy that some of these 'institutions' – universities in particular – might rightfully claim are also established by such governmental regimes (Lefebvre [1974] 1991, pp. 47-8).

The School's 'inner-directedness' – if not its autonomy – is in fact confirmed by the building's rather uninviting Skin. It presents a very dark brick surface. At the front of the building, the lowest row of windows is situated above eye-level, making it impossible to look in from the outside. The front is also marked by two elaborately carved and very heavy wooden front doors; only one of them is usable, as the other is fixed in place. Next to this one entrance are two banners indicating the School's current name and relating it to Utrecht University; a prominent sign commemorating the building's respected past as a rather famous lab is also affixed to the building near this door. But, apart from these outward signs relating to its past and present scientific occupants, the building's Skin seems to successfully resist any attempt at penetration, as does the entrance that the building's physical Structure presents.

THE BUILDING'S STRUCTURE, SPACE PLAN AND STUFF: THE PHYSICAL ACCOMMODATION OF INSTITUTIONAL ACTIVITIES

A Structure may or may not confirm the accessibility of a building's occupant, but, more importantly, together with the building's Space plan and Stuff, the Structure can contribute to the presentation of its organized activities, as well. In fact, it may even organize them in a physical way, by providing the places and the spaces where the occupying organization's population can physically perform their work. Following Augé, the concept of place can be understood as designating 'a culture localized in time and space' (Augé [1992] 1995, pp. 80–81). Accordingly, it can be seen as a specific kind of space, with well-defined properties that are associated with well-defined activities. By contrast, the determination of a 'space' usually relies on parameters that are more abstract or undetermined. As a practical concept, a space can be expected to be more open to a variety of activities.

A Solid Frame

According to Brand, a building's Structure is often quite synonymous with its physical durability: 'The foundation and load-bearing elements are perilous and expensive to change, so people don't. These *are* the building' (Brand 1994, p. 13). In the case of this specific building, its Structure fits this picture. The same holds true for its Space plan, which for Brand means 'the interior lay-out – where walls, ceilings, floors and doors go' (Brand 1994, p. 13). The building contains three massive floors, with lengthy hallways running down the middle of each floor lined on both sides by walls and doors giving access to rooms of various sizes. The stone staircases linking these floors are also quite solid.

However, the staircases are also quite tall and wide. Accordingly, they may also be open to the casual conversations 'on the road' that are so often associated with informal power structures in the workplace. On the first floor, a large, open space in the middle of the building that is supported by rows of rather firm-looking pillars presents itself as a restaurant but also appears to be open to a variety of uses. Generally speaking, however, the inflexibility of this building's structure and space plan seems to prevail.

An Entrance Hall

After having entered the building through its one available door, a visitor is presented with a rather wide set of stone steps leading upwards. These are flanked on both sides by low balustrades that give access to an open space with no apparent purpose. Although this apparently empty space presents itself as quite solid, as well, it may call to mind a non-place of the kind theoretically conceptualized by Augé: 'If a place can be defined as relational, historical and concerned with identity, then a space which cannot be defined as relational, or historical, or concerned with identity will be a non-place' (Augé [1992] 1995, pp. 77–8). To Augé, however, such non-places are not as undetermined as they may seem.

So it is with this entrance hall. First of all, it gives access to the building's front office, which is hidden behind a wall of coloured glass opposite the flight of stairs, with two swinging glass doors providing access. In the managing professor's presentation discussed earlier, this front office was identified as 'the head of the building' (Bovens 2006). It presents the School's central information point where visitors from outside can be informed about what is going on inside.

Second, the entrance hall at times serves as a waiting area. For instance, it is often crowded with students waiting for their classes to start. But its waiting area purpose also frames it as a 'liminal space' in the specific sense proposed by Van Gennep ([1908] 1960). To him, liminality denotes the situation 'in between' two states of being, for instance for young people being initiated as adults. In this intervening, liminal stage, those undergoing such a *rite de passage* would often be held for a while 'in anticipation' of things to come. The same may be said of those visitors who are asked, by the front office, to take a seat in the entrance hall to wait for their appointments, making this ostensible non-place a liminal space.

And, finally, Augé observes that such non-places are often also present to show new visitors the way. To serve this purpose, he observes, they are usually 'defined … by the words and texts they offer us ... which may be prescriptive ("Take right hand lane"), prohibitive ("No smoking") or informative ("You are now entering ...")' (Augé [1992] 1995, p. 96). So it is with this entrance hall. It displays some of the School's house rules on a paper poster. Graphic signs affixed to the walls indicate room numbers and the locations of the staircases, the lift and the restaurant. Moreover, a handwritten blackboard is occasionally put up at the top of the flight of stairs announcing meetings to the School's guests – an expert meeting, a student's presentation, etc. All of this confirms another observation made by Augé, that such non-places may even be intentionally 'formed in relation to certain ends' (Augé [1992] 1995, p. 94). But let us follow the signs and try and find out what is going on inside.

An Educational Landscape

According to the managing professor's presentation, the initial assignment from Utrecht University in 1999 to create a new School was translated by the School into a strategy to create 'a community of scholars and students' (Bovens 2006). The physical building they were given seems not only to support the administrative distance and 'immunity' the School's management aspired to, but also to physically create the inner sanctuary where a community such as this could flourish. Realizing this notion of community was primarily focused on the School's teaching efforts, which, according to the presentation, were very central to the School's work. They were related to an essentially individualizing 'new learning' approach, which is also supposed to improve students' mutual cooperation. These educational objectives were explicitly presented as having governed the building's renovation. Hence, the notion of 'educational landscape' became part of the School's vocabulary-in-use (Verweel 2002). As far as the students are concerned, these learning activities and the spaces designed to help achieve them could also be seen as an example of the kinds of everyday arrangements that are expected to contribute to the 'production of people' described by Dale and Burrrell (2008, xii and pp. 99–134).

For instance, the School's policy objectives in the educational realm amounted to a preference for 'small-scale interaction' and aimed at the development of a 'variety of competences' for individual students. Seminars were to support the School's 'inductive teaching methods', and these would largely rely on 'the students' initiative' (Bovens 2006). Accordingly, the wood-panelled classrooms with long 'demonstration tables' that must have been quite effective for a laboratory of the past were to be refurbished to provide all that was needed for the enactment of the School's innovative teaching: 'A variety of class rooms; One lecture hall only; Ample space for interaction; Rooms for self study and group work' (Bovens 2006). The solidity of the building's original structure, however, prohibited changing some of the spatial arrangements dating from this earlier period. Some spatial aspects of the former laboratory building produce impacts on its occupants' actions that seem at this point in time to be quite old-fashioned.

The single large lecture hall accessible directly from the entrance hall, for instance, is an amphitheatre as of old, its demonstration table down below reinforcing one-way communication only. The instructor's position remains fixed at this lower end of the room, if only because the electronic presentation technologies are now placed there. The rows of fixed chairs leading up from that position to the room's entrance doors direct the students' gazes in one direction and reinforce the one-way interaction. Elsewhere, the new tables in the larger classrooms are also attached to the floors, but that dates from a much later 'old' time. Following the School's educational philosophy, these tables provided students with sockets to connect their laptops to the wired network that was put in place to support a new university intranet. These tables remain fixed to the floor, however, despite the now prevailing, newer, wireless communication. Here, also, the instructor's position is fixed by the positioning of the whiteboards and projection screens at one end of the room.

The movable Stuff that can be observed in these rooms includes the standard equipment accommodating the work of teaching today – flip charts, laptops, projectors and screens. One completely unexpected aspect, however, is presented by an essentially aesthetic intervention. There are enlarged colour photographs affixed to these rooms' walls, opposite the instructor's 'natural' position. They (re)present people from all parts of the world and carry quotes from *Alice in Wonderland,* such as: 'The question is …' or 'Who are you?' The reason for these queries may confuse a casual observer, but, according to the School's academic leadership, they confirm 'the exploratory character of our teaching and research' (Verweel 2002).

The smaller rooms designed for individual study and workgroup activities seem to enact the School's innovative educational approach in a more straight-forward manner. On a tour of the building led by the interior architect who had been responsible for their design, these rooms were presented as 'cosy Dutch living rooms' – drawing on a key component of Netherlands culture, *gezel-ligheid* – with 'lampshades above their round tables in the middle'. By offer-ing round tables in the middle and individual work surfaces along their sides, these rooms provide relatively open spaces that can accommodate a variety of small-scale activities, ranging from student group meetings to one-on-one coaching and consultation, although these efforts may not necessarily substan-tiate the homey metaphor that was applied here. Some paper notices posted on the walls even seem to deny any suggestion of homeliness by insisting that any personal stuff that is left behind will be treated as 'matter out of place' (Douglas [1966] 1991, p. 2).

The Visibility of Teaching

A building's Structure, Space plan and Stuff may not only create degrees of flexibility, they may create degrees of visibility as well. That is why particular attention should be paid, in this case, to the sliding doors of coloured glass that are prominent in this building. They replaced the solid walls of the former teaching labs. They render visible the work processes that are going on inside these rooms to anyone who might pass by in the building's corridors. According to the interior architect, the sliding glass doors are simply there to 'allow some daylight into the otherwise quite dark corridors', but he also related them to the 'transparency' that is so often associated with glass walls, nowadays, both by architects and managers who are involved with the refur-bishment of existing buildings (see also Dale and Burrell 2008, p. 258). But, independent of the architect's motivation, students and teaching staff must now somehow cope with the physical visibility these glass doors produce, although they were made soundproof to ensure that auditory privacy could be maintained. It does not seem to happen very often, but some occupants some-times put up a folding screen in front of the glass doors to re-establish visual privacy.

A comment made by an external PhD student who visited the building draws our attention to another effect that is produced by these glass walls: 'You seem to have these glass cubes all over the place, and they all seem to have to do with teaching. Do you people actually perform any research?' Rendering some activities more spatially visible and others less so seems to echo institutional priorities.

The Invisibility of Research

Indeed, the work activity performed by the School's staff that, in this building, is least visible is its research. An astute observer may notice the masses of paper being printed out on the various copying machines (available to 'staff only'). Among these piles of paper one might find various kinds of printouts that could provide evidence of the School's research work. In a glass case in the entrance hall, some of the books published by School staff are on display. But apart from this, the building does not appear to visibly present the School's research efforts.

There are the specialized research meetings where staff and visiting scholars come together in the glass cubes discussed above. The building also houses the occasional scientific conference. Most research activities, however, seem to be quite invisible, indeed, and for a number of reasons. First, there are the scholarly networking activities which are invisible in most university settings, because they are often performed in the 'absent presence' (Gergen 2002) that has become quite common nowadays as a consequence of the prevalence of electronic communication. The building provides the infrastructure required for these activities to occur, and as researchers are working on their computers, they are focused on 'somewhere else'.

Secondly, the person-to-person networking considered quite essential to scientific performance is usually physically performed elsewhere, such as at conference meetings; the building may at most serve as a home base to support these activities. Moreover, such mostly absent scientific networks are not new to this building. As has been amply documented by his biographers (for example, Snelders and Schuurmans 1980), Buys Ballot, for whom the lab was built, was actively involved in international networks of visiting professors.

Thirdly, a similar absence may also apply to the work involved with the production of scientific data. Again, this can be illustrated by the work performed by Buys Ballot. He may in fact have performed very little experimental research of his own in this university building. For instance, the famous law that has generally been attributed to him, concerning the direction of the wind in relation to high and low pressure areas in the northern and southern hemispheres (Snelders and Schuurman 1980), relied on a worldwide research network performing simultaneous observations. This research process is similar to the productive networks that, nowadays, can also be observed in the physical sciences (Knorr-Cetina 1999). The building was designed to accommodate laboratory functions, but it may not have been used very often for this specific purpose by Buys Ballot.

A similar situation holds for the social scientists who now occupy the building. They do not rely, either, on physical experiments of the kind that would be visually accessible to an outside observer (see also Latour and Woolgar ([1979] 1986). As can be gathered from their publications, most of them do not even rely on questionnaires (Van El 2002), although occasionally a research assistant can be observed filling envelopes, preparing to mail a large number of such forms to prospective respondents. Instead, most of those working in this building conduct qualitative research, and the interviewing and observational work that is characteristic of this kind of research is usually performed 'in the field', that is, outside the building. Again, the building may serve as a home base, rather than providing the open spaces that some find so stimulating to innovative research, itself (Kornberger and Clegg 2003).

Fourth, scientific work also involves the activity of writing up research results. In Latour and Woolgar's famous *Laboratory Life* ([1979] 1986, p. 45), the scientists observed appeared to rely so much on computerized appliances that 'inscribed' their data that they could also be seen physically assembling their publications. With fieldwork data of the kind that is collected by the researchers of this School, however, most of the writing up is performed out of the office or, when researchers are on site, behind closed doors (see also Van El 2002).

The office rooms that are shared by this School's professional staff are actually quite private. Some of these rooms have been personalized with their occupants' personal Stuff: photographs, plants, the occasional piece of art. Moreover, and in contrast with most other rooms that are available in the building, their impenetrable wooden doors are often closed. At first sight, this may only suggest that staff work from home (as is common in the Netherlands' academic culture) or somewhere else outside the building. These closed doors, however, may also be seen as an essential prerequisite to the solitude or 'physical thinking space' that, at least according to Westin's (1970) famous essay on the subject, most people seek out whenever they need to think something through. Although scientific reflexivity may very well be produced in conversation with colleagues, whether face to face or via Internet links, making up one's mind about the meaning of one's data appears to be supported by the other extreme of the communicative spectrum. Some innovative research might actually rely on the solitude and silence enabled by closed doors.

THE IMPACT OF THE SERVICES ON THE ORGANIZATION'S ACCOUNTABILITY AND CONTROL

The managerial activities that are relevant to the School may be organized by the building's Structure, Space plan, and Stuff as well. In this section I shall also focus on the IT formats and other 'material actors' that may contribute to this managerial work. According to Bowker and Star ([1999] 2000) these material actors should be included in the Services which, to Brand, are the 'working guts' of a building (Brand 1994, p. 13). The various human actors who are involved with these IT-supported formats often remain hidden from most of an organization's participants' view as well.

Visible Management

To an external observer, the School's management may be very visible, indeed. Central to the management structure are three full professors who occupy adjacent rooms on the building's ground floor, at the far end of a relatively dark and very long hallway. Next to these rooms are the financial and executive managers' offices, as well as an office for the representative of the university's personnel department. Secretarial support for these positions is also concentrated here. In spite of its seeming secludedness, this physical centre of power is particularly easy for visitors from the outside to reach, and it appears to be quite accessible also to the School's staff and students.

Some of these managers' doors are, for instance, left open most of the time. Moreover, one can often observe them in conversation with other participants in the School, at the far end of their corridor, next to the printer that has been located there exclusively for their use. Such casual meetings can also be observed in other parts of the building, particularly on the flight of stairs that connects this end of the ground floor to the building's restaurant and its upper floors. These stairs in fact constitute the relatively open and undefined space of the kind mentioned earlier, where the informal power relations prevail, and deals can be negotiated and decisions can be confirmed.

Invisible Decision-Making

On closer observation, however, most of the organization's internal decision-making is more likely, in fact, to be invisible to an outside observer because here, as elsewhere, it is usually performed behind closed doors, in so-called 'back stage' situations, to prevent the inevitable power effects from openly frustrating the process (cf. Bailey 1977, Buchanan and Boddy 1992). The outcomes of this decision-making are usually distributed more or less 'after the fact', through the School's internal network, or they are presented to the

School's students and staff in 'front stage' (Bailey 1977) meetings, to encourage public debate.

As for external decision-making that may affect the School on a day-to-day basis, the absent networking described earlier might also apply. The School's representatives may meet the University's various decision-makers at locations outside the building – some of these locations are expressly provided at the *Uithof* discussed earlier. Most of the committees that organize research practices in the academic world today, and governmental policies affecting higher education would also be developed elsewhere. Again, the building may only provide a home base to these activities, which, generally speaking, cannot be expected to be locally visible at all.

Incomprehensible Control

The building not only provides the School's IT-supported infrastructure to support the work processes I described earlier; this electronic support may also be relevant to the managerial efforts related to the School's internal control and external accountability. This infrastructure is often quite invisible to most of the building's occupants, as are the numerous operational managers and coordinating staff who are actually involved in its operation. Their workplaces are mostly relegated to the remotest parts of the building, as they are tucked away on its third floor. And, although their presence can quite often be observed in informal encounters in the building's hallways, the impact of this physical absence may very well be framed by some of the 'end-users' who occupy the building as an incomprehensible kind of 'remote control'.

DISCUSSION: WHAT DO BUILDINGS DO?

The observations that have been made using Brand's six Ss help us to visualize the complex and varied interplay of spatial settings and materiality and those institutional practices that constitute the School's working life. In fact, the data presented here show us that these physical elements can be seen to do things. Following Latour's argument that 'in addition to "determining" and serving as a "backdrop for human action", things might authorize, allow, afford, encourage, permit, suggest, influence, block, render possible, and so on' (Latour 2005, p. 72), I can now present some verbs of my own that articulate what this case discussion has shown: these various material aspects can be seen to affect, take part in, negotiate, make visible, present, provide, organize, accommodate and materialize the School's activities in various ways, but they can be observed to take part in various social networks as well.

To begin with these networks: in relation to them the significance of a building's location stands out. This can also be demonstrated with the present building. So if, at first sight, the building appears to be standing all alone, my data also show that a building's location – or, following Brand, its Site – can be very relevant to determining the School's general position. It also shows, however, that the relevance of a particular Site in this respect may change over time. At one point in time, for instance, the present building could be observed as being a prominent part of a nineteenth-century city expansion which also involved a university expansion. But, after the physical prominence of this nineteenth-century era had become obsolete, this very same building would have been seen as located at the edge of the city's medieval centre, something that later seemed important for the School to point out in its conversations with the university. This obsolescence of its nineteenth-century environment was initially triggered by the university's (and city's) expansion to the *Uithof*, but the relevance of this university building's site was restored by a renewed interest in the medieval city centre, also developed by the university.

This condition, however, does not diminish the fact that, physically speaking, the School and its building appear to be standing all alone in this physical context. But together with the fact that it was located at some distance from the university's administration, this condition seemed to support the School's administrative independence and educative mission. On the one hand, it seems to have materialized this organization's 'immunity' to its university context; on the other hand, it established the 'inner-directedness' the School needed to establish its educational innovations, although the 'new learning' the School presents may certainly have been be reinforced by a number of governmental policies as well. In spite of its obvious nineteenth-century institutionalist origins, the actual physical appearance of this building may very well have reinforced the innovative character of the School's space.

We can also focus, however, on the 'institutionalized' activities the School presents on a day-to-day basis. Then Brand's concepts may help us observe how a building's materialization of places and spaces can both enable and constrain the physical movements associated with them. Although I do not present the actual experiences of the people involved, my data have shown that, although the building's original structural rigidity may at first sight prove a constraint on the School's educational innovations, the building's adaptation may very well have played a considerable part in their actual implementation. Moreover, the application of Brand's work helps us realize that some activities – for instance the ones involved with teaching (and with going to school) – are essentially much more 'local' than others.

It even shows that some activities may suffer more from visibility than others. For instance, this specific School's teaching may actually flourish in the spotlight, but the School's management work may, in fact, present us with a much more contradictory situation: at some moments the local visibility of managers may appear to be essential to their actions, but their invisibility and physical absence may be equally desirable at some other points in time. And, except for the activities involved with writing, the notion of absent networking illustrates, once again, that the notion of visibility may actually be quite irrelevant to the local performance of research. An academic community may in fact rely both on 'local invisibility' and on 'absent networking' for the successful performance of its research.

I have paid very little attention, in the course of my research, to the numerous decision-making processes that preceded the actual (re)construction of the building I have considered in this chapter. These decision-making processes may well have led to interesting observations concerning the educational policies involved or the worldwide development of the various sciences. They may even concern the financial partners, developers, and real estate people who may, for instance, be responsible for the choice of a building's site (Lefebvre [1974] 1991, p. 228), not to mention the architects who are responsible for its actual design and construction (Dale and Burrell 2008, pp. 23–6).

As a consequence, I have refrained, as well, from paying a lot of attention to the various expectations that are so often a part of these decision-making processes (see also Van Marrewijk 2009), although, among other things, I have quoted the School's representatives when they argued that the newly created spaces and places of this building must be particularly conducive to the School's innovative teaching. Surprisingly, such aspirations are often presented as facts in scientific arguments concerning buildings. Kornberger and Clegg (2003, p. 78), for example, argue that undefined spaces, such as those discussed above, can be expected to enhance an organization's creativity, by definition.

And yet, it would not do to simply warn against the temptations that are apparently presented by such aspirations. Nor would it suffice to 'debunk' them by confronting them with the 'reality' of the everyday practices that are actually performed in and around organizations. I would like to suggest here, instead, that a careful consideration of the actual dynamics of such arguments and aspirations may actually open up an interesting field of research (see Yanow 1996; see also Dale and Burrell 2008).

ACKNOWLEDGEMENTS

This paper was presented at the Third Annual Symposium on Current Developments in Ethnographic Research in the Social and Management Sciences, 4–6 September 2008 at the University of Liverpool. I thank the colleagues present for their stimulating input. I also thank the editors of this volume for their thorough editing and valuable comments. Any flaws that may remain are my own!

REFERENCES

Augé, Michel ([1992] 1995), *Non-Places: Introduction to an Anthropology of Supermodernity*, translated by John Howe, London: Verso.

Bailey, Frederick G. (1977), *Morality and Expediency: The Folklore of Academic Politics*, Oxford: Blackwell.

Bovens, Mark (2006), 'Space Matters: Creating an Academic Community', presented at the Space Studies Seminar, 30 November, Utrecht School of Governance, the Netherlands.

Bowker, Geoffrey C. and Susan Leigh Star ([1999] 2000), *Sorting Things Out: Classification and Its Consequences*, Cambridge, MA: MIT Press.

Brand, Stuart (1994), *How Buildings Learn: What Happens after They're Built*, 2nd edn, London: Phoenix Illustrated.

Buchanan, David and David Boddy (1992), *The Expertise of the Change-Agent: Public Performance and Backstage Activity*, New York: Prentice Hall.

Csikszentmihalyi, Mihalyi (1993), 'Why we need things', in Steven Lubar and W. David Kingery (eds), *History from Things: Essays on Material Culture,* Washington, DC: Smithsonian Institution Press, pp. 20–29.

Dale, Karen and Gibson Burrell (2008), *The Spaces of Organisation and the Organisation of Space: Power, Identity and Materiality at Work,* Basingstoke: Palgrave Macmillan.

De Jong, Angeliek and Kees Visser (2008), *De Singel van Utrecht: Een Wandeling* [*The Utrecht Outer Canal: A Walking Tour*], Utrecht, the Netherlands: Gusto.

Douglas, Mary ([1966] 1991), *Purity and Danger: An Analysis of the Concepts of Pollution and Taboo*, London: Routledge.

Gastelaars, Marja (2009), *The Public Services under Reconstruction: Client Experiences, Professional Practices, and Managerial Control,* London: Routledge.

Gergen, Kenneth J. (2002), 'The challenge of absent presence', in James E. Katz and Mark Aakhus (eds), *Perpetual Contact: Mobile Communication, Private Talk, Public Performance,* Cambridge: Cambridge University Press, pp. 227–41.

Ibelings, Hans (2009), *De Architectuur van de Uithof* [*Uithof Architecture*], accessed at www.uu.nl/NL/Universiteitutrecht/CultuurenArchtectuur, 7 January.

Knorr-Cetina, Karen (1999), *Epistemic Cultures: How the Sciences Make Knowledge,* Cambridge, MA: Harvard University Press.

Kornberger, Martin and Stewart Clegg (2003), 'The architecture of complexity', *Culture and Organization*, **9** (2), 75–91.

Latour, Bruno (2005), *Reassembling the Social,* Oxford: Oxford University Press.

Latour, Bruno and Steve Woolgar ([1979] 1986), *Laboratory Life: The Construction of Scientific Facts,* Princeton, NJ: Princeton University Press.

Lefebvre, Henri ([1974] 1991), *The Production of Space*, translated by Donald Nicholson-Smith, Malden: Blackwell.

Reinink, Wessel (1984), *Van Johannapolder tot Uithof:. Ontstaan en Ontwikkeling van een Universitaire Vestiging* [*From Johanna-polder to Uithof: Emergence and Further Development of a University Settlement*], Historische reeks, Utrecht, vol. 4, Utrecht: Matrijs.

Roelevink, Harald (2008), 'Binnenpleinen zijn prettige ruimtes in een stad' ['Inner courts are pleasant spaces in a city'], in *Campus onder de Dom 3*, accessed 22 May at www2.hum.uu.nl.

Sennett, Richard (1974), *The Fall of Public Man: On the Social Psychology of Capitalism*, New York: Vintage Books.

Sennett, Richard (1991), *The Conscience of the Eye: The Design and Social Life of Cities*, New York: Alfred A. Knopf.

Snelders, Harry A.M. and Cor Schuurmans (1980), 'Christophorus buys ballot (1817–1890)', in Anne Kox and Margot Chamalaun (eds), *Van Stevin tot Lorentz: Portretten van Nederlandse Natuurwetenschappers* [*From Stevin to Lorentz: Portraits of Dutch Physical Scientists*], Amsterdam: Intermediair, pp. 123–34.

Van der Woud, Auke (1987), *Het Lege Land: De Ruimtelijke Orde van Nederland 1798–1848* [*The Empty Country: The Netherlands' Spatial Order 1798–1848*], Amsterdam: Meulenhoff Informatief.

Van El, Carla (2002), *Figuraties en Verklaringen: Stijlgebonden Schoolvorming in de Nederlandse Sociologie na 1968* [*Figurations and Explanations: Emerging Genres in Dutch Sociology After 1968*], Amsterdam: Aksant.

Van Gennep, Arnold ([1908] 1960), *The Rites of Passage*, Chicago, IL: University of Chicago Press.

Van Maanen, John (ed.) (1995), *Representation in Ethnography*, Thousand Oaks, CA: Sage.

Van Marrewijk, Alfons H. (2009), 'Corporate headquarters as physical embodiments of organizational change', *Journal of Organizational Change Management*, **22** (3), 290–306.

Verweel, Paul (2002), 'B&O als identiteit' ['B&O as an identity'], unpublished lecture presented at Utrecht University, 27 November, Utrecht, the Netherlands, Utrecht (27 November).

Westin, Andrew (1970), *Privacy and Freedom,* New York: Atheneum.

Yanow, Dvora (1996), *How Does a Policy Mean? Interpreting Policy and Organizational Actions,* Washington, DC: Georgetown University Press.

Yanow, Dvora (2006), 'Studying physical artifacts: an interpretive approach', in A. Rafaeli and M. Pratt (eds), *Artifacts and Organizations,* Mahwah, NJ: Lawrence Erlbaum.

5. The beauty and the beast: the embodied experience of two corporate buildings

Alfons van Marrewijk

The sun was shining brightly when I climbed the stairs to the spacious Moon Plaza and walked towards the number 5 building of Dutch telecom operator KPN. Standing there in the middle of the plaza, I looked up and saw on the top of the building the company's name with the golden crown. This was the logo that has meant so much for me, as for a large part of my professional career I have been working with KPN. In this company I have earned my living, obtained my PhD, come to make friends, and been fired during the collapse of the 'internet bubble'.

(Author's fieldwork notes, 14 May 2007)

This sort of personal interpretation and judgement of the meaning of the Moon Plaza reflects what Taylor (2002) calls the aesthetic experience of spatial settings. Such experience is triggered by an external object or setting (Warren 2008). Aesthetics have the double character of reflecting experience and judgement. Aesthetic experience and its associated judgements are subjective reactions to material things (real or imagined) but cannot be reduced to one or the other (Hernes et al. 2006, Warren 2008). For example, employees judge organizational spaces and construct the meaning(s) of those spaces (Dale and Burrell 2008). Lefebvre (1991) calls this phenomenological experienced space or spatial practice.

Organizational spaces as experienced by those working in them have increasingly received attention from organizational scientists (Gagliardi 1990, Witkin 1990, Strati 1999, Lam 2001, Felstead et al. 2005, Carr and Hancock 2006, Strati 2006, Warren 2008). These studies attend to aesthetic elements of organizational life in order to explore what has otherwise been hidden in mainstream organizational and management studies (Warren 2008). These studies of space as experience can be distinguished from other works on organizational space which study space as distance and space as the materialization of power relations (Taylor and Spicer 2007).

Although organizational aesthetics is a very interesting field, practical research on the topic is still problematic, as employees' perceptions and judgements of spatial (and other) aesthetics are difficult to grasp (Warren 2008).

Strati (2006) challenges organizational scientists to become more sensitive to aesthetics in organizations by studying artefacts in daily use. One example of such a study is Bjørkeng et al.'s (2009) analysis of project managers who preferred to hold meetings at their construction sites as their management practices were intertwined with being close to the work, with the smells and sounds of the site. Emotions linked to aesthetic dimensions of work, such as the feel of building materials, the smell of leather chairs, the beauty of office views, the noise of construction sites, can be experienced. However, although in such studies the researcher's person is often the main instrument of the research, as Van Maanen (1995) has noted, organizational researchers' aesthetic sensitivity is insufficient on its own to understand the aesthetic experiences of members of organizations from their own perspectives (Taylor and Spicer 2007, Warren 2008). The main focus of aesthetic research in organizations should be on how to explore the aesthetic responses of employees, rather than only to challenge researchers themselves to develop an aesthetic sensibility (Warren 2008, p. 564). This chapter contributes to this charge to do aesthetic research among employees by means of an auto-ethnographic account of spatial settings in organizations. The central questions in this chapter are 'What aesthetic experiences do employees have?' and 'How can these be studied?'

This chapter explores the aesthetic experiences of one employee – the author – with two different corporate buildings of Dutch telecom operator KPN. Drawing in auto-ethnographic fashion (Humphreys 2005) on my own personal experience as both telecom engineer and organizational anthropologist, I use the KPN case, on which the opening vignette draws, to discuss my aesthetic experiences of both the Central Work Place (CWP) building and the Moon Plaza building. I have selected these two corporate buildings for my focus as they triggered opposing aesthetic responses within me. They thereby help me theorize about the aesthetic dimensions of organizational spaces.

The chapter is structured as follows. The first section discusses a theoretical framework on the aesthetics of re-materializing organizations. The subsequent section presents methodological reflections on studying aesthetic experiences in organization, as well as the methods used in this case study. Then I introduce the KPN case, describing the aesthetic experiences in the two different buildings. The findings are discussed after that, followed by a concluding section.

THE AESTHETICS OF RE-MATERIALIZED ORGANIZATIONS

The richness of physical and spatial arrangements in organizations has interpretive potential for studying various aspects of organizational life. Organizational spaces and spatial arrangements are slowly drawing more attention in organization and management studies (for example, Steele 1973, Rapoport 1976, Becker 1981, Gagliardi 1990, Nauta 1991, Casey 1993, Yanow 1995, 1998, 2006a; Strati 1999, Clegg and Kornberger 2006, Dale and Burrell 2008). Despite these examples, physical features of the spatial environment have largely been ignored in organizational studies (Kornberger and Clegg 2004, Orlikowski 2007). While organizational researchers may observe visual artefacts when doing research in organizations, they usually don't mention these aspects of organizational life in their research reports (Strati 1999). Kornberger and Clegg (2004) plead for us to bring space back into organizational theory and to explore the interdependencies between physical space and organizational behaviour.

We should stop treating the social and the material as distinct and largely independent spheres of organizational life (Orlikowski 2007). Therefore, a useful starting point for the conceptualization of the social and the material as entwined is the anthropological perspective on material culture (Dale and Burrell 2008). Anthropologists have studied material culture and physical arrangements in local communities for a long time, as they see continuity between the social and the material. To draw on a few examples from well-known classic studies in anthropology, Douglas' (1966) *Purity and Danger* discussed the meaning of the lower positioning of the women's hut on the hill in a village in relation to the men's hut, understanding it as men's fear of women's power over reproduction. Lévi-Strauss (1966) discerned from the circular villages of Central Brazilian Indians a mapping of their basic cosmological principles. Malinowski (1922) perceived the spatial arrangement of the Trobriand village as reflective both of its overall unity and of the partial separation of sub-clan segments. Benedict (1989, p. 59) studied the construction of cliff-dwellings and semicircular valley citadels of the Pueblo Indians in relation to their rituals and beliefs. Latour (1993) has suggested utilizing the rich experience of these anthropological studies to study the social and the material in organizations from a holistic perspective.

During the period of the Enlightenment in Europe, Latour (1993) argues, human and non-human objects were established as two irrevocably sundered realms of knowledge and experience. From his perspective, such a separation imposes a binary division on the world of human experience that is not itself *in* the world. He introduces the concept of symmetric anthropology as a way of making equally problematic the world of people and the world of material phenomena, as well as their intersections and entanglements in social-material hybrids. These are proliferating entities that are made and remade as mixtures of culture and nature (Hubbard et al. 2004). In this perspective aesthetic experiences and spatial settings are not separated into cultural and material entities but are strongly intertwined. Symmetric anthropology assumes that organizational spaces and material objects are connected to aesthetic experiences in a network, without being trapped in vulgar material-ism (cf. Harris 1977) or material determinism, a view that the material world exhibits deterministic influence over the social world.

Based upon the rich experience of anthropological studies, De Certeau (1984) uses the concept of anthropological space to explore notions of built spaces as places of practice. The street, geometrically defined in urban plan-ning, is changed into place by the embodied experience of walkers and then transferred back into space as one moves on (De Certeau 1984). In the anthro-pological space concept, spatial experience entails a holistic relation to the world (De Certeau 1984). Organizational members' aesthetic experiences of spatial settings are expressed through sensations such as hearing, feeling and smelling (Corbett 2006, Warren 2008). To enable a more systematic analysis of the experience of organizational spaces, we might draw on Strati's (1999, p. 187) eight categories of organizational aesthetics:

1. the sacred, which includes legendary, fantastic, and mysterious emotions;
2. the picturesque, which contains colourful and fascinating spatial settings;
3. the tragic, related to heroic, suffering, and routine aspects of organiza-tions;
4. the ugly, as a category of distasteful and repulsive emotions;
5. the rhythmic, which focuses on movement;
6. the comic, concerned with the grotesque, irony, laughter, sarcasm and humour;
7. pathos, embracing the beauty and joy of aesthetics;
8. the graceful, related to elegance, work settings and charm.

These categories have to be understood in the context of power, as managers and architects try to influence the aesthetic experience of organizational employees (Kornberger and Clegg 2004). Dovey (1999, p. 15) analysed three different forms of spatial power related to aesthetic experiences. The first one structures through domination or intimidation: the spatial setting is designed to intimidate the visitor or employee; fascist architecture such as that of Albert Speer comes to mind. The second one is manipulation, where visitors or employees think they have free choice but in fact are guided through the space, as is the case in an amusement park, such as Disneyland, or a department store or supermarket. The third is seduction, the most subtle and embedded form, in which people identify themselves with specific spatial settings. Here one might think of a beautiful upmarket shopping area, a cool and aesthetic space that draws one into its folds through the delights of the market that it contains within its depths – if only one wanders through them and lets oneself go with the unfolding spectacle of beauty, fashion and scents; Galeries Lafayette in Paris would be one example. This third form includes aestheticization, the process of transfer whereby organizational goals and organizational identity are transferred to the employee in a process akin to psychological transference processes (Dale and Burrell 2008).

How can such ideas concerning spatial settings and aesthetics and related meaning-making processes be studied in organizations?

METHODOLOGICAL REFLECTIONS ON PARTICIPATING OBSERVATION IN ORGANIZATIONAL SETTINGS

Corporate buildings are seldom left to speak for themselves; they are described, reviewed and interpreted over and over in discourses in and on organizations (Berg and Kreiner 1990). Interpretive methods seek to define the stories that organizational spaces tell (Taylor and Spicer 2007, p. 333). Built spaces have their own vocabulary of building materials, size, scale, mass, colour, shape, design, and relationship with their environment (Yanow 2006a,b). Interpretive methods try to understand the meanings given to spatial settings in organizations by their employees, clients, customers and other visitors. Warren (2008) found that employees' judgements were often very different from her own as a researcher. The office in which they were co-located was more than an aesthetic object, as it was inscribed with everyday practicalities, joys and frustrations. For the researcher, the perspectives of the participants who are part of the research site are sources of significant insights (O'Toole and Were 2008). Researchers of organizational spaces should therefore focus on the ways in which actors experience and imagine physical manifestations and uses of space (Taylor and Spicer 2007).

If it is indeed the researcher who is key to aesthetic research (Strati 1999, Yanow 2006b), this raises some very important methodological concerns. The ethnographic literature emphasizes the ways in which the researcher him- or herself is the primary research 'tool' (Van Maanen 1995). Empathic understanding presupposes an emic perspective in which the researcher studies the organization 'from within', meaning putting oneself in the shoes of an employee (Bate 1997). Researchers might then gain a 'feel' for organizational aesthetics by sensually experiencing spaces as they carry out fieldwork in organizations (Strati 1999, Warren 2008). By working closely with employees, researchers themselves can become valid sources of data through their own aesthetic experiences, refining their capacity to empathize with others and imagining what it might be like to be them walking through and/or working in these same spaces (Warren 2008, p. 563). However, Strati (2006) values the aesthetic experience of employees over that of researchers.

This calls for an interpretive understanding of artefacts, building and spaces:

> Empathic understanding of intentional action essentially requires the researcher to place him/herself in the shoes of the social actor studied. This process presupposes active willingness, knowledge gathering methods, definition of the empathy situation, the architecture and style of accounts and an option for the dominant character of the knowledge process. (Strati 1999, p. 67)

Researchers access space through observing, with whatever degree of participation, and interpreting spatial vocabularies. Yanow (2006a,b) suggests a systematic analysis of space and physical arrangements through the use of four categories:

1. Design vocabularies concern the shape, height, width, mass, scale and material of the building;
2. Design gestures contextualize the relation of buildings to surrounding spaces;
4. Design proxemics refer to the social and personal space between people that shapes human behaviour;
4. Decor includes furnishing, furniture, art, chairs, statues and photographs.

These four categories provide the ethnographer with spatial vocabularies.

In the writing itself, the ethnographer can introduce meaning and morality into the discourse through the use of an autobiographical style (Van Maanen 1995). The author can be seen as a performer combining arts, science and craft in order to write an autobiographic account (Reed-Danahay 1997, Bochner and Ellis 2002, Ellis 2004). Autobiography enables the writer to present a personal narrative and perspective (Reed-Danahay 1997). The scientific autobiographical account, which is neither a fiction nor an art performance, produces understandings of interpretations and judgement concerning organizational aesthetics. Wallace (2003, p. 12) has called this the 'mazeway', a mental image that includes perceptions of both physical objects (human and non-human) in the environment and one's own body, organized by individual experience. Such auto-ethnography is much more helpful than other methods in accessing experiential data of this sort.

In the study presented here, interpretive methods such as participant observation, participation, observation, and interviewing have been used to collect data over a longitudinal period from 1985 to 2007. Participant observation was possible as I had been working at and studying the KPN organization in intervals from 1985 to 2007. From 1985 to 1988 I worked there full-time as a manager of the computer repair department, which was housed in the Central Work Place (CWP) building. In 1989 I became a project manager at the City of Rotterdam Police and took up the part-time study of organizational anthropology. To combine my professional background and academic interests in organizational anthropology, I returned to KPN in 1995 to do my PhD research on the company's change and internationalization processes. From 1995 until 1999, I took a role as a part-time consultant with International Support (IS). From 1999 to 2001 I worked part-time as a senior consultant with the international consulting department in the number 2 building on the Moon Plaza. In 2001, due to the collapse of the 'Internet bubble', I was dismissed from that position, but I continued to work in different departments at the Moon Plaza site and on international joint ventures as an independent consultant.

To analyse the spatial settings of the KPN headquarters, I have returned to a consideration of my aesthetic responses to the two KPN buildings. I have revisited diaries, field notes, observational accounts, pictures, and interview data generated and collected contemporaneously with my various positions in the company. In the process of analysis a certain reconstruction from memory is inescapable. In the same way Venkatesh (2009, p. 284) used his memory, apart from his field notes, to reconstruct his emotions when doing field work on a Chicago gang. Although memory is not a substitute for field notes, it can at times be a useful addition to them. I have tried to reproduce my aesthetic emotions as faithfully as possible. In addition, in 2008 I did desk research on the two buildings discussed here.

CASE INTRODUCTION: THE SPATIAL SETTINGS OF KPN HEADQUARTERS

The Dutch KPN headquarters consists of different buildings in the city of The Hague (see Fig. 5.1).

Each of these headquarters buildings is an embodiment of the company's change ambitions in its different phases of development. The Central Work Place (CWP) building was constructed in 1918, at a time when the company was a government-owned national monopoly, to be the central repair department for all KPN's equipment. Like the CWP all of the KPN buildings were indicated with abbreviations (see Fig. 5.1). The company's headquarters from 1989 to 1999 was called the AA building; the ARC became the headquarters building for international business, coming to symbolize the company's internationalization period. The Moon Plaza was the new headquarters from 1999 onwards, representing the company's networked period (Van Marrewijk 2009).

Furthermore, KPN's spatial location in relation to the Dutch government buildings in the centre of The Hague is a reflection of the privatization process, as the organization moved away from the city's political centre to a

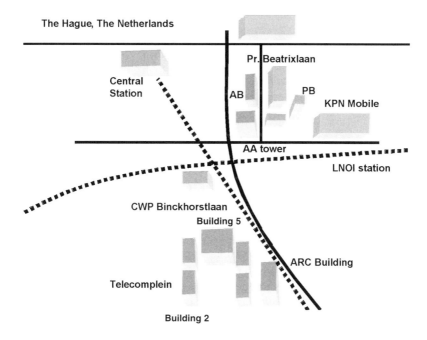

The Hague, The Netherlands

Central
Station

Pr. Beatrixlaan

AB

PB

KPN Mobile

AA tower

LNOI station

CWP Binckhorstlaan
Building 5

ARC Building

Telecomplein

Building 2

Source: A. van Marrewijk

Figure 5.1   Spatial organization of KPN headquarters in The Hague

commercial zone at the city's outskirts (Van Marrewijk 2009). Such introductory description teaches us about the design gesture (Yanow 2006a) of the buildings, but not so much about the aesthetic responses of an employee working in any of them. An aesthetic biography (Warren 2008) promises to obtain the employee's story of buildings, places and experiences. My personal impression of KPN's spatial locations was reflected in field notes from my early research (16 November 1998):

When arriving at the Laan van Nieuw Oost Indië (LNOI) train station at 8.45 a.m., the slender green AA tower and the impressive 133-metre-high telecommunication tower (PB) indicate the presence of KPN. I turn to the left where a beautiful large artistic installation in neon lights attracts my attention. The 30-metre-long wide neon piece of art represents the surface of the earth, with a volcano and two metropolises at each side of a sea. An aeroplane flies in the sky above the sea, and every 15 seconds the bright sun transforms into a blue moon. The neon art in blue, red, yellow and green is located at the KPN mobile network services building (KPN Mobile). To me it symbolizes the international character of KPN, as the organization now [in 1998] has subsidiaries all over the world.

   On my way to the monolithic AA tower I pass the Ministry of Social Affairs. A smaller part of the morning's office crowd enters this building; others continue to the Siemens building or even further on to a large Dutch insurance company. Those who are heading for the AA tower or for other KPN offices follow the turn in the road. I cut across the corner of an empty piece of ground opposite the green tower. A beaten path in the vegetation indicates that the KPN office workers all use this route. I arrive at the broad Prinses Beatrixlaan, nicknamed 'the PTT allee' [Post, Telegraph and Telecommunications Avenue] because of the many telecom buildings located here, such as the AA, AB, AC, ASL, PB, KS, SK, FGH and MBL buildings. This 'PTT allee' makes you feel proud to work in an organization with such an impressive physical presence.

However, when I started to work with KPN in 1985 as a telecom engineer, my judgements on the organization were not at all positive.

The Beast: Aesthetic Experiences of the CWP Binckhorstlaan Building

In 1985 KPN could be characterized as monopolistic, bureaucratic and technology oriented (Van Marrewijk 2003). KPN employed 30 000 civil servants who, as my ethnographic research showed, felt a strong loyalty towards the organization. The CWP was the repair department for all of the telecommunication and post equipment, such as telephones, switches, post sorting machines and office electronics (see Figure 5.2). Large quantities of all kinds of defective equipment were brought in by trucks and repaired by over 500 employees. The CWP was located at the Binckhorstlaan in The Hague in a rather depressing industrial area. Among the neighbours were a car-demolition site, oil distribution tanks, auto breaker yard, and other heavy industrial operations. The CWP building was situated in a remote corner at the cross-road of railways and highways, a relic from the time when post and equipment were transported by rail (see Figure 5.1).

The CWP consisted of two parallel buildings of five floors each, separated by a plaza filled with containers full of electronic and mechanical waste ready for destruction (see Figure 5.2).

At the gate security guards checked all visitors and employees before they entered the premises. In the first building management, administration and some of the repair departments were situated. A connection at the second floor level made it possible to cross the plaza to the second building without going outside when it was raining. Large halls in the second building were where mobile telephones, telecom equipment, and switches were repaired and old telephone exchanges were stripped.

The halls were typically four metres high, 50 metres long, and the full width of the building. I worked in one of these halls together with a team of computer repair technicians. It was a noisy, smelly, dirty environment to work in. The sounds of machines, trucks, forklifts, music and the many employees

Source: A. van Marrewijk

Figure 5.2   The CWP building

reflected off the walls. The odour of solder and synthetic resin, used in the repair of electronics, was mixed with strong smells of Bakelite, a synthetic combined from phenol and formaldehyde, which was a very popular raw material for telephone equipment in the second half of the twentieth century. Bakelite telecom equipment, when demolished, gives off a distinctive sharp smell like burnt rubber. Interestingly, the Bakelite telephones were being destroyed by the CWP as outdated technology, but at the same time they were being taken home by employees as nostalgic symbols of ancient technology. The repair work was dirty as old electronic equipment is always covered with fine dust and cobwebs. However, my colleagues perceived working with computer equipment to be less dirty work than repairing telecom equipment. Dirt piled up in containers in the plaza, and as wind regularly got hold of the materials in the containers, the plaza was filled with plastics, packaging and expanded polystyrene.

The CWP building was a stuffy place to work. Surveillance in the building depended on the arrangement of spatial settings. Managers of repair units were seated at platforms 50 centimetres high to keep watch on employees, providing for constant surveillance, like the panopticon discussed in Chapter 3 (see also Koskela 2003). Clearly, the architects and management of the CWP building designed the platforms both to influence the employees' aesthetic experience of being guarded and to support the power position of managers. Furthermore, at the entrance to the repair hall, employees had to stamp their time registration cards when entering or leaving. Permission had to be asked of the managers when someone wanted to leave, even for going to the toilet. As a consequence of the surveillance and the 'beastly' CWP building, my colleagues and I adapted a '9 to 5' working mentality. I did not want to work with the organization more than 32 hours a week.

KPN headquarters perceived CWP as a relic from 'ancient' times when telecom monopolists did repairs themselves. Increasingly, however, repairs were outsourced as competition was opened up in the telecom market. In 1987, the greater portion of the 500 employees at the Central Work Place was laid off due to Asian competition for repairing peripheral telecom equipment. They were among the first to experience the consequences of the widespread changes in the international telecom market. Interestingly, the building, sold by KPN in 1993, now houses art exhibition halls, architecture firms and new media companies, transforming its unpleasant industrial character into a space for creativity. However, unlike the ending of the fairy tale, *Beauty and the Beast*, CWP remains for me an ugly relic from a monopolistic episode in KPN's history.

The Beauty: Aesthetic Experiences of the Moon Plaza

In 1999 KPN moved its headquarters to the Moon Plaza, a complex of 85,000 sq m spread over 13 offices. The organization was privatized in 1989, taking its place in full international competition in a rapidly growing ICT market. More than 4000 employees worked at the Moon Plaza on top of a parking garage. At that time I worked as an international consultant supporting the implementation of KPN's internationalization strategy in Asia and Eastern Europe. When I walked towards the number 2 building, I crossed large grass fields and an open space with fountains. To me and my colleagues, the Moon Plaza was at that time a 'hot spot', *the* place to be, as it offered many opportunities to be close to top management, to meet a wide variety of colleagues and to be working in a nice, park-like setting (see Figure 5.3).

The number 5 building was, with nine floors, the most important of all buildings, carrying the KPN logo at the top of the building (see Figure 5.3). Its layout was a materialization of power relations as the distribution of floors reflected and supported the position of managers in the organization. The CEOs of KPN occupied the ninth floor, and on the eighth floor the board of directors was located. These executives had their own parking spots with their own separate entrance to the elevator that brought them directly to the eighth or ninth floors. Corporate communication was on the seventh floor; control, the treasury, strategy, and sales were on the fifth; legal on the fourth; the ICT office on the third; billing and auditing on the second; the human resources department on the first; and finally, on the ground floor, the kitchen, restau-

Source: A. van Marrewijk

Figure 5.3 The Moon Plaza

rant, reception and meeting rooms. Here on the ground floor was where my colleagues and I met in the restaurant during lunch. Returning from the number 5 building, employees had to cross the plaza and sometimes had the feeling that they were being watched by top management.

To guarantee the visual unity of the Moon Plaza, all buildings were constructed of English red-brown brick. The raw bricks, however, weren't English but made in the Netherlands and Toscana polished – to make them look older. To overcome the endless repetition of colour, the red-brown brick walls were interrupted with white concrete and sand coloured stones. The architects of the Moon Plaza created the conceptual design of the buildings by combining international ambience with a Dutch flavour, meaning sober colours and style. They monitored the original concept in order to create unity in the diversity, as the complex was designed by five different Dutch architects. All of the buildings have green blocks mounted high in their walls. Green is the colour 'brand' of KPN and is used in all logos, advertising, company cars, etc. Even its employees sometimes make the joke that they are being sprayed green for the company.

My personal impression of the Moon Plaza is reflected in my field notes (4 April 2001):

'Good morning,' I say to a colleague from another department when crossing the Moon Plaza. At the plaza there are clear markers to direct visitors to the different buildings. Each building has a number. I enter the number 2 building, take my electronic pass and hold the card in front of the electronic device. Recently, the doorkeepers situated in each building were replaced by these electronic 'eyes'. I take the elevator to the second floor where the international consultancy department is situated.

Again, I have to use my electronic pass to enter the department. 'Good morning,' I say to the secretary near the entrance to the department. The cleaning employees have just cleaned the wall-to-wall carpet this morning, and it smells of soap. Directly on the right side, the director and the financial manager have their offices. On the left side the business development managers and the human resources managers work. For all other employees there is a large open space in which cubicles are situated on both sides near the windows. The work stations are divided by walls 1.26 metres high. Noise is limited to telephone conversations and colleagues' discussions. For those in need of complete silence there are different workspaces for one or two employees to concentrate or for 'intensive' telephone calls. The open meeting table in the middle of the department room is meant for informal gatherings, ad hoc discussions, and reading. Centrally located in buildings 5 and 7 are meeting rooms that can be reserved at a service desk. Furthermore, there are coffee corners on each floor for informal meetings: the coffee, tea and hot chocolate are free of charge.

It's already 9.30 a.m. and all of the comfortable work spots near the windows are occupied. When moving from the AA tower to the new Moon plaza complex, I was given a map with documentation on the new building, including articles on flexible working and questions and answers on innovative office concepts (The office concept of KPN Telecom 1999). In this Q&A map I could read why the innovative office concept was introduced on such a large scale. The information folder stressed the obligation KPN felt as an ICT company to be at the forefront of innovations. Furthermore, the improvement in communications, the reductions in the high costs of organizational changes, and the more efficient uses of expensive spaces and means were other motives to introduce the innovative office concept. The terms 'high costs' and 'expensive' were mentioned by KPN's CEO, but so was the symbolic importance of the new building: 'Telling people that things are changing is not enough; they have to experience this themselves. To reach this we have used an instrument whose power cannot be underestimated: symbols ... These changes, however superficial they may appear, function as an important symbol of the birth of a new organization.' (Dik 1998, p. 120; author's translation).

In the number 2 building at Moon Plaza I have no personal working place. Other colleagues, who work more often in the department than I do, have their own personal working space with photos of their children, partner, faraway places and some international postcards. This is illicit, as the formal KPN policy requires that desks be empty of personal belongings: 'It is not the intention that employees leave personal belongings at their worksites. If a photo is placed on a desk together with a pile of paper, another colleague will not take that seat. Therefore, clean desks have to be adopted by all of the company.' (KPN Telecom 1999, p. 3; author's translation)

In addition to collective offices with flexible work sites, working hours within the international consultancy department were also flexible. A large part of the assignments were based abroad in foreign telecom markets, so working in the evenings and on weekends was normal for my colleagues and me. By now, I have become a loyal employee of the entrepreneurial KPN (Van Marrewijk 2003) who visits the number 2 building to see colleagues. This is in keeping with Felstead et al. (2005), who argue that the socio-spatial relations and aesthetic order of collective offices are specifically designed to generate intense social interaction among employees. My personal impression of meeting colleagues at the Moon Plaza is reflected in my field notes from 22 November, 2000:

> At 12.30 p.m. I walk with some colleagues across the sunny plaza where some people are sitting on benches and eating lunch in the sun. I enter the number 5 building in which the large canteen with the nickname the 'grub barn' is situated. It is very busy, long lines of people are waiting to scan their chosen products in the scanner and pay electronically. Almost all of the seats are occupied, but I see some people I know from another department and suggest to my colleagues that we sit with them.
>
> On returning to my work site in Building 2, I have the firm intention of arriving next morning as early as possible to occupy one of the nice spaces near the windows overlooking the plaza. It helps to find out if one of the sale managers is on travel assignment, then I can occupy his desk until his return.

These field notes represent my aesthetic experiences of working in the number 2 building at the Moon Plaza. In contrast to the 'beasty' CWP building, the Moon Plaza was a 'beauty': pleasant, modern, clean, relatively quiet, open for making contacts, and serving good food.

DISCUSSION

The exploration of the aesthetic responses of employees triggered by two KPN corporate buildings generates some interesting insights into organizational life in KPN. Treating the social and the material as interdependent spheres of organizational life helps to uncover elements of daily life which normally would have stayed hidden. The everyday experiences with annoying noises, horrible smells, dirty rubbish and ugly halls in the CWP building and with quiet, clean, comfortable and open offices in the Moon Plaza building are the 'mazeways', including both images of physical spatial settings and individual aesthetic experiences, that have built up my experiences of this organization. As an employee of KPN I developed two distinct 'mazeways', one each for CWP and Moon Plaza, in which opposing aesthetic experiences and judgements were strongly intertwined. These led me to distinguish among eight different categories of aesthetics (see Table 5.1).

The empirical data on the two buildings studied do not reflect all eight of Strati's (1999) aesthetic categories. No references to the comic or the rhythmic could be found in my aesthetic experiences of the CWP and Moon Plaza

Table 5.1   Aesthetic categories in the CWP and the Moon Plaza buildings

Aesthetic experience	CWP (1985–89)	Moon Plaza (1999–2007)
Smells	Bakelite, solder, synthetic resin, dirt	Office smell, chocolate, coffee, soap
Sounds	Machines, trucks, forklifts, music in large halls	Typewriting, silence, telephone calls, conversations in muffled voices
Sights	Car destruction industry, oil distribution centre, dirt containers at plaza	New architecture, the plaza fountain, trees, grass, water ponds
Sacred	Relic from monopolistic era, periphery of telecom business	Ambitious international future, sexy, presence of top management
Tragic	Repair, destruction, suffering organization, fixed workplaces	Daily routines at flexible workplaces
Ugly	Industrial waste, dirt containers, halls, site of building	Separate management parking spots
Pathos	Ugly, depressive	Beauty, international, high-tech business
Graceful	Charming old industrial complex	Design furniture, open offices, spacious plaza

buildings. I did, however, experience the materialization of power relations in both buildings. The platforms to keep watch on employees in the CWP building, the distribution of floors in the number 5 building, and the separate entrance and position of top management overlooking the plaza reflected and supported the position of managers in the organization.

The opposing aesthetic emotions of the two corporate buildings are related to two distinct periods of KPN's history. During my experiences with the CWP, KPN was a dull, monopolistic, government-owned telecommunication department. The management and the architect of the CWP building successfully imposed bureaucratic surveillance on my colleagues and me. In this period I was a telecom engineer in public service with a '9 to 5' working mentality. In the period of my experiences with the Moon Plaza, KPN had transformed itself into a 'hot', privatized, international telecom operator. This transformation was embodied in the new Moon Plaza headquarters (Van Marrewijk 2009). The management and architects of the Moon Plaza successfully influenced the aesthetic experiences of my colleagues and me by seducing us to identify ourselves with KPN's internationalization objectives. The aesthetic experiences of the beautiful Moon Plaza buildings stimulated me to work extra hours and weekends and to develop an entrepreneurial working attitude.

In this particular case, these data illustrate the opposed aesthetic emotions that can be observed in ways strongly related to the organization's change process and the ethnographer-author's position in the organization. Furthermore, the data show the close relation of aesthetic emotions and spatial power as managers and architects of CWP and Moon Plaza transfer, for each building, different organizational goals and organizational identity to the employees. In this way, aestheticization (Dale and Burell 2008) supported KPN's organizational change process.

These elements of daily life would normally have stayed hidden in organizational studies. The auto-ethnographic method is a valuable extension of research instruments for studying aesthetic experiences of spatial settings in organizations. Although regarded as self-indulgent by mainstream academics (Warren 2008), this approach meets a need for practical research on aesthetic experiences that employees, clients, customers and others have of organizational spatial settings, something that has, on the whole, been understudied. The auto-ethnographic method enables the participating observer to make a systematic analysis of his/her experiences, at different moments in time, of the organizational spaces experienced as a researcher and, in this case, as an organizational member in various roles. The auto-ethnographic method gains a view that otherwise is not available: the researcher is aware of the interdependency of his/her own body and the surrounding world, the 'body in-the-world' (Merleau-Ponty 1962, p. 101). In this respect the body is the primary bearer of intentionality and the subject of perception. The body is the origin of the object at the very centre of our experience (Merleau-Ponty 1962, p. 71).

CONCLUSIONS

The aim of this chapter has been to explore the aesthetic experiences and judgements made by employees of two corporate buildings of Dutch telecom operator KPN, through the reflective auto-ethnographic account by the researcher of his own experiences.

The chapter has uncovered some challenges for scientists studying spatial settings in organizations. If researchers are to grasp aesthetic experiences of employees and so overcome the 'aesthetic muteness' (Taylor 2002) among organizational members and scientific community, the reading of spatial vocabularies needs interpretive methods in which the researcher is central. This is what an autobiographical method enables, as it allows the researcher to present a personal account of organizational life that includes senses such as seeing, hearing, smelling and feeling, as appropriate to the research setting. Here, the researcher is not only studying the spatial settings employees work in; the researcher *is* an employee.

This doubling of identity, as KPN engineer and organizational anthropologist, is of key epistemological importance. It makes reflexivity on the role and position of researcher of utmost importance when studying aesthetic experiences.

ACKNOWLEDGEMENTS

I want to thank Dvora Yanow, Stewart Clegg, Marianne Stang Våland and Karen Smits for their useful comments on earlier versions of the chapter.

REFERENCES

Bate, Paul (1997), 'Whatever happened to organisational anthropology? A review of the field of organisational ethnography and anthropological studies', *Human Relations*, **50** (9), 1147–71.

Becker, Frank (1981), *Workspace: Creating Environments in Organisations,* New York: Praeger.

Benedict, Ruth (1989 [1934]), *Patterns of Culture*, Boston, MA: Houghton Mifflin.

Berg, Per Olaf and Kristian Kreiner (1990), 'Corporate architecture', in Pasquale Gagliardi (ed.), *Symbols and Artifacts,* New York: Aldine de Gruyter, pp. 124–45.

Bjørkeng, Kjersti, Stewart Clegg, and Tyrone Pitsis (2009), 'Becoming (a) practice', *Management Learning*, **40** (2), 145–59.

Bochner, Art and Carolyn Ellis (eds) (2002), *Ethnographically Speaking: Autoethnography, Literature, and Aesthetics*, Oxford: Alta Mira Press.

Carr, Adrian and Philip Hancock (2006), 'Space and time in organization change management', *Journal of Organizational Change Management*, **19** (5), 545–57.

Casey, Edward (1993), *Getting Back into Place,* Bloomington, IN: Indiana University.

Clegg, Stewart and Martin Kornberger (2006), *Spaces as Process: Developing a Recursive Perspective on Organisational Space*, Oslo and Copenhagen: Liber and Copenhagen Business School Press.

Corbett, Martin (2006), 'Scents of identity': Organisation studies and the conundrum of the nose, *Culture and Organisation*, **12** (3), 221–32.

Dale, Karen and Gibson Burrell (2008), *The Spaces of Organisation and the Organisation of Space: Power Identity and Materiality at Work,* Basingstoke: Palgrave Macmillan.

De Certeau, Michel (1984), *The Practice of Everyday Life*. Berkeley, CA: University of California Press.

Dik, Wim (1998), 'Cultuur door de bocht' ['Culture at change'], in C. Quarles Van

Ufford (ed.), *De Ideologie van de vrije markt* [*The Ideology of the Free Market*], Amsterdam: VU Uitgeverij, pp. 180–205.

Douglas, Mary (1966), *Purity and Danger,* Baltimore, MD: Penguin Books.

Dovey, Kim (1999), *Framing Places: Mediating Power in Built Form,* London: Routledge.

Ellis, Carolyn (2004), *The Ethnographic I: A Methodological Novel about Autoethnography,* Oxford: Alta Mira Press.

Felstead, Alan, Nick Jewson, and Sally Walters (2005), *Changing Places of Work,* New York: Palgrave Macmillan.

Gagliardi, Pasquale (1990), *Symbols and Artifacts: Views of the Corporate Landscape,* New York: Walter de Gruyter.

Harris, Marvin (1977), *Cannibals and Kings: The Origins of Cultures,* New York: Random House.

Hernes, Tor, Torre Bakken, and Per Ingvar Olsen (2006), 'Spaces as process: developing a recursive perspective on organisational space', in Stewart Clegg and Martin Kornberger (eds), *Space, Organizations and Management Theory,* Oslo and Copenhagen: Liber and Copenhagen Business School Press, pp. 33–63.

Hubbard, Phil, Rob Kitchin, and Gill Valentine (2004), *Key Thinkers on Space and Place,* London: Sage Publications.

Humphreys, Michael (2005), 'Getting personal: reflexivity and autoethnographic vignettes', *Qualitative Inquiry,* **11** (6), 840–60.

KPN Telecom (1999), *The Office Concept,* internal document, The Hague: KPN Telecom.

Kornberger, Martin and Stewart Clegg (2004), 'Bringing space back in: organizing the generative building', *Organization Studies,* **25** (7), 1095–114.

Koskela, Hille (2003), '"Cam era" – the contemporary urban panopticon', *Surveillance & Society,* **1** (3), 292–313.

Lam, Shun Yin (2001), 'The effects of store environment on shopping behaviors: a critical review', *Advances in Consumer Research,* **28** (2), 190–207.

Latour, Bruno (1993), *We Have Never Been Modern,* London: Harvester Wheatsheaf.

Lefebvre, Henri (1991), *The Production of Space,* Oxford: Basil Blackwell.

Lévi-Strauss, Claude (1966), *The Savage Mind,* Chicago, IL: University of Chicago Press.

Malinowski, Bronislaw (1922), *Argonauts of the Western Pacific: An Account of Native Enterprise and Adventure in the Archipelagos of Melanesian New Guinea,* London: George Routledge & Sons.

Merleau-Ponty, Michel (1962), *Phenomenology of Perception,* London: Routledge.

Nauta, Rein (1991), 'Symboliek in organisaties' ['Symbolism in organisations'], in J. Van Grumbkow (ed.), *Cultuur in Organisaties* [*Culture in Organisations*], Assen, The Netherlands: Van Gorkum, pp. 55–80.

O'Toole, Paddy and Prisca Were (2008), 'Observing places: using space and material culture in qualitative research', *Qualitative Research,* **8** (5), 616–34.

Orlikowski, Wanda J. (2007), 'Sociomaterial practices: exploring technology at work', *Organization Studies,* **28** (9), 1435–48.

Rapoport, Amos (1976), *The Mutual Interaction of People and Their Built Environment,* Paris: Mouton Publishers.

Reed-Danahay, Deborah (ed.) (1997), *Auto/Ethnography: Rewriting the Self and the Social,* Oxford: Berg Publishers.

Steele, Fritz (1973), *Physical Settings and Organization Development,* Reading, MA: Addison-Wesley.

Strati, Antonio (1999), *Organization and Aesthetics,* London: Sage.

Strati, Antonio (2006), 'Organisational artifacts and the aesthetic approach', in Anat Rafaeli and Michael Pratt (eds), *Artifacts and Organizations: Beyond Mere Symbolism,* Mahwah, NJ: Lawrence Erlbaum Associates, pp. 23–41.

Taylor, Scott (2002), 'Overcoming aesthetic muteness: researching organisational member's aesthetic experience', *Human Relations,* **55** (7), 821–40.

Taylor, Scott and Andre Spicer (2007), 'Time for space: a narrative review of research on organisational spaces', *International Journal of Management Reviews,* **9** (4), 325–46.

Van Maanen, John (ed.) (1995), *Representation in Ethnography,* Thousands Oaks, CA: Sage.

Van Marrewijk, Alfons H. (2003), 'New forms of organisational identification in a fragmented society: the case of telecom operators', in Wim Koot, Peter Leisink, and Paul T. Verweel (eds), *The Meaning of Organisational Relationships in the Networking Age,* Cheltenham, UK and Northampton, MA, USA: Edward Elgar, pp. 377–413.

Van Marrewijk, Alfons H. (2009), 'Corporate headquarters as physical embodiments of organisational change', *Journal of Organisational Change Management,* **22** (3), 290–306.

Venkatesh, Sudhir (2009), *Gang Leader for a Day,* London: Penguin.

Wallace, Anthony (2003), *Revitalizations & Mazeways: Essays on Cultural Change,* Lincoln, NE: Nebraska University Press.

Warren, Samantha (2008), 'Empirical challenges in organisational aesthetics research: towards a sensual methodology', *Organization Studies,* **29** (4), 559–80.

Witkin, Robert (1990), 'The aesthetic imperative of a rational-technical machinery: a study in organisational control through the design of artifacts', in Pasquale Gagliardi (ed.), *Symbols and Artifacts: Views of the Corporate Landscape,* New York: Walter de Gruyter.

Yanow, Dvora (1995), 'Built space as story: the policy stories that buildings tell', *Policy Studies Journal,* **23** (3), 407–22.

Yanow, Dvora (1998), 'Space stories; or, studying museum buildings as organizational spaces, while reflecting on interpretive methods and their narration', *Journal of Management Inquiry,* **7**, 215–39.

Yanow, Dvora (2006a), 'Studying physical artifacts: an interpretive approach', in Anat Rafaeli and Michael Pratt (eds), *Artifacts and Organizations,* Mahwah, NJ: Lawrence Erlbaum Associates.

Yanow, Dvora (2006b), 'How built spaces mean: a semiotics of space', in Dvora Yanow and Peregrine Schwartz-Shea (eds), *Interpretation and Method: Empirical Research Methods and the Interpretive Turn,* Armonk, NY: M E Sharpe, pp. 349–66.

6. Space as context and content: the *diwan* as a frame and a structure for decision-making

David Weir

It is by now quite well agreed that space is a core dimension of organizational analysis (Kornberger and Clegg 2004), but it is by no means equally clear how space works in organizational life. Nor are definitions of space universally accepted and used among ethnographic researchers. Earlier work has tried to codify the different ways in which locational concepts have been used in the 'community studies' tradition in ethnographic work in Britain (Lambert and Weir 1976). Space can be seen, for example, as a frame within which organizational events occur or as a location, defined by other social or organizational parameters, at which organizationally significant occurrences happen.

In this chapter I argue that space is indeed both of these but that the way it is organized in different cultures conditions certain types of organizational behaviour and that these conditionings are both cause and consequence of other aspects of organizational structure. Thus, where in one culture it is the external framings and structures that are organizationally significant, in another it may be more illuminating to consider the ways in which apparently 'free' space, unencumbered by structural divisions or boundaries, is used in a variety of contexts.

In this interpretation I follow the proposal of Castells (1996, p. 410) who argues that space is 'not a reflection of society, it is its expression. In other words: space is not a photocopy of society, it is society'. Lefebvre (1991, p. 73) goes even further: 'social space is not a thing among other things, nor a product among other products: rather it subsumes things produced and encompasses their interrelationships in their coexistence and simultaneity, their (relative) order and/or their (relative) disorder'.

In the spatial swirl of the *diwan* in the contexts of decision-making in the societies of the Middle East and North African (MENA) region, we can see the relevance of Castells' and Lefebvre's observations. The *diwan* is a widespread phenomenon in these societies (though it may be known under other names, such as *majlis*). *Diwan* embodies and focuses other aspects of culture and behaviour, including the reaffirmation of hierarchy coupled nonetheless with personal access to decision-makers. It utilizes the ambiguous and uncertain aspects of organizational life in ways that permit effective resolution of differences. The decision-making style known as *diwan* takes place in an organizational space also known as *diwan*, which has a physically real as well as a virtual symbolism.

Maruyama (1992) offers a system of classification of social spaces that distinguishes four basic types of what he calls 'mindscapes'. The H-type mindscape is characterized as classifying, sequential, competitive, and focused at one truth. The I-type is randomizing, independent, makes issues and problems unique, and is subjectivity-oriented. The S-type is contextual, simultaneous, cooperative, and poly-objective, capable of handling uncertainty and diversity. The G-type is oriented towards the discourse of others, what Maruyama describes as hetero-geneistic, interactive, and pattern-generating. These 'mindscapes' aim to link personal behaviours with aspects of social functioning, and behavioural styles with distinct spatial contexts. Maruyama clearly implies both that individuals use organizational space differently and that these usages are identified with more generic and deeper, culturally-rooted predispositions, for example to the use of symbols, the generation of acceptable knowledge and ultimately to aspects of cognitive functioning. But these typological classifications seem not to be rooted in comparative empirical ethnographic fieldwork. They may nonetheless be provocative and intriguing, as well as influential and relatively unusual coming from a theorist of architecture and cybernetic systems who has attempted to link macro- and micro-levels of analysis.

Another attempt at a comprehensive typological overview of social structures comes from Douglas's grid-group cultural theory, in which these terms have spatial connotations. Group refers to the extent to which an individual is incorporated into bounded units, such that the greater the incorporation, the more the individual's choice is subject to group determination; grid denotes the degree to which an individual's life is circumscribed by externally exposed prescriptions. These 'external prescriptions' include the constraints of space. The more binding and extensive the scope of these prescriptions, the less life is open to individual negotiation (Douglas and Wildavsky 1982, Thompson et al. 1990). Mars (2008, p. 185) links these definitions of grid and group and the four kinds of cultures their intersections produce to the problems of organizational space in corporate environments, demonstrating four different uses of space that link it integrally to information flow and control.

Space, time and the tropes of interculturality are linked, because, as Homi Bhabha (1994, p. 293) notes, 'no single explanation sending one back immediately to a single origin is adequate'. Yet whereas each of the preceding typological systems provides insights into the ways in which the uses of organizational space may be linked to wider aspects of social structure, their weakness lies in their lack of basis in empirical fieldwork. This chapter contributes to such accounts by reporting on a use of space in organizational settings in a distinct cultural context, that of the MENA region.

Space, site and place and their representations may carry different connotations in the post-Cartesian Western and the Islamic traditions. Casey (2002, p. 222) dates this to the seventeenth-century Western idea of site beginning to crowd out the notion of place, an idea honoured by the ancient Greeks and many in the Middle Ages. The relation between site and place is also questioned by anthropologists like Clifford (1997) who think of the 'field' as a habitus (Bourdieu 1990) rather than a place or as a cluster of embodied dispositions and practices.

This implies the need to move beyond suggestions of a universal applicability of any currently available typological system, for organizational space is by no means culturally neutral. In this chapter I will look at the differences between the representations of spaces of decision-making in traditional Anglo-Saxon depictions and those prevalent in the MENA region. I focus on a style of decision-making that occurs throughout the latter in one guise or another, characterized as the '*diwan* model' (Weir 2008, 2009). The spatial organization of this style of decision-making carries over from domestic to business settings and embodies similar connotations in both. This is not to make exaggerated claims that this is the only style of decision-making in these cultural contexts or that variations do not exist. *Diwan* is not perceived or enacted in precisely the same way throughout all the cultures of the region, and no two examples of *diwan* in action cited in this chapter come from the same country. But in principle, the uses of space described in this chapter are recognizable throughout the MENA region.

For studying the interweavings of structures, in particular spatial structures, cultures, and, *a fortiori*, behaviours in organizational spaces, ethnographic methods are particularly appropriate. Over a period of some 40 years I have been a participant-observer in many formal and informal *diwaniah* (plural of *diwan*) in many locales throughout the region, including the United Arab Emirates, Kuwait, Oman, Jordan, Saudi, Libya, Yemen, Morocco, Egypt and Lebanon. My initial role in these situations has been varied, as researcher, consultant, family friend or teacher. My experiences of *diwan* have occurred within the regular practice of my own social roles in their settings rather than as pre-planned occasions for objective research. This 'naturalistic stance' (Schütz 1967) assumes intersubjectivity, with the researcher acting as normally as seems natural in such situations. I have tried to follow Malinowski's famous dictum that the ethnographer should 'relinquish his comfortable position on the verandah' (Malinowski 1926, p. 146) and study practices that are 'significantly divergent from the "normal" practices and mores of Western society' (Giulianotti 1995, p. 2). *Diwan* is indeed significantly divergent from prevailing mores and practices of Western organizational life and hardly reported on in the contemporary organizational or general ethnographic literature. I did not initially problematize these experiences from the perspective of a desire to test or confirm any propositions derived from organizational or sociological theory. It was not until I had experienced *diwan* from the inside over a long period of time that I started to understand what it was that might be different and significant about the way space is used in *diwan* and the way in which the *diwan* style of decision-making embodies other features of these societies.

A central feature of ethnographic writing is its extensive description of the place or space in which the research was conducted, as well as its context – that is, not only what the inside of the organization looked like, but also how it is situated in its historical, national, 'industry', and/or neighbourhood 'space' (Ybema et al. 2009, p. 65). After additional theoretical discussion and an account of the concept of *diwan*, I turn to a micro-level description of several *diwan* spaces encountered in a historically- and geographically-specific region, the contemporary Arab Middle East.

SPACES OF DECISION-MAKING IN ANGLO-SAXON ORGANIZATIONS

It is common in the West, and specifically in 'Anglo-Saxon' organizations – those located in such countries as the USA and the United Kingdom, as well as those located in other parts of the world but run by the kinds of executives and managers who have been trained and socially conditioned in the West – to find spaces that are internally structured with furniture items like the 'executive desk' and the 'boardroom table', both of which have physical and symbolic significance in organizational terms. Positionings of these furnishings – and indeed, of the desks and tables within office or meeting spaces – are often fixed, so verbalizations like 'take a seat' and 'head of the table' connote expectations not only of movement and behaviour but also of organizational role and status. There are expectations of ownership, hierarchical position and status in these spatial divisions.

When decision-spaces and locations are fixed, liminal behaviours – those at the borders, boundaries or intersections of fixed spaces – may be intrinsically regarded as problematic. Turner (1964) characterized the liminal phase of adolescent male development as an 'interstructural situation', created between different positional structures as these individuals became free from pre-existing social expectations but before they were eligible to adopt those appropriate to their new roles. For example, among the Ndembe people Turner studied, the pubertal boys were taken physically out of the normal spaces of daily tribal activity into a specially constructed place, where the potential danger and social pollution in a situation where social actors are between categories or at the boundaries of defined social spaces could be controlled and averted by ritual.

In this sense, the concept of social actors existing in a liminal state constitutes an essentially structural problem for individual actors, as well as for the wider organization that has to create special spaces at which these interstitial events occur. Liminal roles create specific difficulties for role-occupants, as they facilitate the experiences of social marginality, ambiguity, openness, feelings of indeterminacy, disorientation and lack of acceptance that typically characterize such transitions from one structural situation to another (Turner 1964).

In general, organizational analyses have treated structure positively as an aspect of organization that offers participants stability and opportunity to participate in a system of roles that gives social and personal reassurance and confirms organizational identity. Liminality may, however, also create special opportunities for social learning. Tempest and Starkey (2004), extending liminality to organizational learning, examine individual and organizational learning in the context of organizational re-composition where learning increasingly occurs at the limits of organizations within networks and teams that cross organizational divides. Furthermore, Cornis-Pope (1997, p. 27) postulates the dynamic possibilities in liminality in cultural systems:

> As with a natural system, which needs … heat regulation, cultural systems also need a regulating balance in order not to collapse or disappear. This regulating balance is manifested in the stratificational oppositions. The canonized repertoires of any system would very likely stagnate after a certain time if not for competition from non-canonized challengers, which often threaten to replace them.

Thus liminality, per se, constitutes if not a structural problem, then at least something that needs to be explained or interpreted. Derrida, according to Shakespeare, has argued that the discourse of metaphysics in Western philosophy has been organized around the notions of structured knowledge (Shakespeare 2009, p. 50). In turn these structures of knowledge are given order and unity by a centre, 'a point of presence, a fixed origin' (Derrida 1978, p. 278). Knowledge, arguably, is always and essentially spatially manifested, both in terms of the overall structurings of the spaces in which decisions are characteristically made, but also in terms of the decorations, furnishings and internal divisions of the decision-making space.

These distinctions may be especially important when 'decisions' take place in 'meetings'. Discussions can occur around whether a particular manager or co-worker is 'in or out of this meeting'. Questions or statements such as the following can be heard in the workplace: 'Why are you hovering at the door? Can't you see we are having a meeting?' or '*We* are having a meeting in here' or 'One meeting at a time, please!' These discourses imply that meetings typically should take place in spaces that are bounded and temporally and spatially constrained, often in a linear fashion. The discourse forms part of a wider set of expectations that temporal and spatial structurings are intrinsic to the organizational validity of decisions. They also imply, for example, that it is appropriate to demand, 'Has a decision been taken?' or to use phrases like 'We need to make a decision here', or 'Is this the right room? Shouldn't we be in the boardroom?'

It is also characteristic of these modes of decision-making in many societies that physical space often operates to divide decision-makers from subalterns [a point discussed in Panayioutou and Krini's analysis of films, chapter 9 this volume. Eds]. In terms of individual behaviours it would be normally seen as inappropriate for a subordinate to offer to occupy an organizational space normally privileged for a superior. Great care is often taken to make these spatial demarcations in organizational life. One might hear, for example, of the 'top corridor' where the rector and sub-rectors have their offices in a university – a clear link between organizational spaces and hierarchy. Other examples include 'the corridors of power', 'the boss's inner sanctum', 'the top table' and so on. For an organizational participant to be 'in' these spaces is distinct from being 'out' of them.

In organizational life in such cultures, certain spaces are conventionally reserved for certain modes of social performance. So in business organizations, decisions are not supposed to be taken in corridors or on staircases but in boardrooms; indeed 'corridor politics' and 'backstairs manoeuvres' are somewhat derogatory terms used when such spatially inappropriate decision-making behaviours are suspected. But these characteristics, while often presented as universal, are decidedly not so. Not all cultures have the same orientation towards temporal and physical structures, and their notions of decisions and decision-making are also different, as are their spatial manifestations. In cultures where decision-making is expected to be definite, precise and recordable, the appearances of ambivalence and indeterminacy – that is, the occurrence of liminal situations – may pose intrinsic analytical and behavioural problems (Dench 1986). In other cultures the internal organizational space tends to be free and uncluttered by comparison with Western norms; and within these spaces personal physical mobility is possible in ways that are comparatively more fluid. The values embedded in arrangements of the spaces allow individual access to key agents of decision in a fluid mode. This mobility is important to the operation of decision-making: indeterminacy, ambivalence and liquidity – all those characteristics of liminality, in fact, that appear to cause trouble – may be central to these decision-making tropes. In *diwan*, 'Whose space?' is not so readily determined as in the Western designation of meeting and office rooms.

CONTEMPORARY ISLAM AND MUSLIM PRACTICE: *DIWAN* AND ITS MEANINGS

The influences of Arab and Muslim cultures (although these two are not precisely synonymous) are prevalent throughout the MENA region, which also comprises a diversity of other cultures and ethnicities, including the Turkish, Christian, Judaic, Persian and Egyptian. *Diwan* practices are widespread throughout all of these. Many texts and sources describe and interpret the practices of these cultures (see for example, Rahman 1979, Ahmed 1993, Siddiqui 1997, Naipaul 1998, Weir 1998, 2000, 2003), and although there are variations, some features are reasonably well agreed.

In relating to this literature, however, there is one aspect that should be avoided: the discourses of 'traditionalism' and 'underdevelopment', for as Gole (2002, p. 173) reminds us:

> New faces of Muslim actors using both secular and religious idiom are appearing in public life; the terms of public debate are being transformed by the eruption of religious issues; Islamic films and novels are becoming popular subjects of cultural criticism; new spaces, markets, and media are opening up in response to the rising demands of recently formed Muslim middle classes.

These debates extend to the arenas of business and management, and it would be quite misleading to present *diwan* decision-making as in any sense uncontested. Indeed, in principle business and management as social phenomena are vigorously contested domains in contemporary Muslim discourse. Some see the adoption of typical Western practices as emblematic of modernity itself, for others the goal is to achieve a meld of what is useful in these new ways with what is central to traditional practice.

Contemporary Islam and contemporary Muslim practice are both very complex and dynamic arenas of discourse and analysis, and simplification, while necessary to make the analytic point here, is also inevitably dangerous. Nevertheless, it is generally agreed that status, position and seniority tend to be more highly regarded in business and management throughout the MENA region than ability and performance. Decision-making is usually located in the upper reaches of the organizational hierarchy, with authoritarian management styles predominating. Subordinates tend to appear deferential and obedient, especially in public. Autocratic decision-making is tempered with an emphasis on consultation, which is typically practiced on a one-to-one basis.

Decisions appear to emerge, rather than to issue explicitly from formal decision-making processes. Prior affiliations and existing obligations, whether these originate in familial or business milieus, may be more influential than explicit performance objectives (see, for instance, Al-Faleh 1987).

In one guise or another – in public and private spaces alike, in offices as well as in homes – a particular spatial arrangement can be observed: the *diwan*. The term refers to a rectangular room with low seats around the walls. Within this space the movements of people tend to describe characteristic patterns. 'Diwan' can also signify a couch, a room, the holder of an office of state, a place, an organization, and a style of decision-making. It can also be a historical account, a collection of poems, a journal or a mode of literary production. The word has been known in English since at least the sixteenth century, but its origin is claimed in Arabic, Turkish and Persian. Its multiplicities and connotations are understood by practically everybody in the Middle Eastern Arab, Turkish and Islamic worlds.

Within the MENA region the precise terms for *diwan* can vary. In Iran, *majlis* (literally, 'a place of sitting') may refer to informal gatherings like those found among desert Bedouin or Touareg, when people gather around a rectangular space outside their familial tents, as well as to more formal parliamentary or representative bodies. While the *majlis* may be more akin to a town hall or government office in terms of function and formality, *diwan* connotes a more regular and casual gathering place for families and invited strangers. In Malaysia and in Indonesia, *dewan* is the more usual spelling.

Diwan is a dominant term in the history of Islam and of Muslims and in the territories where their regimes have ruled. In the Mughal period in India from 1526 onwards, the term identified the head of the revenue department, while the *diwan-i-aam* (literally, the hall of public audience) was the assembly or court for ordinary matters and people, and the *diwan-i-khaas* was the court or assembly for special matters and people. Edwardes and Garett (1995, p. 247) offer a graphic description of the public *diwan* of the Shah Jehangir: 'At 7.40 he held his public durbar in the *diwan-i-am* followed by the private audience in the *diwan-i-khass* at 9.30 … [A]t 4 pm the public audience again took place and lasted until 6.30 pm when he presided over administrative matters in the *diwan-i-khass.*'

The use of the term '*diwan*' to denote a governmental department is still common throughout the region. For example, the administrative offices of the *emir* (ruler) in Kuwait – the Amiri Diwan – consists of both the core administrative support for high-level strategic decision-making and the repository of various projects and activities in which the ruler and his family take a special interest. A similar connotation is found in describing contemporary ministries in many MENA countries (Schimmel and Waghmar 2004).

In the Western literature and pictorial representations of the Orient, of

'Orientalist' tradition, the divan – its Westernized spelling – has been conventionally portrayed as a type of low, backless couch on which partly-clad females loll in languorous poses while richly dressed Sultans feast their eyes on the concupiscent scene of a dimly lit chamber sweet with the perfumes of *nargileh* smoke and a pervading air of decadence. Saïd has criticized the subtle and persistent Eurocentric prejudice embodied in such popular images and social science representations that militate against Arabo-Islamic peoples and their cultures, claiming that these representations comprise 'a kind of intellectual authority over the Orient within Western culture' (Saïd 1978, p. 19). Although Saïd's generic analysis is now viewed as debatable and contentious (Varisco 2007), to understand *diwan* the discourses of imperialism, orientalism and post-modernism all have to be transcended. In doing so, I wish to extend the tropes of decision-making that have embodied and 'embrained' – in the sense used by Blackler (1995) – their spatial framings on the basis of their usages in the individual-centred, hierarchical and top-down cultures that have been most influential in Western managerial theory.

Diwan is not, then, an archaic term, in use only in scholarly discourses. In contemporary descriptions of Islam and the vital central institutions of a Muslim society, as well as in ethnographic studies within this region, there is usually an account of or reference to *diwan*. Al-Naser (2002), for example, argues that it was through the discussions in *diwan* that ordinary Kuwaitis derived the communal support and coping strategies that enabled them to survive during the Iraqi occupation. Historically, a *diwan* could be either an individual or a collective term, as well as describing a process and the results of or the structure of a system of administration. It could refer to the court of a ruler or the familial decision-making on routine domestic matters. These multiple uses survive with similar connotations to the present day.

In sum, the *diwan* is both the characteristic place of meeting in this region and also a generic idea that relates to many different aspects of communal life, integrating other social practices and performances that are associated with its spatial practices in a wide range of social settings. It constitutes, in Maruyama's terms (1992, p. 3), an 'epistemological metatype' in that it provides a relational link between seemingly disparate activities in many distinct contexts. This chapter focuses initially on the core sense of *diwan* as a rectangular room, with little or no furniture other than cushions, chairs or benches around the walls. Figure 6.1 shows such a room, at the Beiteddine Palace, a nineteenth-century building in Lebanon. This is evidently a rather grand room, but the inner space fulfils the same functions in *diwaniah* great and small.

Source: Photo by David Weir

Figure 6.1   A diwan in the Beiteddine Palace, Darmour, Lebanon

Diwan in Operation

Within the *diwan* space the movements of people tend to describe characteristic patterns, because *diwan* signifies a process as well as a location. It is common in a public *diwan* for the swirl of mobility to form a counter-clockwise pattern as people approach the leading person – the *shaykh* – or persons, who are typically to be found seated on the far side of the entrance, and engage them in discussion before moving on. An implicit hierarchy is inscribed on the space and underpins the spatially located activity. While the more important people may initially be seated, they will move to greet, welcome and involve newcomers in the swirl of the *diwan*. A *diwan* in action is a scene of mobility rather than stasis.

As Simmel (1950) points out, the ways in which societies provide for the role of the stranger can be central to an understanding of their structures and functioning. The special duties of care owed to strangers are well understood within this region. In Kuwait a family might build a special room adjacent to their main dwelling place in order to have a place where they could meet as family, but also host other people, whether friends, guests or strangers. But the distinction between what is familial and private and what is political or public may not be tightly drawn.

The Marafie family in Kuwait, for example, provide a very detailed, clear history and evolution of their family *diwan*:

> This separate yard or room is a public place where guests are received, neighbours, friends and relatives get together. During these leisurely meetings people would discuss daily events, exchange ideas, news and narrate episodes. Most of the *diwans* remained open the whole day long to receive guests and elderly people. The *diwan* is usually rectangular in shape, where seats are arranged on both sides, and sometimes includes a guest house for those who need to stay overnight or longer in the city. Further, seats also are extended on either sides of the main door, where pedestrians may rest, or guests may enjoy the sea breeze if the *diwan* is located on the sea front, especially in summer time. (Marafie family 2009)

Three examples from my field experiences illustrate the *diwan* in operation.

Diwan 1

A couple of years ago, I visited a Gulf state to undertake a consultancy assignment and took the opportunity to have lunch with a friend. He invited me to spend the evening with his family at the home of his father as head of the extended family. In due course I arrived at the house and was ushered into a small, rectangular and quite sparsely furnished *diwan*, laid out in the customary way, with cushions everywhere around the walls and no chairs except for one low couch at the far end of the room. As soon as I entered, having left my shoes at the door, I was asked to sit on the couch next to my friend's father, who was sitting at the centre of the short side of the rectangular space already in conversation with a well-dressed man in a Western business suit. All the other men were in the local *dishdasha* attire.

I sat as requested between the two of them. They seemed at first to be discussing the general situation of higher education in the kingdom, but after several iterations it became apparent that they were discussing plans for a new private university that was thought to be a possibility in the light of new decisions from the government. I was introduced into the conversation at first in a tangential way, but then was mercilessly quizzed about my experiences as a business school dean. Thereafter the discussion segued into references to quite specific people, their qualifications, standing and appropriateness for becoming part of a project. At various times when names of local people were mentioned, I was talked over and around rather than directly included.

The conversation was direct and to the point, very business-oriented, and intensely political, but as well as the small knot of us who seemed to be centrally involved, other participants rotated throughout the space during the evening in a counter-clockwise swirl. Some participants paid their courtesies, stayed briefly and then left. I watched as men entered the doorway and made their way, gradually, to the 'head' of the room, where I continued to sit next to my friend's father. Arriving to sit near him, a participant proposed the name of a member of a leading family with whom participants had worked on another project. 'Oh, he is nothing!' interjected my host. 'He is out of this altogether. He has no place here and he will go away, perhaps to London. He does not work. His father knows he is not working so he will send him away, perhaps to London. Yes, to London. He can do something there. Perhaps to America.'

I was surprised at this line of argument and the personalization involved, perhaps because I would have expected more deference to be shown towards a member of the elite. I was also subconsciously rather surprised (miffed, indeed) to understand that London or America were considered appropriate destinations for the not-quite-good-enough members of the elite!

As the evening progressed new people joined our small group. One picked my brains about where his son should go to do his Masters in Management and what were the relevant differences between the USA and the UK. Another joined the conversation and wanted to enquire about undergraduate medical programmes in UK compared to North American medical schools. When I protested that this was outside my specific field of expertise, my new acquaintance retorted, 'Oh, you are well connected. You can find out. It will be helpful to me. Please let me know what you think.' I realized then that my attendance at this *diwan* implied acceptance of the social and personal obligations implicit in being included in this gathering as a friend of the family and thus implicated in its social networks.

Another discussion occurred with a lawyer who wanted to talk about issues concerning political representation. I realized that I had not been so intensively involved for a long time in discussions about live political situations in which real outcomes were being discussed. In fact, *diwan* can often have an explicitly political aspect. It reminded me somewhat of discussions of the 1960s in UK trade union settings about the merits of worker control of Clydeside shipyards or of the 1970s in Scottish universities about the advantages of home rule. The participants were a mixture of young and old, including some who were clearly not only not family members but had been relatively unknown themselves to the core members of this family before this particular *diwan*. But in being invited because of their special expertise and then by participating, they were *becoming* connected.

Other conversations involving younger participants, contemporaries of my young friend who had been my doctoral student some time previously, returned to the matter of higher education, and I found myself thinking and feeling that the very directness of the argument and the specificity and personalization of some of the comments could be considered to open up the speakers and listeners to some vulnerability if they were to become known outside of this context. Later I realized that these suspicions were needless. Only the honestly expressed personal truth was of interest, for in *diwan* what in the British Civil Service code of conduct are called 'Chatham House Rules' govern the discourse. Whatever is said within the room may be open and indiscreet, if necessary, but none of it can be broadcast outside under penalty of being excluded from the inner circle. Nonetheless, most people listened rather than talked, and the head of the family seemed to be the quietest and least-voluble participant.

As we walked finally to the door to the main street at the conclusion of what had, after all, been a pleasant and sociable as well as challenging evening, my host took my arm and said quite firmly, 'Perhaps we will not do this business school thing. It will be hard to do it properly. We need bigger investment. We need a different kind of people. Perhaps in some years... You are right, Professor!'

I paused, uncertain what had been directly said that he could be so forcefully agreeing with. Then I realized that in an indirect way, he had distilled the essence of my unspoken, opaque, even subconscious conclusion, and that the sum total of all that had been said, with respect to many different aspects of the situation, was that it was too soon to make such a decisive move into a new business area and because they were not ready, they should stick to their own knitting. The real business of this *diwan* had been something akin to a preliminary project review meeting of the board of a venture capital house with limited disposable funds for investment in an uncertain project.

Within the swirl of the *diwan* many voices had been heard and many interests recognized and perhaps many competing interests pacified, though the existence of possible tensions was not blatantly obvious to me. The intense internal politics of the evening had come to a definite conclusion. Minutes were not taken; reports were not written; accounts had not been presented; there had been no papers on the table. But face had been saved and reputations honoured. This was essentially a family meeting, and it would undoubtedly meet again, later, perhaps directed to a different project and undoubtedly with different participants relevant to other concerns. An opportunity not to take an opportunity had been taken, and life in its political, organizational, business and familial aspects would go on.

Diwan 2

On another visit in another country, I had been undertaking a strategic consulting assignment for a major industrial group, of whom the members of the board were all closely connected family members of several generations. After a conventional morning of detailed work on the project, we adjourned to the house of one of the leading members of the family. I was accompanied by my company host who was a divisional head in the company and also the nephew of the board member whose home this was.

We went immediately into *diwan*, and my companion took me straight away to the far side of the room where the older, senior man was clearly engaged in conversation with another company person. He broke off to greet me, enquired how the project was going and then initiated a new conversation with me, asking about other work I had been doing in the region. As we were talking, I noticed a party of American managers enter. I knew that they had come especially for a meeting with the top team of the company to discuss a big project that was not connected with my business. But seeing us talking, they sat down in a group near the entrance, did not mingle, and carried on discussing their business, even referring to documents and plans as they did so.

It seemed clear to me that this placed my host in a difficult situation, and I backed away slightly to permit him to move closer to them and greet them. But he did not do so, preferring to await their pleasure. In the meantime, he carried on two conversations simultaneously, with me and with his original conversant, and others were added in as they came up to greet him. In due course a junior member of the *diwan* brought the American party over and they were formally introduced and joined our conversation; but it was evident from their body language that they had expected the meeting to be more formal and to be concerned with their business only.

Afterwards, as we mingled in the adjacent room to eat, one of the Americans remarked to me, 'These are hard guys to do business with. They don't like to do one thing at a time, so you never know quite where you are with them.' He was clearly surprised and somewhat discomfited at my presence in *diwan* and repeatedly asked 'who I was' and 'what I was doing there' and 'whether I was advising them or what …'.

Diwan 3

On another occasion in yet a third country, I was a member of an official party on a week-long educational mission. Towards the end of the week we were invited to the family home of the father of one of the young scholars who had accompanied our visit. We went into a *diwan* that was very traditional, with no furniture, only cushions on the floor.

As I sat with a mixed group of hosts and team members, I noticed, quite late in the evening, an older man enter and sit near the door and converse with family members. After a while he made eye contact with me and then came over to sit next to me. After a short while he announced, 'I understand that you are a poet.' I demurred, explaining that this was too much honour, although it was true that I did write poetry. 'Ah!' he responded, 'that is what I say, too! I am not a poet but I do write poetry.' We proceeded to discuss the ways in which our two styles of poetry differed, and it subsequently became clear that he was the brother of the man whose *diwan* this was and therefore the uncle of the young scholar. We enjoyed our discussion and parted at the end of the evening.

The next day I thanked the young man for the introduction, and he said: 'Oh, he is my uncle so he can come any time to our *diwan*; but he especially wanted to come to meet you. But it was a long journey for him because his work is in another city.' Naturally, I enquired what this work was and was stunned at the response: 'He is the CEO of the State Oil Corporation.'

In some ways this example indicates the ways in which familial roles and behavioural styles are perceived as primary and occupational and hierarchical ones are secondary. In a Western context the role of 'CEO of the State Oil Corporation' might have been the primary point of reference, and as a guest, I might have expected to be formally introduced to this person, and thereafter poetry would probably not have constituted the focus of our discussions. But even as a high-ranking official, such a person was content to sit on the floor, adopt a liminal position in relation to what was already going on, join in the conversational swirl and wait his turn. In accepting his presence and respecting his agenda, and in not pressing to move on to business matters, I was entering into a *diwan* style of informality. Nonetheless, I knew that thereafter any expectation that either I personally or our team might have for the support of his organization would very probably be facilitated.

Familial discourse is quite usual even during formal business and management settings. On one occasion in another country, I was introduced by the head of a family as 'my son's second father' at a grand *diwan* ostensibly called to celebrate this son's attainment of a doctorate that I had supervized. During the course of the evening others to whom I had not been formally introduced used this designation in a quite natural and unforced way. On another occasion in quite a formal *diwan* in a banking house I was introduced as '*amo* David' (Uncle David) to a group of business people. When I questioned this, I was told, 'Well, you are like an uncle to our business and everybody knows that he can trust his uncle.'

The examples presented above indicate the lack of precise spatial or temporal framing of agenda in *diwan*, quite a different style from typical meetings in Anglo-Saxon organizations. It is possible for more than one meeting to be going on in the same space and with some variation in the participants who may be involved. But *diwan* is in principle inclusive rather than divisive, so non-planned participation is not explicitly discouraged. I never discovered in the case of *Diwan* 1 whether it had been merely opportunistic that the topics of discussion were related to my own expertise or whether that had been the plan all along. But the spontaneous interaction facilitated by the *diwan* space created a discourse that might not have been achieved with much pre-planning and advance notification.

Diwan as a Decision-Making Style

Diwan styles thus operate in both family and business situations, and the dynamics are similar in both. The space is used in a way that is quite different from a Western office, dining room, meeting room or boardroom. It is effectively not a fully public meeting space, and movements are far from random. Indeed, quite clear and firm, though unverbalized rules of order apply. There is a pattern to the movements and a structure to the timings as participants move through the space.

Hierarchy is a feature of the *diwan*, both in its spatial layout and in moving and interpreting others' movements through these spaces. While the hierarchical structures are modified by fluid movement or 'liquidity', it is not clear that this manifests the implications that Bauman (2005, p. 1) draws in concluding that in contemporary society, 'all boundaries are tenuous, frail and porous. ... Geographical discontinuity no longer matters'. One wonders if his observation might characterize Western society more than MENA region organizational society.

Sociological analyses often incline towards binary models and a tendency for concepts as well as structural depictions to be 'one thing or the other'. But *diwan* transcends the binary and potentially oppositional features of organizational spaces which obtain in business and decision-making contexts, where typically it is binary distinctions between 'decision-makers' and 'operatives' and between 'boardroom' and 'shop floor' that divide the space. For in *diwan*, the middle is not excluded. Where ambiguity is not construed as a threat to identity, as is the case in *diwan*, the dangers perceived in liminality are much diminished. This means that the questions implied in making the distinctions between 'empty and full space(s), open and closed, public and private, intimate and expansive, negative and positive, narrative space and production space' (Deflem 2002, p. 24) are limited in scope and effect.

Because *diwan* in business settings is modelled on activities that occur primarily within families and generalized into both a physical space and a pattern of activity that can be virtual as well as actual, the liminality that one experiences in entering a room and making one's way gradually around it towards the key figure with whom one came to speak may operate as a strength of the spatial framing of the organizational action. As in familial settings, members can be both present and absent, responsible and irresponsible. Likewise, as in familial settings, role-based behaviours may be motile and emergent. Deniability is always an option, but never to be counted on. 'Telling it like it is' can be countered by 'listening to what makes sense to you'.

In familial settings there is no need to work to a specific, pre-ordered agenda; indeed, attempts to do this are often resisted as inappropriate. But familial roles may be quite tightly defined, although this may not be immediately apparent to outsiders. As a newcomer in a family, for example through marrying in, one has both to make the effort to play according to the local familial rules and to be accepted as a player, but these acceptances are conditional on performance and will probably evolve over a period of time. In the Western executive world, by contrast, if one is defined formally as having authority in that particular bureaucratic context, one can usually exercise that authority *ab initio*, without waiting to be accepted. In *diwan*, individual social action becomes collective responsibility and the personal option becomes the networked opportunity. For while *diwan* is a highly ordered interactional event, it is also a model for virtual bonding and extension, because *diwan* manifests the spatial focusing of characteristic patterns of social networking that reinforce existing strong bonds of family and kinship while drawing trusted newcomers into a pre-existing network. These more extensive social networks are described as *wasta*. *Wasta* carries the connotation of connectedness, contacts, network-brightness, mediation, influence, interpersonal respect and organizational trust. *Wasta* and *diwan* are mutually supportive processes that create the spatial manifestation of a method of managing and generating social knowledge that can lead to business and political opportunity.

Indeterminacy is both an organizational and an individual advantage in this context. If it seems essential to a newcomer to ask questions like, 'Why am I here?', 'What is my role?' or 'What do these people expect of me?' the expected clarification may in fact weaken one's position. In *diwan* spaces it is better not to ask questions, but to take advantage of unexpected or undeserved opportunity. This use of space may also represent a location for the development and use of social capital, as the *diwan* space brings together members of networks linked by shared norms and values and offering opportunities for both 'bonding' and 'bridging', by sustaining existing bonds and facilitating their extension into new ones.

Experiences of space and time in business and managerial decisions in this region enact relevant characteristics of the *diwan*. Because it permits both openness and closure, *diwan* is a matrix for knowledge-management that embodies openness to the possibility of new knowledge that can emerge as the activity progresses. The bounds of interaction are self-limiting, and an interactional homeostasis is the outcome of events that may, in precise terms, be unplanned. An agenda is not issued, nor are minutes taken, and although decisions may have implicitly been taken, what has happened may only later become transparent, as *Diwan* 1 clearly shows.

What makes *diwan* of especial interest for theorists of organizational spaces is that it provides a physical matrix for a type of decision-making that is non-linear and non-hierarchical, discursive and recursive, self-limiting but co-extensive with the range of interactional possibilities available. The swirl of the *diwan* permits an order to emerge that is not rigid and pre-imposed, and it opens up possible new frameworks of decision, creating potential as well as reinforcing existing social categories. The swirl is a temporary structure that can persist as long as the need for the activity persists. A *diwan* finishes when the participants leave, and attempts to enquire ahead of time 'How long will this last?' – in a very Western manifestation of time – will probably receive only vague answers.

The processes of decision-making tend to appear characteristically prolonged because the swirl of the *diwan* imposes its own pace and the assemblage of persons may vary both situationally and temporally. Nonetheless, the *diwan* as a spatial context preserves an appropriate ambiguity about the precise roles played by specific participants while ensuring that outcomes may in fact be quite decisive. *Diwan* is neither unambiguously 'autocratic' nor 'democratic', 'consultative' or 'participative', as these terms are conventionally understood. Rather, *diwan* offers a special melange of autocracy and consultation as a dynamic listening 'machine' through which diversity and difference may obtain their opportunity equally with hierarchical authority. At the same time, while consultation in *diwan* is both one-to-one and through group discussion, direct access by individuals to the shaykh is of the essence. The designation of 'shaykh' can identify a specific person in *diwan* as role-occupant; but it can also be a term of art applied to those who hold senior positions in a particular *diwan*. In one *diwan* in an academic setting I was startled when a participant referred to 'Shaykh David', and when I enquired who this person was, I was told, 'It is you, in this *diwan* you are the shaykh!'

Diwan decisions are the outcome of processes of information exchange, practiced listening, questioning, and the interpretation and confirmation of informal as well as formal meanings. The implication of 'informal' in this context is that ambiguity and ambivalence, indeed liminality itself, are central to the operation of the *diwan*, such that it may in practice be difficult, if not impossible, to ask for a formal record of events either before or after, even though participants may sense informally what the outcome may have been and may be perfectly prepared to act on these presumptions.

That there are differences of power and status in organizations is, of course, equally true in Western and *diwan*-styles of management, but the boundaries of action are differently drawn. Cornis-Pope (1997) has argued that 'stratificational opposition' helps to regulate opposition and deal with complexity; but although this may be correct in Western organizations, elsewhere this may not be the only or best method of internal system regulation or of framing complexity in social action. Canonized repertoires of organizational action that permit dynamic co-evolution exist in *diwan* and similar spatial framings.

In *diwan* the informality as well as the liminal nature of the experience is advantageous to participants because it preserves the status of all participants, who leave no worse off than when they came in, and may well have learned something. However, the contrast between Western and *diwan* expectations can sometimes cause offence. I have heard anecdotal stories of executives being in *diwan* situations with superior managers or directors and, having been assured that all was well and that their services were valued, have returned to their desks to find dismissal notices. To the Western manager this causes outrage, and the ensuing discourse can include statements like 'He didn't have the guts to tell me face to face' and 'How two-faced is that!' But to the Arab manager, all the proprieties have been observed, and it would have been indecent to sully the respect and informality appropriately shown in *diwan* with the formal business of a dismissal notice.

CONCLUSIONS

The exploration of the spatial settings of *diwan* shows that organizational spaces are by no means culturally neutral. This means that our theorizing of them needs similar differentiation and nuancing. The spatial settings in *diwan* contrast with the spatial settings of Anglo-Saxon organizations, as do their respective uses of and mobilities through the spaces and their associated processes of decision-making. *Diwan* decision-making is unmediated by intermediate spatial positionings such as desks, chairs or office furniture or any pre-figured expectations of the ownership of particular spaces. It is through the open and temporary spaces of *diwan* and its organic, emergent mobility that is, in principle, inclusive rather than exclusive that the structural features of a hierarchical-autocratic society can be moderated and made effective.

The organizational consequences for Western managers of encountering the *diwan* styles of decision-making are that decisions may appear to take longer than anticipated, personal relationships and their consequential obligations are paramount, and a penumbra of uncertainty may arise concerning, what if anything, has been specifically decided in a particular situation. These create predictable frustrations for Western managers and business-people. The spatial swirl of the *diwan* is effective because it is both open outward, as in Maruyama's G-Mindscape, and enclosed, as in his H-Mindscape, which also embodies respect for existing spatial orders while combining those features with the 'outside-absorbing space of S-Mindscape' (Maruyama 1992, p. 18). Yet although Maruyama's typology is intriguing and provocative, it is not clear that it is precisely suitable for the analysis of *diwan*, which does not fall squarely and unambiguously into any particular one of the four types. But this is not to say that it is pointless to seek to link explanations at the cultural, organizational, psychological and cognitive levels; further research will doubtless illuminate the possible range of these linkages.

Diwan embodies the virtues of what Thompson et al. (1990) termed 'clumsy institutions'. It is precisely because it is clumsy that it survives; because it is indeterminate that it is useful; because it is opaque that its outcomes can be viable; because of its ambiguity that it effectively links the domains of control and openness of information. Liquidity, contained within the rectangular space that permits internal fluidity, becomes an organizational advantage permitting learning. It allows authority not merely to be reinforced creatively in spatial process, but for participants to emerge from that process with the potential to deal with the real uncertainties of business, political and managerial life, with the concurrent consensus of those likely to be implicated already pre-figured. The indeterminacy of *diwan* constitutes the kind of temporal and spatial 'in-between' (Bhabha 1994).

Diwan's strength resides in a spatial manifestation of the ambiguity and disruption of presence that permeates decision-making in these cultures, and its decision-making style can be perceived, in turn, as an embodiment of the spatial representation of these values: the two are mutually constitutive. *Diwan* thus embraces the possibility of 'the ambivalent and chiasmatic intersections of time and place' (Bhabha 1994, p. 140), as there are always potentials for the play that permits the chance and the inventive that creates the opportunity for 'the dissolution of structuralist ambitions towards certainty' (Shakespeare 2009, p. 49).

The habitus of the *diwan* is thus embodied in the characteristic use of space and in the social practices of neo-familial behaviours, mobility, opacity and uncertainty that are embodied in other structures and symbols in these societies. The structural constraints of *diwan*, learned first in familial and tribal contexts, translate into the social practices of decision-making in more formal organizational and business contexts. These practices are fundamentally different from that which obtains in Western organizations. Understanding *diwan* helps to understand why strategy and implementation are different in these cultural settings and why the rhythms and pace of management are distinct and ultimately irreducible to the abstractions of Western management theory.

ACKNOWLEDGEMENTS

This chapter is based on a paper originally presented at the Asia-Pacific Research in Organizational Studies Conference in Melbourne in December 2005 in the stream on 'Spaces as settings and stages: physical settings in the study of organizations'. I give sincere thanks for the helpful feedback provided by colleagues at that conference and colleagues at CERAM, ESC Rennes and Liverpool Hope University, and most especially and with deep gratitude to Dvora Yanow and Alfons van Marrewijk for their forthright and supportive critique and endless patience. Nicolas Rolland, Taran Patel, Nabil Sultan and David Torevell also gave helpful comments on earlier drafts. Any mistakes are my own.

REFERENCES

Ahmed, Akbar. S. (1993), *Living Islam*, London: Penguin Books.

Al-Faleh, Mahmoud (1987), 'Cultural influences on Arab managerial development', *Journal of Management Development*, **6** (3), 19–33.

Al-Naser, Fahad (2002), 'The diwaniah: a traditional Kuwaiti social institution in a political role', *Domes*, January 31, pp. 11–32.

Bauman, Zygmund (2005), *Liquid Life*, London: Polity Press.

Bhabha, Homi (1994), *The Location of Culture*, London: Routledge.

Blackler, Frank (1995), 'Knowledge, knowledge work and organizations: an overview and interpretation', *Organization Studies*, **16** (6), 1021–46.

Bourdieu, Pierre (1990), *In Other Words: Essays Towards a Reflexive Sociology*, translated by Matthew Adamson, Stanford, CA, Stanford University Press.

Casey, Edward (2002), *Representing Place*, Minneapolis, MN: Minnesota University Press.

Castells, Manuel (1996), *The Rise of the Network Society*, New York: Blackwell.

Castells, Manuel (1997), *The Power of Identity*, Oxford: Blackwell.

Castells, Manuel (1998), *The End of Millennium*, New York: Blackwell.

Clifford, James (1997), *Routes*, Cambridge, MA: Harvard University Press.

Cornis-Pope, Marcel (1997), 'Rethinking postmodern liminality: marginocentric characters and projects in Thomas Pynchon's polysystemic fiction', *Symploke*, **5** (1–2), 27–47.

Cornis-Pope, Marcel (2001), *Narrative Innovation and Cultural Rewriting in the Cold War Era and After*, New York: Palgrave.

Deflem, Mathieu (2002), 'Ritual, anti-structure, and religion: a discussion of Victor Turner's processual symbolic analysis', *Journal for the Scientific Study of Religion*, **30**(1), 1–25.

Dench, Geoff (1986), *Minorities in the Open Society: Prisoners of Ambivalence*, London: Routledge.

Derrida, Jacques (1978), *Writing and Difference*, London: Routledge.

Douglas, Mary and Aaron Wildavsky (1982), *Risk and Culture*, Berkeley, CA: University of California Press.

Edwardes, Stephen M. and Herbert L.O. Garrett (1995), *Mughal Rule in India*, New Delhi: Atlantic.

Giulianotti, Richard (1995), 'Participant observation and research into football hooliganism: reflections on the problems of entrée and everyday risks', *Sociology of Sport Journal*, **12** (1), 1–20.

Gole, Nilufer (2002), 'Islam in public: new visibilities and new imaginaries', *Public Culture*, **14** (1), 173–90.

Kornberger, Martin and Stewart Clegg (2004), 'Bringing space back in: organizing the generative building', *Organization Studies*, **25** (7), 1095–114.

Lambert, Camilla and David T.H. Weir (1976), *Location*, in E. Gittus (ed.), *Key Variables in Sociological Research*, Oxford: Basil Blackwell.

Lefebvre, Henri (1991), *The Production of Space*, translated by Donald Nicholson-Smith, Oxford: Blackwell.

Malinowski, Bronislaw (1926), *Magic, Science and Religion*, New York: Doubleday.

Marafie family (2009), 'The Dawaween of the Marafie Family', accessed 27 September at www.diwanmarafie.com/En/Diwn_marafie_3.htm, 27 September.

Mars, Gerald (2008), 'Corporate cultures and the use of space: an approach from cultural theory', *Innovation: The European Journal of Social Science Research*, **21** (3), 185–204.

Maruyama, Magoroh (1992), 'Interrelations among science, politics, aesthetics, business management, and economics', in Magoroh Maruyama (ed.), *Context and Complexity: Cultivating Contextual Understanding*, New York: Springer-Verlag, pp. 1–34.

Naipaul, Vidiadhar S. (1998), *Beyond Belief: Islamic Excursions among the Converted Peoples*, London: Little, Brown.

Rahman, Fazlur (1979), *Islam*, Chicago, IL: University of Chicago Press.

Saïd, Edward (1978), *Orientalism: Western Conceptions of the Orient*, London: Penguin.

Schimmel, Anne-Marie and Burzine K. Waghmar (2004), *The Empire of the Great Mughals: History, Art and Culture,* London: Reaktion Books.

Schütz, Alfred (1967), *The Phenomenology of the Social World*, Evanston, IL: Northwestern University Press.

Shakespeare, Stephen (2009), *Derrida and Theology*, London: Continuum Books.

Siddiqui, Ataullah (1997), 'Ethics in Islam: key concepts and contemporary challenges', *Journal of Moral Education*, **6** (4), 423–31.

Simmel, Georg (1950), *The Sociology of Georg Simmel*, translated by Kurt Wolff, New York: Free Press.

Tempest, Sue and Ken Starkey, (2004), 'The effects of liminality on individual and organizational learning', *Organization Studies*, **25** (4), 507–27.

Thompson, Michael, Richard J. Ellis and Aaron B. Wildavsky (eds) (1990), *Cultural Theory*, Boulder, CO: Westview.

Turner, Victor W. (1964), 'Betwixt and between: the liminal period in rites de passage', in June Helm (ed.), *Symposium on New Approaches to the Study of Religion: Proceedings of the 1964 Annual Spring Meeting of the American Ethnological Society*, Seattle, WA: American Ethnological Society, pp. 4–20.

Varisco, Daniel M. (2007), *Reading Orientalism*: *Saïd and the Unsaid*, Seattle, WA: University of Washington Press.

Weir, David T.H. (1998), 'The fourth paradigm', in Ali A. Shamali and John Denton (eds), *Management in the Middle East*, Kuwait: Gulf Management Centre, pp. 60–76.

Weir, David T.H. (2000), 'Management in the Arab world', in M. Warner (ed.), *Management in Emerging Countries: Regional Encyclopaedia of Business and Management*, London*:* Business Press/Thomson Learning, pp. 291–315.

Weir, David T.H. (2003), 'Human resource development in the Middle East: a fourth paradigm', in M. Lee (ed.), *Human Resource Development in a Complex World,* London: Routledge, pp. 69–82.

Weir, David T.H. (2008), 'Cultural theory and the diwan', *Innovation: The European Journal of Social Research*, **21** (3), 253–65.

Weir, David T.H. (2009), 'Liminality, sacred space and the diwan', in Steve Brie, Jenny Daggers and David Torevell (eds), *Sacred Space: Interdisciplinary Perspectives within Contemporary Contexts*, Newcastle: Cambridge Scholars Publishing, pp. 39–54.

Ybema, Sierk, Dvora Yanow, Harry Wels and Frans Kamsteeg (eds) (2009), *Organizational Ethnography: Studying the Complexities of Everyday Life*, London: Sage.

PART III

Thinking organizational spaces

7. Giving voice to space: academic practices and the material world

Dvora Yanow

> We shape our buildings, and afterwards our buildings shape us.
> (Winston Churchill, to the House of Commons, 28 October 1943)

Organizational scholars studying spaces have a 'science problem': to analyse experiences of, in and with organizational spaces, scientific discourse requires words; but space is wordless, as are our experiences of it, overall. Because spaces do not announce themselves through verbal language, they are more easily rendered 'neutral' for academic practice, beyond the analytic gaze (by contrast with such fields as human or social geography, architecture and planning, where spatial elements are the raison d'être of the field). So the first difficulty is to de-neutralize them and focus attention on spatial elements in organizational studies domains – to develop a spatial sensibility.

Once spatial elements are on the research radar screen, the second problem is to figure out how things have, and convey, meaning, as well as what they mean in specific organizational circumstances. This requires not only attending to space, in a hermeneutic fashion, but also 'feeling' space – an intentional act, of imagination, perhaps, but certainly a bodily one of in-dwelling and through-moving, in a phenomenological attitude, attending to one's sensing. For certain kinds of science, this raises its own issues: these are subjective and largely non-verbal ways of knowing, achieved through the experiences and understandings of a particular knowing subject, which pose challenges for those insisting on more objective ways of knowing that are external to and detached from the knowing scientist (on objectivity, see Bernstein 1983; on methods, Yanow 2006a). From the perspective of interpretive science, drawing on a hermeneutic phenomenology, issues such as the procedural rationales underlying what philosophy of science terms 'truth claims' are engaged through an aspired-for transparency of reasoning and research process achieved through reflexivity. But this methodological turn itself poses problems for the kind of science for which reflexivity appears a nonscientific indulgence.

Calling for studies of organizational space is not new (Hernes 2004 and Kornberger and Clegg 2004 are two recent examples). Neither is theorizing about why spatial and other objects have been omitted from an organizational studies agenda: Gagliardi (1990) took this up two decades ago, in his introduction to the book of papers resulting from the 1987 Milan Standing Conference on Organizational Symbolism (SCOS) gathering which called attention to the symbolic role of artefacts in communicating organizational meanings. One wonders why, five to 20 years later, attention to the spatial is still marginal(ized).

Moreover, something has happened in the development of organizational studies in recent years that makes it worth sounding the call once again – the rise of discourse analysis and other analytic forms that privilege explicit language over other modes of meaning-making. As part of the various 'turns' taking place in the social sciences, including organizational studies, in the last decades of the twentieth century – the interpretive turn (for example, Hiley et al. 1991), the linguistic turn (for example, Van Maanen 1995), the argumentative turn (Fischer and Forester 1993), the narrative turn, the practice turn – 'taking language seriously' (White 1992) has occasioned a shift towards discourse analysis and other treatments that focus on written or spoken texts, such as interviews that can be recorded, transcribed and formally coded (for example, with ATLAS.ti or other such software, thereby bringing a hint of quantitative methods to qualitative research).

While such a focus is to be applauded over one that treats theories as 'mirroring' the social world (to borrow Rorty's term, 1979), it runs the risk of privileging language – more commonly, the written word, but also the spoken word treated as a 'text analogue' (Taylor 1971; see also Ricoeur 1971) – over acts, and even more so, over objects, the physical artefacts we create in organizations (and other settings) and vest with meaning. One effect of such privileging seems to be that organizational researchers and many practitioners lose sight of the fact that meaning is communicated, organizationally and otherwise, through more, or other, than just words. The non-verbal is particularly active in the realm of space. Indeed, why has discourse analysis taken hold, whereas spatial analysis has not, in the same period of time?

Framing organizational studies' space problem from the perspective of science studies (or the sociology of knowledge), which would investigate the academic practices of organizational studies scholarship in creating 'facts' and knowledge, sheds light on the causes of this gap and suggests different paths towards a remedy. From this perspective it becomes clear that a reasoned argument that points to their absence and calls for research to fill that void is not likely on its own to bring spatial analyses to the organizational studies table. Instead, that will require the community of organizational studies scholars to reconceive several aspects of its understandings of what it means to do work that is scientific and of its practices in doing so. Those are the aspects that are fundamental to the study of space and which pose equally fundamental challenges to a particular view of science: the non-verbal character, the role of the researcher's body, and the matter of researcher reflexivity in the communication and analysis of spatial meanings.

Before engaging those issues, we need to be clear on what a spatial sensibility entails. I begin with a field research narrative that illustrates some of its key parameters, in a way that shows how a spatial sensibility can heighten a researcher's awareness of and attention to the non-verbal and the bodily in spatial meaning-making. I then turn to academic practices to see why they do not foster such a sensibility or might even inhibit its development.

HANGING REPRODUCTIONS: SPATIAL SENSIBILITIES AT WORK

Returning from a trip to Tel Aviv, Beny [a pseudonym], director of a community centre in an immigrant town, brought back a half dozen poster-sized reproductions of Impressionist 'best-sellers' – Van Gogh's *Sunflowers* and *Self-Portrait*, a Picasso, several Matisses – to decorate the walls of the alcove off the centre's main entrance hall, which housed the television and the armchairs. Coming in to work that day, I found him standing on a ladder, hanging them within inches of the ceiling. The bottoms of the posters were shoulder height for me, such that in order to look at them, I had to tilt my head back to a very uncomfortable position.

I asked him why he was hanging the reproductions at that height, without mentioning the common gallery advice to hang artwork at eye level and work with 'negative space' surrounding its placement. He explained, in confidence, that he feared for their safety at a lower height. The room was commonly occupied by a group, a 'gang', of young men in their late teens to early 20s, most of them not working but also ineligible for (mandatory) army service because they were school dropouts (and, hence, had poor reading and writing skills) or had served jail time (for petty theft, disrupting the peace, or smoking hashish), or both. Beny feared they would trash the posters.

I used to hang out with these guys, drinking coffee and chatting at the centre, or I would see them at the beach during my lunch break. They could be a bit rough around the edges, but one on one, they expressed concerns about not fitting in – not having jobs, not serving in the army, not having a place in society. They were aware that Beny didn't trust them, and they volunteered the thought that he was intentionally hanging the posters out of their reach. 'What do you think,' they asked me, 'we couldn't scratch them if we wanted to?'

Three women used to come into the centre to use the library. Originally from England, they came to town for the shops and services lacking in the nearby upscale enclave where they lived. They were initially drawn into the centre by its library's small English language collection. Eventually, they spoke with me about volunteering, and we set up a tutoring programme for them to help schoolchildren in the afternoons. On their visit after Beny's 'gallery work' in the alcove, I saw them looking askance in its direction. Not wanting to be impolite, they were

guarded in their comments, but it became clear to me that they thought Beny –
European-born, city-bred, with a postgraduate degree – 'uneducated' and 'uncul-
tured'. That was what they inferred from the height at which he had placed the
posters – he didn't know any better. They extended that inference to the rest of the
centre's staff, and the townspeople beyond it.   (From author's field notes, Spring
1973)

Space and its appurtenances – furnishings, decor, construction and design
materials, wall colour or decorations, and the other objects or 'props' that
decorate or clutter it – are decidedly not neutral with respect to power, values
and other meanings. Organizational spaces are not empty shells forming the
backdrop to or stage-setting for the rest of human activity. The meanings – the
values, beliefs, and feelings or sentiments – that those designing organizational spaces embed in them are 'read' by others passing through, looking on
(both, more passive usages), and/or stopping, sitting, acting, using, interacting
in and through the spaces (more active engagements). Such 'designers' can be
not only architects working with policy-makers or executives on new
construction, but managers and other employees redesigning the spaces they
are given or inherit from prior occupants. 'Readers' of their intended meanings
can include clients and customers, as well as investors, neighbours, voters and
other onlookers. But intended meanings do not control interpreted meanings
(which we know in broader organizational cultural terms; see for example,
Kunda 1992). 'Beny' may have had one thing in mind in hanging the artwork,
but neither gang members nor the volunteers saw matters as he did, and he
could not control their interpretations. Nor did they need to respond to that
arrangement of space and the objects in it as he intended them to: gang
members could still have defaced the posters at that height.

Unlike many organizational studies scholars, for whom spatial elements are
still, at most, a research afterthought, Winston Churchill appreciated the
significance of built space in communicating meaning and in shaping people's
actions and even lives. Yet Churchill's dictum (the epigraph to this chapter)
requires an addition: … and afterwards – after we have shaped our built spaces
and after they have shaped us – we act right back on those shapes and that
shaping. Or we at least have the capacity to do so, reshaping spaces when their
designs and/or intended uses do not fit our needs or enable us to do what we
want or need to do. There is nothing, in other words, in human-spatial relations
to suggest either interpretive monophony or determinism (nor do different
readings of spatial elements need to be harmonious, as we see in the English
women's interpretations of Beny's actions). Spatial analysis needs to engage
human agency, including on the part of those on the receiving end of others'
designs and space use intentions who may have very different readings and
reactions.

Not only are spatial elements not *tabulae rasae*, devoid of meaning, or filled with necessarily singular meanings; spatial shapings – their design, arrangement, and/or use – and readings can manifest power/powerlessness dimensions. For example, gang members and volunteers had their own inter-pretations of the paintings' heights. Yet at the same time, neither group took action with respect to their interpretations: gang members didn't deface the paintings, nor did they or the volunteers re-hang them at a lower, more engag-ing (and comfortable) and less insulting level. (And neither did I.) Some intended uses of space carry more weight than reactions against them, whether because of the relative power positions of their creators and interpreters or some other factor; some spatial interpretations are more powerful – more enabling or more injurious – than others. And these are conveyed without resort to explicit language.

We are not born knowing how to 'read' spatial elements; such interpreta-tion is learned, and it is culturally specific. Consider the fine 'water ballet' of Amsterdam bicyclists or Manhattan pedestrians navigating bike paths or side-walks past cars, buses, trams and tourists during rush hour, getting to work mostly without crashing into each other. What keeps brand-new, first-year students entering a classroom they have never seen before from taking their places at the professor's table? The unspoken, unwritten, involved choreogra-phy of a job interview, with respect to who welcomes whom, who takes whose coat, who offers coffee, who gestures to places in the interview room, who sits where, is also learned.

Spatial learning begins in infancy, via direct physical contact with the mate-rial world, largely through touch and taste.[1] Much of child development concerns learning how objects occupy space; their size and position are learned in relation to 'me', as children use their own bodies as measurement devices, drawing on all senses. The things that are learned include location, position, distance; shape; quantity, volume; direction; interval; time; and movement. These are learned and known by building systems of relationships. A gradual shift takes place from tactile 'assessment' to visual assessment, at ever growing distances, as children form visual memories of these relation-ships as well as muscle memories (both in the form of motor actions involved and the required exertion of force necessary to achieve an intended purpose). The older child shifts further from physical interaction with material elements to the symbolic representationality of language. Consider:

- Spelling is an activity of ordering;
- writing on the line anchors that ordering to space;
- punctuation (for example , ; : ? ! and so forth) puts 'the spaces of oral language into written form' (Stockdale and Possin 1998, p. 7];
- possessives (for example, 'Dvora's chapter') link owners and objects.

Even grammar is relational: subjects relate to verbs; adjectives to nouns; adverbs to verbs. Children learn to understand *order* from elements' position in a sequence: meaning is conveyed through the order of letters in a word ('on' is not the same as 'no') and words in a sentence. The position of numbers adds value to meaning: 17 is not the same as 71, nor is it the same as 117. *Size* and *distance* are also learned, via comparison to a standard ('me', Uncle Jeff); this is the beginning of methods of comparison and contrast. And children learn to understand *shape*: b is not the same as d. Spatial skill, in other words, has both visual and motor components. Marching together in time, as in a military troupe or a marching band, is a vivid example: it requires both visual and muscular effort to maintain formation (cf. McNeill 1995).[2]

Spatial knowledge, ability or reasoning is an intelligence, in Gardner's (1983) sense. Spatial intelligence leads a researcher to attend to the layout of the community centre building, its radio, television and 'paintings' in the alcove, and the height of the latter. We register their presence. Drawing on some expectations we bring to the situation, based on some prior knowledge (for example, what galleries consider 'appropriate' height), we register this height as a surprise. We sense something 'strange' about the posters; we notice their height, and we sense and register a puzzle there; and that then leads us to wonder both at our surprise and at the reason for it, and to seek an explanation for a display that we *experience*, sensately, as unusual.[3]

Treating built space as an artefact embedded with meaning(s) draws on a hermeneutic perspective on human action. Admitting of one's bodily experience of spatial elements draws on a phenomenological perspective (Casey 1993, 1997). Part of what renders this experience of the paintings' height surprising is its bodily basis – the physical experience of having to lean backwards as one tilts one's head back to capture the poster's full image. By grounding theorizing in surprise (rather than, for instance, in a formal hypothesis), we are following an abductive logic of reasoning (Van Maanen et al. 2007, Locke et al. 2008, Agar 2010): we start from a surprise, or a puzzle, or a tension between expectations and experience, and we try to figure out what meanings, what human choices and what reasons for those choices, would make that surprise – here, that height – less surprising.

In organizational and other forms of ethnography, it is becoming more common to note that 'ethnography' means not only a set of methods and a form of writing, but also a particular orientation towards the social world – an 'ethnographic sensibility' (Pader 2006, Ybema et al. 2009). This is a hermeneutic-phenomenological orientation towards the meaning-filled 'underlife' of human acts, language (including written, oral, and non-verbal), and objects – their situationally common-sensical, unwritten, unspoken, everyday, tacitly known textures. We might speak in this sense of a 'spatial sensibility': a hermeneutic-phenomenological orientation towards the spatial dimensions of the material world, in which we act and through which we move, and the physical objects in that world, and towards their meaningfulness and ability to convey meaning. That sensibility extends also towards researchers' and others' ability to interpret those meanings.

Different people marshal spatial intelligence with different degrees of ability. Might this mean, though, that it can be forgotten? And if so, can it be recovered? Can all of this characterize a discipline – an epistemic community – as a whole? If so, what keeps its development from happening? Can it be systematically 'destroyed'? More specifically, what keeps such a sensibility out of organizational studies research? To suggest answers that go beyond what has already been offered requires apprehending the non-verbal character of spaces and their elements.

ANALYTIC VERBALITY AND THE NON-VERBAL CHARACTER OF SPATIAL EXPERIENCES: SCIENCE, LANGUAGE AND THE RESEARCHER'S KNOWING BODY

After spending three years as a participant-observer based in a community centre – a *matnas* – in two locations and visiting several others, I felt that I was intimately familiar with the physical plant. In an ordinary day, I would engage the centre building in many different ways, from walking past or through it to visiting its various rooms and areas and interacting there with staff and visitors, all the while watching and listening to those entering and engaging the space – in short, by 'in-dwelling' with others in the centre spaces, following the dictates of my role as community organizer.

But I had not thought much about the buildings as an artefact communicating meaning until reading in agency archives one day during the second research phase some years later. I came upon copies of some letters written by the founding chairman of the board during the period of the organization's creation which referred to the design of the *matnas* buildings. These letters made reference to overall scale, building materials, specific design elements (for example, the kinds of rooms) and to the fact that useful models for community centre construction existed in the US.

Not long after that, I set out to interview the director of the community centre in a place I'd never visited before. As I entered the town where it was located, I realized I didn't have an exact address for it. I told myself to head toward the town centre area, near the town hall and the open-air market, and to look for 'a *matnas* kind of building' – although in that moment, I could not have spelled out what that meant. I found the centre in minutes.   (From author's field notes, December 1980)

What led me in that research moment to think that there might be such a thing as 'a *matnas* kind of building'? Although they do not use words, spatial elements communicate. They do so through their own kinds of 'vocabularies' (Yanow 2006b): overall design elements, such as shape, height, width, mass, and their historical or aesthetic reference points; construction materials (glass,

wood, cement, stone, shingle) and their colour, tone, texture; siting considerations, such as echoes of or contrasts with surrounding spaces, relative proximity to or distance from these, or setbacks from streets and property lines; usage
designations; furnishings/decor and their designs, materials, usages, etc.; the
ambient environment these create, such as the quality of light and dark, airi-
ness and coziness; landscaping; and so on. But as they articulate these
elements through a kind of sign language, without resort to spoken words (or
written words, usually, other than in signage of various sorts[4]), built space
vocabularies are one of the elements of non-verbal communication.

Language – spoken or written – rarely works alone to communicate meaning. Some research suggests that spoken words convey only 7 per cent of the
meaning of a 'message' in situations where meaning is ambiguous (Mehrabian
1981[5]). Elements of non-verbal communication – bodily stance and movement
in acts and interactions, hand and facial gestures, paralanguage (the tone of
voice, vocalizations, etc.), and personal 'décor', such as uniforms – have occasionally received attention in organizational studies (for example, Pratt and
Rafaeli 1997, Rafaeli et al. 1997, Rafaeli and Pratt 2006). Analyses of non-
verbal behaviour, however, have been rather widely dismissed, along with
extrasensory perception, in the social sciences in general (until recently:
research in linguistics is reclaiming at least the domain of gesture studies; see
Cienki and Müller 2008). Although built spaces have, in general, not been
disparaged as much, one explanation for their having been, with rare exception (for example, Guerreiro Ramos 1981, pp. 144–5, Goodsell 1988, 1993,
Gagliardi 1990), largely ignored in organizational studies might be because of
their association with the non-verbal.

A significant portion of non-verbal communication includes the body. In
order to make sense of and talk about spatial meanings, the researcher draws
on her own personal, bodily experience of them in an act of empathic imagination concerning their meaning to those who engage them regularly. As Van
Maanen (1996, p. 380) has noted with respect to ethnography, the researcher's
self is the primary instrument of research. This requires making room for
bodily experience and meaning within the realm of science.

Carl Rogers, an American phenomenologist albeit better known as a theorist of psychotherapy, described the process this way. One first forms inner
hypotheses, in a subjective mode of knowing within oneself, 'from within my
own internal frame of reference' in which 'I consult my experiencing of the
situation' (1964, pp. 110–111). For example, my efforts to answer my own
question: what made me think there might be a '*matnas* kind of space'? Rogers
describes this as the researcher 'making patterned sense out of his experiencing' (1964, p. 112). This provisional sense-making must then be subjected to
further exploration in observations of others' uses and responses and/or in
conversations with those others about their uses and responses and/or in docu-

mentary sources through an intersubjective knowing and meaning-making process. For example, my observations of townspeople entering the centres (or not), the correspondence I found in the archives, subsequent interviews with townspeople and organizational members interacted with my own meaning-making of those same spatial elements. This entails 'translation' by both researcher and situational actor of their own experiences, meanings and frames of reference into the other's terms. In the process, the researcher's initial personal knowledge, based on his or her own and observations of others' initial bodily sense-making, is rendered mutually comprehensible, and inter-subjective knowledge is developed.[6]

These interpretive processes are characterized by the indeterminacy of language and the academic discomfort with bodies and 'embodied' meaning, which shifts attention away from the mind, in a Cartesian duality. Although we might say that the meaning of all language is indeterminate (Harshav 2003), the meaning of physical artefacts has a double indeterminacy. First, the meanings of objects are experienced without words. Spatial vocabularies exist largely in the perceptual, non-linguistic world. But in order to communicate explicitly about their objectual referent, these implicit meanings, usually known tacitly and communicated non-verbally, must be translated into language. If linguistic meanings are themselves indefinite, then the meanings of objects are twice removed from definitiveness.

It is, I think, relatively easy to see why positivist-informed science would be uncomfortable with such a research practice. Positivism presupposes a correspondence theory of truth or meaning: a one-to-one correspondence between the artefact and its meaning based on an objective reference point (see Rorty 1979). The indeterminacy of spatial meanings twice removed from their sense-based experience – personal experience to personal sense-making, to a narrative presented to another person – eliminates this separation of 'research object' from researcher (one of the definitions of objectivity; Yanow 2006a). As symbols (including words) accommodate multiple meanings, this indeterminacy cannot be eliminated. This is quite aside from the role of tacit knowledge, including of the bodily and other non-verbal sort, in this sense-making. This poses a problem for a science still under the sway of requiring verifiable and generalizable data collected in an objective – physically and intellectually-emotionally detached – fashion (Yanow 2006a), which requires that meanings be made explicit and that explicit meaning not be ambiguous.

But what would make interpretive scholars uncomfortable dealing with the spatial? Understanding built spaces draws on bodily experience, but, at least in Western science, body has been severed from mind. English-language terms for *organ*ization, *corpora*tion, *head*quarters, however, do not sever the relationship between organizational spaces and human bodies; it is also present in the root of *man*agement – the 'hands on' activity of horsemanship (Jaques

1996); and it resides in the orientational aspect of a considerable part of American English, which accords status to one word in several matched pairs (for example, *up*–down, *front*–back, *central*–peripheral; Lakoff and Johnson 1980). These values are built in to North American, UK and European spatial designs. For instance, one commonly looks for high status individuals on the top floor of a building. To say that buildings 'embody' meaning, then, may have a quasi-literal sense as well as a figurative one. In linguistic and design practices, bodies are intertwined with the spatial, such that studying organizational spaces requires bringing the body back into the research picture, something that challenges this longtime understanding of what it means to be 'scientific'.

But the non-verbal does not fully explain organizational studies' neglect of the spatial. It is ironic that even while limiting scientific study to the realm of 'directly observable' data, positivist-informed organizational studies have, by and large, turned a blind eye to the very observable world of physical objects, while favouring the printed word and human action. But even more ironic is that studies informed by meaning-focused, interpretive presuppositions, such as constructivist participant observations, ethnographies, content and discourse analyses, and so on, have done so as well. One might suppose, for example, that hermeneutics' original textual orientation might explain why objects are not routinely included in organizational analysis. But hermeneutic analysis was long ago extended beyond texts to conversations, acts and other non-literal texts. Like them, built spaces, design elements, furnishings and other decor, dress, trophies, and so on are susceptible to rendering as 'text analogues' (Taylor, 1971) that might be subjected to word-based analysis. Why, then, privilege words, and acts rendered as words, over physical artefacts rendered similarly? If hermeneutic approaches (including a critical hermeneutics that attends to questions of power) have been extended beyond literal texts to acts rendered as texts, why have they not also been extended among organizational scholars to spaces (and other objects) so rendered? An explanation for this silencing must be sought elsewhere than in ontological and epistemological reasoning *tout court*.

SILENCING OBJECTS: THE NORMATIVITY OF ACADEMIC PRACTICES

> The invention of the scientific laboratory was 'a conscious effort to create a "placeless" place' for the conduct of science.
> (Livingstone 2003, p. 3)

Gagliardi (1990) offered several explanations for the absence of scientific engagement with the material world in general: the relative prominence of theoretical attention to explaining human *behaviour*; the relegation of material culture to the past, where and when it is the sole source of information available for analysis (as in archaeology); the extent to which artefacts take on a 'common sense' invisibility; difficulties in developing interpretation skills; and a general orientation, inculcated through our professional training and practice as academics, that privileges mental processes and cognition. He remarked on the extent to which even organizational culture studies, which at least in some of its aspects promised a more meaning-focused, interpretive approach, focused on beliefs (cognitive experience; logos) and values (moral experience; ethos), neglecting sensate experience (pathos) – 'the way we perceive and "feel" reality' (Gagliardi 1990, p. 13), rendering it less than an equally central aspect of the meaning dimension of human action. He postulated that this was due to academics' heightened focus on the rational dimension of human life and their greater comfort in the logos and ethos of existence.

There is much to be said for these explanations, which still hold today. But why has there been so little change in the field since Gagliardi sounded them? Reframing these concerns in terms of the character of the work practices of academic life, and the creation of knowledge and knowing in that practice, explains that as well as the comparative success of discourse analysis. A science studies perspective focuses on academic practices. What binds the several explanations offered by Gagliardi is an underlying sense about the character of knowing that is accepted, still, within organizational studies, together with a normative stance towards that particular form of knowing and the kind of knowledge it affords. This form of knowing embedded within academic work practices privileges words, from actual texts to interviews and other text analogues that inscribe ideas on paper. It highlights the extent to which they engage ideas and words, as communicated through written texts and through lectures, seminar discussions, and collegial or advisory conversations. This is what discourse analysis joins; it explains its rise in the last two decades and the ongoing neglect of spatial analysis.

Academics traffic in words: that begins with our earliest education and training for the practice of our profession. The primary mode of socialization to the profession is hermeneutic and textual. Students read and analyse written texts and lecture notes, write course papers and dissertation drafts. 'Journeyman' assistant professors or lecturers write and evaluate article drafts, reviewers' critiques and editors' comments. Master professors maintain these practices. 'Academic *talk*' is a close second socialization mode.[7] This orientation towards language may be the single characteristic common across the academic practices of all disciplines, including the arts.

After language, acts come next in importance: orientation rituals for new 'apprentices'; defending general exams or dissertations; graduation ceremonies for those moving on to successive ranks and new settings. Although these are also widely participated in, and one might even argue for their disciplinary universality as well (despite the variance in particular forms and sequences), the difference is that their meanings are tangential for the research practices that lie at the core of academic life. Whereas they may model for apprentices what teaching and advising should look like, they do not model its 'core business' practice: the conduct of research.

Physical objects come last. Settings, too, might be thought to have a kind of universality: classrooms, laboratories, offices, campuses, living spaces, dining halls. But these are not universally shared experiences in their forms, nor are the experiences of the spaces part of the research process. From the perspective of learning a research practice, the lived experience of a lab lies in partaking of the scientific activity that takes place in it. That is what is being modelled, and learned. Spatial characteristics – the shape of the room, the arrangement of the furnishings and decor, and so on: the 'geographies of science' (Livingstone 2003, p. 1) – are, or are treated as if they were, incidental to the major activity taking place within and before them: the acts of doing science.

This heightened comfort level in dealing with texts and acts both reflects and further underscores an overall practice-based (and perhaps personal) disinclination to attend to the physical world, starting with academics' own research spaces, as Livingstone's comment (in this section's epigraph) on the laboratory points up. (Those disciplines whose 'laboratory' is spatial, in which physical settings are germane to the research itself – social geography, archaeology, cultural anthropology, city planning, and the like that attend to spaces and other objects and their central role in the communication of meaning – are at least a partial exception.) The spatial's non-verbal character, which draws on and calls attention to bodily experience, strengthens the aversion. Both may underlie the analytic invisibility of space and its appurtenances in organizational studies; and the putative difficulties in developing interpretive methods skills may arise more from a disinclination to do so that derives from these explanations, than from any innate intricacy or arduousness. Socialization to organizational scholarship practices is largely blind to the physical surroundings in which organizational life takes place; these are treated, instead, as invisible containers for the focal activities being researched. This is the case regardless of the researcher's ontological and epistemological presuppositions.

WAYS OF KNOWING: FORMS OF KNOWLEDGE AND REFLEXIVITY

What underscores these various attitudes inculcated through professional socialization and practices – including a discomfort with non-verbal media and the bodily focus in spatial sense-making – is a division between two different kinds of knowing, one of them more highly prized within academic practices because of its association with the understanding dominant in organizational studies of what it means to do science and to be scientific. Linked to the politics of 'expertise' and of science, this form of scientific knowing became associated with university training, positioning the mode of knowing associated with mind-based, intellectual work ('I know') against the one associated with physical ability ('I can') (Yanow 2004; see also Hummel 2001).

Each of these modes is affiliated with a different type of knower and the latter's occupational and gender characteristics. Mind-based work is linked to the kind of knowledge that characterizes technical-rational expertise: knowledge is made up of detached, universal, generalizable facts capable of being rendered explicitly and without ambiguity, which can be known objectively, absent the context of their origin. By contrast, the realm of physical objects requires a more 'intimate', insider's knowing, drawing often on tacit knowledge that is characterized by the indeterminacy and ambiguity of meaning and non-verbal 'feel' (in both kinesthetic and affective meanings of the word). This is the realm of 'practical knowledge' that is tied more closely to physical work and the domain of spatial knowing.

The heritage of this distinction joins organizational studies' academic practices, privileging texts over objects; and this operative definition of knowledge creation – that is, of what it means to do science and to be scientific – is powerful enough to carry over even into interpretive modes of knowing that might be expected to be sympathetic to the study of physical spaces as meaning-carriers. Spatial modes of knowing – non-verbal and body-based – challenge perceptions of the very character of science and 'truth claims'. Interpretive science's answer to the question of how knowledge is produced and how knowledge claims are substantiated is to turn to reflexivity. Interpretive researchers try to make the research process as transparent as possible, due to an understanding articulated by reader-response theory (see Iser 1989) – that interpretations are not controlled. Researchers strive to be transparent about the bases for their interpretations – their research process, what and to whom they did and did not have access, what voices might have been silent, or silenced – in short, the characteristics under which the researcher produces knowledge, scientifically (that is, systematically, and within an attitude of doubt), including his/her own personal circumstances (known as positionality) to the extent that these may have affected the generation of data and subsequent knowledge claims.

How much more necessary this aimed-at transparency is when it is the researcher's own body that is in play in the process of making sense of things. But this very openness looks to many like self-obsession, rather than as a concern for knowability – the production of knowledge claims. From the perspective of traditional scientific practices – that is, from the vantage point of doings, action, conduct, rather than reason – its engagement looks like personal indulgence and idiosyncracy, rather than like an effort to achieve research trustworthiness (see Schwartz-Shea 2006). If spatial meanings cannot be studied and analysed absent the researcher's body, and if the use of and attention to that body and its sensate experiences is perceived as a fundamental challenge to the conduct of science, it is no wonder that organizational spaces and their objects are still being silenced, even across methodological divides.

SILENCING SPACE AND OBJECTS: AT WHAT COST?

Presenting spatial research and theory to organizational studies scholars, I continue to encounter such comments such as: 'Now that you mention it, it's obvious to me that space matters – it's right under my nose whenever I go interview someone! But I never paid attention to it before.' (Colleague, pers. comm.). Organizational studies scholarship, as a whole, needs to develop a spatial sensibility.

One might expect that a call to engage the spatial might be addressed to organizational ethnographers and others doing field research; but in light of recent theoretical and methodological developments, I extend it to those engaging in textual analyses, including discourse analysis but also narrative or storytelling analysis, whose definitional starting point insists on the linearity and temporality of beginnings, middles and ends. In this, I draw on Soja (1989), whose central concern is to 'spatialize the historical narrative':

> The discipline imprinted in a sequentially unfolding narrative predisposes the reader to think historically, making it difficult to see the text as a map, a geography of simultaneous relations and meanings ... tied together by a spatial rather than a temporal logic.   (Soja 1989, p. 1)

Space does not follow the linear logic of time and historical chronology, even when those histories are present-day narratives that seek to answer 'And then what happened?' To the extent that discourse analysts and others close their eyes to the spatial geographies of organizational life, they – we; the discipline – are losing out on much that is of importance.

Recognizing that spatial settings and their accoutrements are significant actors in the creation and communication of meaning is the first step towards developing a spatial sensibility.[8] Knowing what vocabularies are available to use in these non-verbal communicative processes is a second step. To this might be added a spatial mapping of movement within organizations, for what it can reveal about interactions, relationships, power and powerlessness (such as the movements through doors discussed by Panayiotou and Kafiris in Chapter 9), and so forth. Adding a comparative orientation moves analysis further: asking how some spaces are alike and others different, using those spatial vocabularies to focus attention. But even this may not be enough to overcome obstacles to developing that spatial sensibility in the first place.

Those of us studying organizations ignore space at our analytic peril. Privileging language over other sources of meaning in an organizational context artificially and unnecessarily limits the range of research questions that might be asked about meaning-related matters, thereby narrowing our potential understanding of a wide variety of processes that affect organizational life. But there is another, potentially even more serious cost to the ignoring of non-linguistic sources of data, in terms of methodological arguments and procedures themselves. The same characteristics of ambiguity and indefiniteness seen to mark the study of physical objects, and the same discomfort (at best) with the bodily associations and experiences that mark those studies, are central characteristics of interpretive empirical research methods. And so an entire range of methods for accessing data, along with tools for analysing them, which depend on reflective introspection and self-awareness for the understanding of others' experiences, is ruled out of existence by this orientation towards that which originates in words. That is, it is not just physical objects that are lost in the study of organizational realities; it is processes and methods of study themselves that are lost. For instance, ethnographic work, which would put researcher bodies in organizational spaces and attend to both, is still a marginal and marginalized undertaking in organizational studies and, I am guessing, in required methods courses in management curricula (cf. Schwartz-Shea 2003 for the comparable study in US political science curricula).

As organizational discourses, as well as acts, take place within settings and often engage other material objects that 'people' those settings, it has been something of a puzzle that spatial sources of meaning continue to be marginalized as a focus of study in the organizational field – but only if one focuses on the content of research. Moreover, it is curious that critical studies scholars, in taking up the works of Foucault and Bourdieu (among others), have engaged them more on their discussions of power and control than of the spatial matters that both engaged (for example, Bourdieu 1989), even when it comes to the former's engagement with Bentham's panopticon (Foucault 1977; Kenis et al., Chapter 3 in this book, illustrate such an engagement from a more spatial perspective). From the perspective of the practices of science, such silencing will continue to take place as long as that mode of knowledge, with its associated scientific practices, that turns its back on researchers' bodies, the non-verbal, including gestures, and other spatially oriented ways of knowing continues in the hegemony. Learning to 'speak space' is but one step on the road away from silencing spatial discourses; challenging understandings of science is the perhaps more fundamental one.

For that to take place may require a 'duck-rabbit' sort of gestalt shift, rather than a process of reasoning alone. My abilities to trigger such a shift through the print medium are, I fear, limited; but perhaps some readers might be induced to reflect on their own space-related analytic practices by considering why the privileging of text over space (and other objects) might be a normative practice in academe and what is being lost in doing so.

This blinkered silencing has costs, then, not only for the 'production' of knowledge and understanding but, in terms of the sociology of the discipline, for scholars who prefer and are more adept at that mode of study. Such methods enable, certainly, a focus on built space and other physical artefacts and their roles in communicating organizational meanings. But they also facilitate studies of meaning-making and interpretive processes far more broadly, including of language in all its forms and acts. If this is the cost of the privileging of texts, we all lose.

ACKNOWLEDGEMENTS

The two field research narratives have appeared in previously published work (Yanow 1996, 2006b). I thank my co-editor, Alfons van Marrewijk, for his careful reading of earlier drafts of this chapter, the first of which was presented in the 'Discourse analysis and management practice' stream at the 10th APROS (Asian and Pacific Researchers in Organizational Studies) International Colloquium, Oaxaca, Mexico (7–10 December 2003). Thanks also to David Knights and Ola Bergström, co-convenors of the stream, for their comments on that version, and to those at the Euroqual Programme, 'Spatial and Network Analysis in Qualitative Research', European University Cyprus, Nicosia (25–27 November 2009), where a more recent version was presented as the keynote address.

NOTES

1. The next paragraph draws on Stockdale and Possin (1998).
2. Piaget's experiments with children learning prepositional relationships – the cup is on/under/next to, etc. the table – is further evidence of the fact that spatial sensibility can be learned. Moreover, blind children can be, and are, taught how to navigate through space. That some children and adults develop social interactive limitations due to their lack of spatial understandings – dyssemia (Nowicki and Duke 1992) – points to the fact that these are learned skills.
3. Strati (2003) might say that this is an aesthetic experience. To the extent that that word derives from a root that means perception through the senses – the *American Heritage Dictionary*

(2004) traces it to the 'German *ästhetisch*, from New Latin *aesthēticus*, from Greek *aisthētikos*, *of sense perception*' – this line of reasoning makes sense to me; but as I cannot divorce my understanding of the word from its English language meaning of beauty, and as a spatial sensibility, as discussed below, is not restricted to the beautiful, I do not follow his theoretical lead.

4. I have in mind also the use of typefaces in annual reports, prizes, and other things lying on tables or shelves or displayed on walls. Clearly, these use words; but much of their meaning is carried in their fonts, colours and other textual design elements as much as in the words themselves.

5. Under conditions of ambiguity – when verbal and non-verbal elements conflict – Mehrabian argues that the non-verbally communicated meaning is more likely to compel, with 55 per cent being expressed through facial and hand gestures and 38 per cent through tone of voice. The research is not unproblematic, methodologically: he combined findings from two separate studies; the research was based on female subjects; he did not consider posture; etc. Subsequent research produced different relationships between non-verbal and verbal communication of meaning; but the substance of the argument – that non-verbal elements carry and convey significant parts of the meaning of an exchange – is increasingly supported by contemporary research (see Cienki and Müller 2008).

6. Drawing on Polanyi's (1962) notions of personal knowledge, Rogers (1964, p. 113) defines objective knowledge as 'publicly validated knowledge': hypotheses 'checked both by externally observable operations and by making empathic inferences' about their acceptance within the researcher's community (much in the way that Kuhn, 1970, described a scientific paradigm, or in the sense of a hermeneutic circle, more broadly). For Rogers, then, objective knowledge is about things 'observable by others', which observations 'can be checked by another' (p. 113). The intersubjective knowing that I am describing here is what Rogers terms interpersonal or phenomenological knowing, in which the researcher uses 'whatever skill and empathic understanding' she has 'to get inside [the other's] private world of meanings, and see whether [her] understanding is correct' (p. 115). This may be done through direct inquiry or by inferring from acts (including non-verbal behaviours) and language used. Corroboration of the validity of the inference comes either from direct acknowledgement or by confirmation from third parties articulating similar interpretations, possibly supported by logical claims ('it is the most reasonable and most parsimonious explanation of the behavior'; p. 116).

7. I am thinking here, analytically, of Phyllis Chock's (1995) analysis of 'Congressional "talk".' I have not seen any similar analysis of academic talk practices, although Latour's (1987) and Traweek's (1992) work comes close, both of them looking at lab scientists. The same attention that philosophers, sociologists, and historians of science and technology have paid to work practices in the natural and physical sciences has not been directed at social scientists, with the exception of works in anthropology and organizational studies looking at the production of texts (Clifford and Marcus 1986, Van Maanen 1986; Geertz 1988, Golden-Biddle and Locke 1993, 1997) and studies of rhetoric in economics and political science (Brown 1976, Edelman 1977, McCloskey 1985, Schwartz-Shea and Yanow 2002).

8. Actor-network theory (ANT) extends these arguments further, arguing that objects are themselves 'actants' that need to be taken into account in any analysis (for example, Engeström et al. 2003, Latour 2005, Miettinen and Virtunnen 2005, Orlikowski 2007). I do not have space to explore the parallels and differences, especially given differences among ANT scholars themselves. But increasingly, I see few differences: whether one takes a more or less radical ANT position, it is clear that the social and the technical or technological are intertwined, mutually constitutive, and in need of theorizing and analysing together.

REFERENCES

Agar, Michael (2001), 'On the ethnographic part of the mix: a multi-genre tale of the field', *Organization Research Methods*, **13**, 286–303.

Bernstein, Richard J. (1983), *Beyond Objectivism and Relativism: Science, Hermeneutics, and Praxis,* Philadelphia, PA: University of Pennsylvania Press.

Bourdieu, Pierre (1989), 'Social space and symbolic power', *Sociological Theory*, **7** (1), 14–25.

Brown, Richard Harvey (1976), 'Social theory as metaphor', *Theory and Society*, **3**, 169–97.

Casey, Edward S. (1993), *Getting Back into Place*, Bloomington, IN: Indiana University Press.

Casey, Edward S. (1997), 'By way of body', in *The Fate of Place*, Berkeley, CA: University of California Press, pp. 202–42.

Chock, Phyllis Pease (1995), 'Ambiguity in policy discourse: Congressional talk about immigration', *Policy Sciences*, **18**, 165–84.

Cienki, Alan and Cornelia Müller (eds), (2008), *Metaphor and Gesture*, Amsterdam: John Benjamins.

Clifford, James and George E. Marcus (eds), (1986), *Writing Culture: The Poetics and Politics of Ethnography*, Berkeley, CA: University of California Press.

Edelman, Murray (1977), *Political Language*, New York: Academic Press.

Engeström, Yrjö, Anne Puoni and Laura Seppänen (2003), 'Spatial and temporal expansion of the object as a challenge for reorganizing work', in Davide Nicolini, Silvia Gherardi and Dvora Yanow (eds), *Knowing in Organizations,* Armonk, NY: M.E. Sharpe, pp. 151–86.

Fischer, Frank and John Forester (eds), (1993), *The Argumentative Turn in Policy Analysis and Planning*, Durham, NC: Duke University Press.

Foucault, Michel (1977), *Discipline and Punish: The Birth of the Prison*, New York: Pantheon Books.

Gagliardi, Pasquale (ed.), (1990), *Symbols and Artifacts*, New York: Aldine de Gruyter.

Gardner, Howard (1983), *Frames of Mind: The Theory of Multiple Intelligences*, New York: Basic Books.

Geertz, Clifford (1988), *Works and Lives*, Stanford, CA: Stanford University.

Golden-Biddle, Karen and Karen Locke (1993), 'Appealing work: an investigation in how ethnographic texts convince', *Organization Science*, **4**, 595–616.

Golden-Biddle, Karen and Karen Locke (1997), *Composing Qualitative Research*, Thousand Oaks, CA: Sage.

Goodsell, Charles T. (1988), *The Social Meaning of Civic Space*, Lawrence, KS: University Press of Kansas.

Goodsell, Charles T. (ed.), (1993), 'Architecture as a setting for governance', themed issue, *Journal of Architectural and Planning Research*, **10** (4) (Winter).

Guerreiro Ramos, Roberto (1981), *The New Science of Organizations,* Toronto: University of Toronto Press.

Harshav, Benjamin (2003), 'Language beyond linguistics', The Herman P. and Sophie Taubman Lectures in Jewish Studies, Program in Jewish Studies, 30 September, 1 and 8 October, University of California, Berkeley, CA.

Hernes, Tor (2004), *The Spatial Construction of Organisation,* Amsterdam: John Benjamins.

Hiley, David R., James F. Bohman and Richard Shusterman (1991), *The Interpretive Turn*, Ithaca, NY: Cornell University Press.

Hummel, Ralph (2001), 'Kant's contributions to organizational knowledge: do workers know something managers don't?' presented at the Annual Conference of the Public Administration Theory Network, 21–23 June, Leiden, NL.

Iser, Wolfgang (1989), *Prospecting: From Reader Response to Literary Anthropology*, Baltimore, MD: Johns Hopkins University Press.

Jaques, Roy (1996), *Manufacturing the Employee: Management Knowledge from the 19th to 21st Centuries*, Thousand Oaks, CA: Sage.

Kornberger, Martin and Stewart Clegg (2004), 'Bringing space back in: organizing the generative building', *Organization Studies*, **25** (7), 1095–114.

Kuhn, Thomas S. (1970), *The Structure of Scientific Revolutions*, Chicago, IL: Chicago University Press.

Kunda, Gideon (1992), *Engineering Culture,* Philadelphia, PA: Temple University Press.

Lakoff, George and Mark Johnson (1980), *Metaphors We Live By*, Chicago, IL: University of Chicago Press.

Latour, Bruno (1987), *Science in Action*, Cambridge, MA: Harvard University Press.

Latour, Bruno (2005), *Reassembling the Social: An Introduction to Actor-Network-Theory*, Oxford: Oxford University Press.

Livingstone, David N. (2003), *Putting Science in its Place*, Chicago, IL: University of Chicago Press.

Locke, Karen, Karen Golden-Biddle and Martha Feldman (2008), 'Making doubt generative: rethinking the role of doubt in the research process', *Organization Science*, **19** (6), 907–18.

McNeill, William H. (1995), *Keeping Together in Time: Dance and Drill in Human History*, Cambridge, MA: Harvard University Press.

McCloskey, Donald (1985), *The Rhetoric of Economics*, Madison, WI: University of Wisconsin.

Mehrabian, A. (1981), *Silent Messages: Implicit Communication of Emotions and Attitudes*, 2nd edn, Belmont, CA: Wadsworth.

Miettinen, Reijo and Jaakko Virkkunen (2005), 'Epistemic objects, artefacts and organizational change', *Organization*, **12** (3), 437–56.

Nowicki, Stephen and Marshall Duke (1992), *Helping the Child Who Doesn't Fit In*, Atlanta, GA: Peachtree.

Orlikowski, Wanda J. (2007), 'Sociomaterial practices: exploring technology at work', *Organization Studies*, **28** (9), 1435–48.

Pader, Ellen (2006), 'Seeing with an ethnographic sensibility: explorations beneath the surface of public policies', in Dvora Yanow and Peregrine Schwartz-Shea (eds), *Interpretation and Method: Empirical Research Methods and the Interpretive Turn*, Armonk, NY: M.E. Sharpe, pp. 161–75.

Polanyi, Michael (1962), *Personal Knowledge*, London: Routledge & Kegan Paul.

Pratt, Michael J. and Anat Rafaeli (1997), 'Vested interests: dress as an integrating symbol', *Academy of Management Journal*, **40**, 860–96.

Rafaeli, Anat, Jane Dutton, C.V. Harquail and Stephanie Lewis (1997), 'Navigating by attire: the use of dress by female administrative employees', *Academy of Management Journal*, **40**, 9–45.

Rafaeli, Anat and Michael Pratt (eds), (2006), *Artifacts and Organizations*, Mahwah, NJ: Lawrence Erlbaum.

Ricoeur, Paul (1971), 'The model of the text: meaningful action considered as text', *Social Research*, **38**, 529–62.

Rogers, Carl (1964), 'Toward a science of the person', in T.W. Wann (ed.), *Behaviorism and Phenomenology*, Chicago, IL: University of Chicago Press, pp. 109–32.

Rorty, Richard (1979), *Philosophy and the Mirror of Nature*, Princeton, NJ: Princeton University Press.

Schwartz-Shea, Peregrine (2003), 'Is this the curriculum we want? Doctoral requirements and offerings in methods and methodology', *PS: Political Science and Politics*, **36**, 379–86.

Schwartz-Shea, Peregrine (2006), 'Judging quality: evaluative criteria and epistemic communities', in Dvora Yanow and Peregrine Schwartz-Shea (eds), *Interpretation and Method: Empirical Research Methods and the Interpretive Turn*, Armonk, NY: M.E. Sharpe, pp. 89–113.

Schwartz-Shea, Peregrine and Dvora Yanow (2002), '"Reading" "methods" "texts": how research methods texts construct political science', *Political Research Quarterly*, **55**, 457–86.

Soja, Edward W. (1989), *Postmodern Geographies: The Reassertion of Space in Critical Social Theory*, New York: Verso.

Stockdale, Carol and Carol Possin (1998), 'Spatial relations and learning', ARK Institute of Learning, accessed 15 October 2009, at www.newhorizons.org/spneeds/inclusion/teaching/stockdale.html.

Strati, Antonio (2003), 'Knowing in practice: aesthetic understanding and tacit knowledge', in Davide Nicolini, Silvia Gherardi and Dvora Yanow (eds), *Knowing in Organizations*, Armonk, NY: M.E. Sharpe, pp. 53–74.

Taylor, Charles (1971), 'Interpretation and the sciences of man', *Review of Metaphysics*, **25**, 3–51.

Traweek, Sharon (1992), *Beamtimes and Lifetimes: The World of High Energy Physicists*, Cambridge, MA: Harvard University Press.

Van Maanen, John (1986), *Tales of the Field*, Chicago, IL: University of Chicago.

Van Maanen, John (1995), 'Style as theory', *Organization Science*, **6**, 133–43.

Van Maanen, John (1996), 'Commentary: on the matter of voice', *Journal of Management Inquiry*, **5**, 375–81.

Van Maanen, John, Jesper B. Sørensen and Terence R. Mitchell (2007), 'The interplay between theory and method', *Academy of Management Review*, **32** (4), 1145–54.

White, Jay D. (1992), 'Taking language seriously: toward a narrative theory of knowledge for administrative research', *The American Review of Public Administration*, **22**, 75–88.

Yanow, Dvora (1993), 'Reading policy meanings in organization-scapes', *Journal of Architectural and Planning Research*, **10**, 308–27.

Yanow, Dvora (1996), *How Does a Policy Mean? Interpreting Policy and Organizational Actions*, Washington DC: Georgetown University Press.

Yanow, Dvora (1998), 'Space stories; or, studying museum buildings as organizational spaces, while reflecting on interpretive methods and their narration', *Journal of Management Inquiry*, **7**, 215–39.

Yanow, Dvora (2004), 'Translating local knowledge at organizational peripheries', *British Journal of Management*, **15**, special issue, S15–S25 (March).

Yanow, Dvora (2006a), 'Neither rigorous nor objective? Interrogating criteria for knowledge claims in interpretive science', in Dvora Yanow and Peregrine Schwartz-Shea (eds), *Interpretation and Method: Empirical Research Methods and the Interpretive Turn*, Armonk, NY: M.E. Sharpe, pp. 67–88.

Yanow, Dvora (2006b), 'How built spaces mean: a semiotics of space', in Dvora Yanow and Peregrine Schwartz-Shea (eds), *Interpretation and Method: Empirical Research Methods and the Interpretive Turn*, Armonk, NY: M.E. Sharpe, pp. 349–66.

Ybema, Sierk, Dvora Yanow, Harry Wels and Frans Kamsteeg (eds) (2009), 'Studying everyday organizational life', in *Organizational Ethnography: Studying the Complexities of Everyday Life*. London: Sage, pp. 1–20.

8. Virtual worlds for organizational spaces

Mark Mobach

The study of organizational space deals with the mutual influences of the physical environment and human behaviour. It can be seen as the place where organization and space analytically meet face to face (Dale and Burrell 2008). In many cases organizational space studies focus on the effects that architectural structures have on social structures and behaviour. As such, organizational space combines organizational design with architectural design. Organizational design entails the constructing and changing of an organization's structure in order to achieve the goals of the organization (Bowditch and Buono 2005), and, in the particular case of organizational space, architectural design deals with the constructing and changing of buildings and related physical structures for organizational purposes (Handler 1970). However, analysis of organizational space is not limited to organizational and architectural design. Organizational spaces produce meaning and may therefore also be regarded as an expression of organizational identity (Rapoport 1982), and changes in such spaces can be seen as a reflection of intended change processes (Van Marrewijk 2009).

When plans for new organizational spaces are discussed, at least two professions will always meet: the manager and the architect. The collaboration of these two roles is central to this chapter. Managers and architects try to influence the aesthetic experience of employees in organizations (Kornberger and Clegg 2004). In a process of aestheticization, organizational goals and organizational identity are transferred to the employee in a process akin to psychological transference processes (Dale and Burrell 2008). This is what they share; but there are also differences that hinder cooperation in the design process. Even though the shared task of designing organizational spaces requires both kinds of professionals to communicate and cooperate in order to find design solutions, in practice they do not always work together well (Wolthuis 2003, Ree 2004, Hulsman 2006, Van den Boogaard 2007). Problems may arise because managers and architects come from two different professional practices with different expertise, needs and priorities. This chapter describes some of these problems and explores 'virtual reality', a technology that can help to mediate these cross-professional difficulties, as a possible solution to these problems.

Only very rarely do organizations integrate visualization techniques, such as virtual worlds, for supporting the communication and cooperation of managers and architects (for exceptions see Brogan et al. 1998, Rickel and Johnson 2000). The concept of virtual worlds refers to an application of virtual reality in which the users are immersed in a complex spatial scene with a large number of dynamic objects which can be explored and interacted with (Poot and Mesters 2005). Users of virtual worlds can, for instance, observe a design of a building, navigate through it via synthetic characters, and manipulate the objects present in it in real time. The literature on virtual reality presents evidence that an application of virtual worlds to the design of organizational spaces may be a fruitful path. Furness (1987), for instance, states that virtual worlds have a positive influence on the qualities of organizational space designs. The use of that tool stimulates managers and architects to include behavioural issues in the architectural design of organizational spaces, offering the possibility of capturing a high degree of realism in interactions between the behaviour of staff and customers and a planned physical environment, as design changes can be made instantly (Airey et al. 1990). Further, virtual worlds allow organizations to catch a glimpse of their possible futures and to assess the quality of their behavioural and spatial ideas (Lansdown 1994). Finally, and perhaps most importantly for organizations, virtual worlds can stimulate cooperation within the organization (Frazer 1998). However, the 2005 and 2006 Virtual Concept conferences confirmed that the application of virtual worlds in the design of organizational spaces remained limited (Fischer and Coutellier 2005, Fischer and Coutellier 2006). Given the potentialities that virtual reality tools bring to manufacturing processes (Rigot-Müller 2005) and to airport design (Lourdeaux et al. 2005), it is surprising how little organizations use the full potential of such technologies when designing or re-designing their spaces in practice.

Bringing visualization tools into the design of organizational spaces may allow managers to improve the efficacy of their physical settings for organizational purposes. The use of virtual worlds in the context of organizational space design can improve the managers' understanding of the consequences of the intended change processes. Before the actual changes have been realized, managers can connect empirical evidence with perceived realities from the organizational and architectural designs both in present time and in the imagined future. This connection allows managers to compare old and new organizational spaces, to assess if existing situations can be improved, and to change the plans if their improvements remain insufficient.

This chapter focuses on the use of virtual reality to support managers' and architects' cooperation and collaboration in what would then be participatory processes of designing and changing organizational spaces, involving both designers and users. It seeks to describe some of the collaboration problems in the design process and discuss the use of visualization techniques, illustrated by a case example. The chapter is structured as follows. In the next section, I discuss the differences that can be observed in collaborations between managers and architects. Then, I explore whether virtual reality indeed is a possible solution for mediating these cross-professional differences. In conclusion, I will discuss to what extent new visualization techniques may be supportive in designing better organizational spaces.

ARCHITECT–MANAGER INTERACTION IN DESIGN PROCESSES

Even though managers and architects may share common goals for a building's design, their practices differ substantially, potentially hindering the successful completion of a design process. Six main differences which may complicate their cooperation can be distinguished here.

A first difference lies in the perspectives of managers and architects with respect to the desired outcome of the design process. In the managerial perspective the targeted outcome of the design process is a physical environment that supports organizational structures and identities (Mobach 2009a). In contrast, most architectural perspectives, while aiming at designing a building in relation to its users, direct their primary efforts towards physical design elements – a combination of materials, colour and light – rather than towards human activities. These differences emerge from and are enforced by differences in education, professional terminology, and experience of the two professional groups. For instance, business school curricula tend to educate managers in the design of organizational structures, management processes, organizational culture, marketing, business development, information and communication technology, finance, human resources, etc.: a degree programme tries to cover the full range of managerial issues. By contrast, schools of architecture concentrate on methodologies, methods and techniques for architectural design, interior design, real estate and project management, structural and mechanical engineering (for example, for load-bearing structures), installation technology, etc.; this curriculum is mainly technical in its orientation, rather than focused on human social processes.

A second difference is in the perspectives of managers and architects on the function of a building. In its extreme version, the architect is engaged with form, especially as manifested in the building's external aspect, which is very rarely discussed in terms of its function for the organization (by contrast with the building's interior design). Although many architects claim that form will always follow function, as expressed by renowned US architect Louis Sullivan (1896), not all architects support this opinion (Hulsman 2004). For many of them, form may precede function (Handler 1970), but it becomes separated from it as design progresses. In this perspective the design is not based on the value for the user, apart from those buildings where management and architect share their interest in communicating a message to the world. This is architecture for its own sake. It is an attitude that reflects the architect's reaction against the long tradition of pure functionalism that organizational management often seeks in architecture (Sharles 1923). Their preference for form allows architects to express their own identities through building design, which then becomes part of the architect's portfolio. Rather than being 'enslaved' to the client's ideas, architects create corporate identities for their own firms through the buildings they design for others. From architects who take such a perspective, managers can expect intelligent and experienced opposition to a functionalism that would tie design to organizational needs.

Third, the orientation of architects' and managers' methods for creating a design is different. Most design methods in architecture have a technical orientation which supports identifying the best solution to a design problem (Gregory 1966, Broadbent and Ward 1969, Jones 1992, Van der Voordt and Van Wegen 2000). Roughly speaking, after the design problem is defined, the methods support a process in which architects seek to generate as many potential solutions as possible and select the best one (Jones 1992). Even though architectural design methods incorporate the human aspect (Collins 1970, Schön 1983, De Jong et al. 2002) and many management design methods embrace a technical orientation at least in part, for instance in product development (Pahl and Beitz 1996, Rosenau 1996), neither focus is primary for either of them. The focus of architects is primarily of a technical nature, they spend only 1 per cent of their time discussing with customers (Broadbent 1988), and one of the biggest challenges confronting managers is that of creating time for human contacts in the organization (Urwick 1956). Managers primarily seek to influence human behaviour, whereas architects primarily seek to solve technical design problems; and the two realms are exceedingly different.

A fourth difference between managerial and architectural practices lies in the different properties of the things that managers and architects design. The manager designs for human factors, trying to influence and structure human behaviour. The architect uses non-human materials to create a design, trying to accommodate human factors. The number and diversity of forms and materials for building construction is enormous. New materials and technologies are developed every day, and computer design programmes enable the consideration of countless forms. Some architects even appear to tease the law of gravity. But at the end of the day, bricks themselves neither argue nor change.

Once chosen, the properties of materials themselves, apart, perhaps, from erosion, will not change. Buildings are basically fixed, whereas human behaviour is in a state of flux and transformation (Morgan 1986), although many organizations do have administrative structures that are stable over time, and buildings can change through redesign and reconstruction. But the basic problem of 'fix versus flux' is central to any design of new organizational buildings.

A fifth category of difference is a direct consequence of the different properties of the things that managers and architects design, and it concerns the respective 'process needs' of each practice. As noted above, managers' needs relate to the state of organizational flux, whereas architects' needs relate to fixedness of the building design. Consequently, where the architect seeks to freeze the situation as soon as possible, management will continuously try to unfreeze it and include organizational changes up to the last moment. The pressure this puts on the architect to incorporate the latest organizational developments, even after contracting out the construction of the building, is strong. The unfreezing of design decisions that had been agreed upon earlier in the design process disarranges the logical sequence in the design process of the building and in many cases is also very expensive.

A final difference between the two professions is in the targeted design transformation. In organizational change, managers primarily deal with transformations from current to desired organizational states. The ideal is a clear and consistent vision of the future state of the organization, understanding its full complexity and consequences, and respecting its current position. Ideally, the architect will use the managerial information about a desired change as a basis for the building design. However, although managers may be the alleged organizational experts, their information is usually far from complete and may at times have become invalid by the time it comes to design implementation. Their expertise is subject to 'bounded rationality' (Simon 1945). In addition, managers can never foresee all possible future states of the organization (Mintzberg 1994). Moreover, small enterprise strategies are seldom made explicit (Mintzberg 1979), leaving the architect working in the realm of implicit meanings, trying to get strategic ideas out of the chief executive's mind. Bounded rationality and implicit meanings make it hard to transform organizational goals and objectives into concrete architectural forms expressed in materials, colour and light.

Given these six professional differences, managers need to understand spatial arrangements or re-arrangements, including their effective use, while architects need to understand the effects of their spatial designs on human behaviour. New visualization techniques may be very helpful in bringing about this needed mutual understanding of architects and managers. Visualization has significant potential for making the above-mentioned differences explicit and workable for both professions, thereby enabling understanding and improving the design of future organizational spaces.

VIRTUAL WORLDS

What kinds of techniques are encompassed in this notion of virtual worlds? Visualization techniques such as virtual reality, augmented reality, and virtual worlds, which will be discussed below, are examples of the kinds of possibilities organizations can draw on to represent possible futures of organizational spaces. All three techniques accommodate the three-dimensional worlds of organizational space; they can represent a possible spatial future and, by doing so, allow organizations to debate that intended future in ways they cannot otherwise do as easily with regular architectural devices such as floor plans, perspective drawings, photography or scale models (Brill et al. 1985). Such representations can be manipulated or not, depending on whether they are interactive or spectator models. With these techniques, organizations can evaluate their plans, decide to change them when necessary, and hope for a better future in the real world. Let me give a brief account of the first two of these visualization techniques and then elaborate on virtual worlds, the third form.

Virtual reality (VR) allows a three-dimensional representation of any object. Such representations can be projected on flat screens such as a computer monitor or regular beamer (or projection) screen, but also on large curved screens and on wall-like screens in a small room with beamers above, behind or below (Karaseitanidis et al. 2006). With the latter two representation techniques managers and architects are 'immersed' in a digital world as they evaluate their organizational spatial plans, meaning that they are almost completely surrounded with digital representations. Users wear special glasses to allow three-dimensional graphics to be seen. Applications of these can be found in a computer-aided virtual environment (CAVE) (a room with walls that are made up of rear-projection screens and projectors that display images on each of the screens, allowing users to get a proper view of the building details and interact with it), or in an immersive virtual theatre (a larger room like a cinema, in which groups of up to 20 people can view the building simultaneously and interact with it).

Augmented reality, the second types of visualization technique, mixes virtual reality with the real world. It might allow people in organizations to walk through a current real-world office or factory environment with digital devices, such as a head-mounted display. What the individual sees mixes the real world she or he is walking through with the digital envisioning of a new workplace layout. One might also walk through an empty lot to determine how a building created in virtual reality might be best embedded in a real setting, such as an industrial zone.

The third form of visualization, virtual worlds, seeks to represent the real world through digital hyperrealism, which produces a similar experience to the real world. Digital models for virtual worlds might include industrial zones, organizational buildings, humans, and organizational behaviour. Such models are the most advanced and realistic of the three visualization techniques because users are immersed in a complex real-life scene with a large number of dynamic objects, which can be explored and interacted with. To achieve full immersion, techniques such as head-mounted displays and head tracking are employed.

With respect to the six professional differences discussed in the previous section, how can organizations benefit from an application of virtual worlds techniques to the design of organizational spaces? With their architectural walk-throughs, virtual worlds involve organizational members in discussions that were formerly only available in the architectural domain. These can stimulate a participatory design process approach which has several advantages.

First, the involvement of workers is a serious design test. The organizational changes that are planned through new building designs will affect their future work, not necessarily that of the designers who planned the organizational spaces (Davies 2004). Workers on the work floor have the expertise and the motivation to make thorough assessments of design quality. By exposing the intended design plans to the workers, organizations can improve the functionalism of the architectural design (Larijani 1993, Zahniser 1993, Mahony 1994).

Second, virtual worlds can emancipate managers from architects in several respects. While virtual worlds help in foreseeing the organizational consequences of a planned spatial layout (Pialot et al. 2006), these worlds also enable understanding and improving the design of future organizational spaces by non-experts in design and construction, such as managers. This may lead to financial advantages for organizations: if the new design is not entirely functional for the work that needs to be done there, virtual worlds can prevent costly reconstruction after completion of the building. Virtual worlds for organizational spaces can avoid a situation of an undesired misfit between organizational activities and spatial design, which then requires architectural correction (Mogensen and Shapiro 1998, Büscher et al. 2001).

Third, virtual worlds can give people in organizations a voice (Bruno et al. 2005) in the design process that they do not otherwise have. Participation in design processes offers new opportunities for those who are affected by spatial redesign, who were at least initially not involved in it (Ulrich 1983), including the possibility to discuss its consequences. In many organizations, participation in such processes might include not only members of the workforce, but also customers or clients, visitors, and passers-by. As such, virtual worlds for designing organizational spaces have the potential to involve and enthuse very different stakeholders.

To illustrate the possibilities and benefits that virtual worlds offer for designing organizational spaces, I will use a case from my own research.

From Virtual to Real Worlds

Over a period of four years, between 2004 and 2007, I studied organizational spaces together with a consortium of researchers and organizations involved with primary health care provision in the Netherlands. The basic idea of the research was to find differences in the performance of two pharmacies after they occupied new organizational spaces, through a pre-test, post-test experimental design. Action research (in this case understood as a participatory process in the pursuit of practical solutions to issues of pressing concern to people; see Reason and Bradbury 2001) was performed between the pre-test and post-test phases. In this approach managers, architects, workers and researchers participated in the evaluation of the organizational spatial design. This approach sought to solve these issues of pressing concern that emerged in the pre-test. We hoped to solve those most urgent problems with the re-design of organizational spaces and to prove progress in the post-test.

The pre-tests showed that patient privacy was a major problem at the counter areas of both health care organizations. In those spaces patients were mutually exposed, visually and acoustically. In health care, such counter areas are regarded as spaces where multiple patient–staff communications routinely occurred and where patient privacy is an important issue (US Department of Health and Human Services 2007). Before the new construction projects began, at a time when organizational members were satisfied with their designed and intended futures, we presented them with representations of their chosen futures in a virtual organizational world. The researchers sought to determine whether the chosen futures would solve the problems of these organizations, and if not, to explore what properties of organizational spaces should still be changed.

The virtual worlds of these two organizations were displayed in a virtual reality theatre space which allowed 20 people to assess the design quality simultaneously. In this theatre stereo images were projected on a cylindrical screen with three projectors. These were placed above the audience, as they would be in a regular cinema. The stereo effect was created with shutter glasses, which can switch from fully transparent to opaque. The right glass was transparent when the right-eye stereo image was projected, and the left glass was transparent when the left-eye stereo image was projected. This technique created an illusion of three dimensions in the workplace design of the two primary health care organizations. The software allowed for visualizing architecture interactively. It allowed architectural elements to be relocated, rotated, duplicated or removed, interactively, and it also allowed the changing of colours and materials. The model included the behaviours of synthetic characters, hereafter called agents, representing working staff and customers. The routeing pathways taken by the agents, the timing of agents' interactions at the counter, their waiting times, and agent behaviours during the wait were based on a mix of estimates from the newly designed working systems and data from the pre-test phase.

The use of this virtual worlds technique invited organizational members to intervene in the planned design and, by doing so, to improve the fit between the existing organizational structure and the planned spatial redesign. The results were improved staff satisfaction with the design and a reduced necessity to reconstruct the building after completion in order to correct an undesired misfit between organization and space (Mobach 2008). The immersion in this virtual world made very clear, however, that the two organizational designs were not capable of sufficiently solving the problems of privacy that existed in the two organizations. The distances between patients were so small that they were exposed to each other's private conversations: they could listen in on conversations, and the view between patients at different counters was still on the whole unobstructed. The designs that had been created without the use of the virtual worlds technique did not achieve the sense of privacy that the organization sought to create with the new design.

In the first organization, virtual worlds techniques became useful in helping managers, architects, and workers to work together to trace misfits between organizational activities and spatial designs. Four days after the action research project took place, concrete was poured, thereby fixing the interior space and leaving almost no flexibility to alter the plans. In advance of the action research phase of the project, management had asked all participants not to unfreeze the agreed design decisions made earlier in the design process or alter the design plans, because doing so would disarrange the logical sequence in the building design process and add to the expense of the project. However, management could not resist the seductive powers of the virtual worlds tools, as the main privacy problems remained. Given the tight time schedule and the significant cost of any intervention at that point, it was striking that management still demanded that the architect make changes in the plan.

However, even though this organization had learned something new about its future space through the virtual representation of its design and made some interventions in the design plans, the interventions were superficial. They did not touch the main counter design, something that had the potential to really solve the privacy problems, due to what was perceived as a fixed time schedule. The full potential of virtual worlds was not realized in this case. The organization missed an opportunity to solve one of their main problems by 'simply' changing the things they wanted to change.

In the second organization there was more time and flexibility to change the plans after the use of virtual worlds techniques. This intervention took place relatively early in the design process, approximately six months before the actual construction began. It allowed the organization not only to learn from facts and values of both present and future spatial designs, but, by contrast with the first organization, to intervene in the main plans for the counter design. Management and workers seriously scrutinized the privacy problem and sought improvements. Their re-design measures proved successful. The organization improved the privacy problem at the counter area: the application of virtual worlds techniques generated a completely new counter design which significantly improved patients' perceptions of privacy (Mobach 2009b). Clients are much more at ease during sensitive exchanges of information in conversations at the counter. In the newly enclosed counters, they benefit from the design interventions provoked by virtual worlds techniques that enabled managers and architects to interact in ways they otherwise had not.

DISCUSSION

This chapter argues that in the collaboration of managers and architects, both professions try to influence the aesthetic experience of employees, but at the same time there are differences that hinder cooperation in the design process. These differences pose two important challenges in the building design process. First, both types of professionals need to incorporate human perspectives in the design process. Both managers and architects have to make accommodations on non-human materials *and* human factors in order to create efficacious organizational spaces. Second, concerning the connection between the fluidity of organizations and the fixity of buildings, organizations need adaptive capabilities with respect to future changes such that the need for reconstruction of their physical 'container' is not immediate, similar to the concept of the generative building (Kornberger and Clegg 2004). Through the use of virtual worlds techniques, managers and architects may have the possibility to rise to these challenges.

To solve the two challenges, virtual worlds techniques, for instance, offer advantages over more traditional design tools, especially in the layering of information on paper, such as with floor plans, perspective drawings, or even photography (Brill et al. 1985, Tufte 1990). Paper makes it hard to include people in organizational space design as well as to connect between the fluidity of organizations and the fixity of buildings. Lifting a paper flap, laying over a spatial scene with a before/after presentation of an architectural redesign, does bring about a nearly simultaneous visual comparison of the old and new buildings exactly in position (Tufte 1997). But virtual worlds can do better than that. Modern visualization techniques can enable designers to create virtual three-dimensional representations of a variety of organizations and their physical environments, such as airports, factories, health care institutions, museums, offices, penitentiaries and stores. They can also focus on special organizational spaces, like entrance halls, canteens, meeting rooms, escape routes, and passageways. A multi-screen theatre also allows for a comparison of organizational data and digital images of existing organizational spaces with those of a new building and expected human behaviour. Organizations can not only assess the functionality of the architectural design of these spaces but also experience the aura and atmosphere of their spatial future, perhaps not bodily but actually almost as if they were in real spatial settings. This approach also allows constant interaction and changes to be made.

But such applications showing possible future states of organizational spaces are still a surprisingly scarce phenomenon. The use of virtual worlds techniques enable non-designers' understanding of spatial design and construction, thereby allowing for more thorough debate between managers and architects over plans. Moreover, by combining different sorts of facts, expertise and opinions with digital images of a possible future state, virtual worlds can increase the mutual and common understanding of management and architect. Given many architects' preference for form over function, virtual worlds also force architects to make spatial functions explicit. Such visualizations allow organizations to determine what is or what is not the case, what ought or ought not to be the case, and the best means available to reduce the mismatch between is and ought (Vickers 1965). Consequently, virtual worlds for changing organizational spaces can stimulate the communication among managers, architects and organizational members, with improved coherence of organization and space as a possible result.

Furthermore, virtual worlds have the potential to bring human and technical orientations together because they can represent building and human behaviour at the same time. Issues related to the building design are often kept apart from organizational decision-making, bearing the risk of a relatively poor fit between organization and space. By showing (even rudimentary) human behaviour in spatial representations, the relationship between organization and space can be improved substantially (Mobach 2008). Virtual worlds may also help to support cooperation between managers and architects in design processes as digital images invite debate, thereby allowing for a more thorough exploration of both technical and human aspects of the building design.

At some point in time organizational facts and figures have to be frozen in order to bridge the gap between the dynamic organization and the static architecture and enable construction to proceed. Exactly where, what and how these are frozen is very important. A wrong estimation, for instance on the spatial needs for staff, customers or patients, could lead to spatial overcapacity (and relatively high real estate costs) or, in contrast, to spatial scarcity and annoying human density. As a consequence, the pressure on both kinds of professionals to design a building that creates freedom for managerial intervention after the physical plant is in place needs to be high. With virtual worlds the necessary flexibility of the interior to allow for possible organizational changes in the future can also be easily represented and determined in advance.

CONCLUSION

Virtual world techniques may prove to be a fruitful intervention in promoting design solutions because they can help mediate existing cross-professional difficulties between manager and architect. Every day in countless numbers of organizations all over the world, managers in organizations make decisions during the design process about new buildings. Many of them struggle with such decisions: the project preparations for construction often come on top of a manager's regular workload, and building projects can turn into financial disasters. Managers have difficulties cooperating with architects due to professional differences. Virtual worlds can support the cooperation of managers and architects in a participatory design process. New visualization techniques allow organizations to plug in computer-animated human behaviour in these virtual spaces. By doing so, they allow for a truly participatory design process in which the planned spatial layout, including the expected human behaviour, is confronted with the opinions of managers, architects, and workers. Organizations that design or re-design their spaces may profit from these developments because spatial representations in virtual worlds allow them to scrutinize the quality of their planned future spaces, in advance of occupation. In addition, by using virtual worlds, the complexity of the organizational consequences of spatial re-arrangements can be more easily understood by design laypersons such as managers, which creates an opportunity for broad participation in and around organizations. Virtual worlds stimulate the convergence of the professions of manager and architect and allow the finding of common ground for a truly interdisciplinary design of organizational space.

Societal developments show that future demands for visualization can be expected to grow. In many areas of organized human activities organizations may turn away from textual and numerical flatlands and rely instead on the convenience and multidimensionality of digital worlds. Virtual worlds used for organizational space design processes have an enormous potential to help organizations find the right spaces that fit the human activities they perform and converge the meeting of management with architects. Although a major uptake of virtual worlds for organizational space has not yet come about, perhaps such applications, interweaving virtual and real worlds in order to design better organizational spaces, are at their beginning stages. Future research should illuminate these processes, as well as investigating whether virtual worlds for organizational space design can create benefits for other professions, as well.

REFERENCES

Airey, John, John Rohlf and Frederick Brooks Jr. (1990), 'Towards image realism with interactive update rates in complex virtual building environments', *Computer Graphics,* **24** (2), 41–50.

Boogaard, Raymond van den (2007), 'MIT spant proces aan tegen architect Gehry' [MIT institutes proceedings against architect Gehry], *NRC,* 9 November, p. 8.

Bowditch, James L. and Anthony F. Buono (2005), *A Primer on Organizational Behavior*, Hoboken, NJ: Wiley.

Brill, Michael, Stephen T. Margulis and Ellen Konar (1985), *Using Office Design to Increase Productivity: Volume Two*, Buffalo, NY: BOSTI/Workplace Design and Productivity.

Broadbent, Geoffrey and Anthony Ward (eds) (1969), *Design Methods in Architecture*, London: Lund Humphries.

Broadbent, Geoffrey (1988), *Design in Architecture: Architecture and the Human Sciences*, revised edn, London: Fulton.

Brogan, David C., Ronald A. Metoyer and Jessica K. Hodgins (1998), 'Dynamically simulated characters in virtual environments', *IEEE Computer Graphics and Applications*, **18** (5), 58–69.

Bruno, Fabio, Rosa M. Mattanò, Maurizio Muzzupappa and Marco Pina (2005), 'A new approach to participatory design: usability test in virtual environment', in Xavier Fischer and Daniel Coutellier (eds), *Research in Interactive Design*, Paris: Springer.

Büscher, Monika, Satinder Gill, Preben Mogensen and Dan Shapiro (2001), 'Landscape of practice', *Computer Supported Cooperative Work*, **10** (1), 1–28.

Collins, Peter (1970), *Architectural Judgement*, London: Faber.

Dale, Karen and Gibson Burrell (2008), *The Spaces of Organisation and the Organisation of Space: Power, Identity and Materiality at Work*, Basingstoke: Palgrave Macmillan.

Davies, Roy C. (2004), 'Adapting virtual reality for the participatory design of work environments', *Computer Supported Cooperative Work: The Journal of Collaborative Computing*, **13** (1), 1–33.

Fischer, Xavier and Daniel Coutellier (eds) (2005), *Research in Interactive Design*, Paris: Springer.

Fischer, Xavier and Daniel Coutellier (eds) (2006), *Research in Interactive Design*, vol 2, Paris: Springer.

Frazer, John H. (1995), 'The architectural relevance of cyberspace', in Martin Pearce and Neil Spiller (eds), *Architects in Cyberspace*, Chichester, UK and New York: John Wiley.

Furness, Thomas A. (1987), 'Designing in virtual space', in William B. Rouse and

Kenneth R. Boff (eds), *System Design: Behavioral Perspectives on Designers, Tools, and Organizations*, New York: North Holland.

Gregory, Sydney A. (1966), *The Design Method*, London: Butterworth.

Handler, A. Benjamin (1970), *Systems Approach to Architecture*, New York: Elsevier.

Hulsman, Bernard (2004), 'Een sublieme fantast die niets normaal doet' ['A sublime visionary doing nothing normal'], *NRC*, 16 February, p. 2.

Hulsman, Bernard (2006), 'Te klein, te gehorig en te benauwd, opstand tegen gebouwen van kunstacademies' ['Too small, too noisy and too narrow, uprising against buildings of art academies'], *NRC*, 21 July, p. C4.

Jones, John C. (1992), *Design Methods*, 2nd edn, New York: Wiley.

Jong, Taeke M. de, Ype Cuperus and Theo J.M. van der Voordt (eds) (2002), *Ways to Study Architectural, Urban and Technical Design*, Delft, the Netherlands: Delft University Press.

Karaseitanidis, Ioannis, Angelos Amditis, Harshada Patel, Sarah Sharples, Evangelos Bekiaris, Alex Bullinger and Jolanda Tromp (2006), 'Evaluation of virtual reality products and applications from individual, organizational and societal perspectives', *International Journal of Human-Computer Studies,* **64** (3), 251–66.

Kornberger, Martin and Stewart R. Clegg (2004), 'Bringing space back in: organizing the generative building', *Organization Studies*, **25** (7), 1095–114.

Lansdown, John (1994), 'Visualizing design ideas', in Lindsay MacDonald and John Vince (eds), *Interacting with Virtual Environments*, Chichester, UK and New York: John Wiley.

Larijani, L. Casey (1993), *Architectural Walkthrough: The Virtual Reality Primer*, New York: McGraw-Hill.

Lourdeaux, Domitile, Bogdan Stanciulescu and Philippe Fuchs (2005), 'Collaborative decision in shared environments: airport management application', in Xavier Fischer and Daniel Coutellier (eds), *Research in Interactive Design*, Paris: Springer.

Mahoney, Diana P. (1994), 'Walking through architectural designs', *Computer Graphics World*, **17** (6), 22–30.

Marrewijk, Alfons H. van, (2009), 'Corporate headquarters as physical embodiments of organizational change', *Journal of Organizational Change Management*, **22** (3), 290–306.

Mintzberg, Henry (1979), *The Structuring of Organizations: A Synthesis of the Research*, Englewood Cliffs, NJ: Prentice-Hall.

Mintzberg, Henry (1994), *The Rise and Fall of Strategic Planning*, New York: Prentice-Hall.

Mobach, Mark P. (2008), 'Do virtual worlds create better real worlds?', *Virtual Reality*, **12** (3), 163–79.

Mobach, Mark P. (2009a), *Een Organisatie van Vlees en Steen* [*An Organization of Flesh and Stone*], Assen, the Netherlands: Van Gorcum.

Mobach, Mark P. (2009b), 'Counter design influences the privacy of patients in health care', *Social Science & Medicine*, **68** (6), 1000–1005.

Mogensen, Preben and Dan Shapiro (1998), 'When survival is an issue: PD in support of landscape architecture', *Computer Supported Cooperative Work Journal of Collaborative Computing*, **7** (3/4), 187–203.

Morgan, Gareth (1986), *Images of Organization*, Beverly Hills, CA: Sage.

Pahl, Gerhard and Wolfgang Beitz (1996), *Engineering Design, A Systematic Approach*, London: Springer.

Pialot, Olivier, Jérémy Legardeur and Jean F. Boujut (2006), 'Model and tools for collaborative design', in Xavier Fischer and Daniel Coutellier (eds), *Research in Interactive Design*, vol. 2, Paris: Springer.

Poot, Hedi and Manoe Mesters (2005), *Programme Text I-Science Cluster*, The Hague: Netherlands Organization for Scientific Research.

Rapoport, Amos (1982), *The Meaning of the Built Environment: A Nonverbal Communication Approach*, Beverly Hills, CA: Sage.

Reason, Peter and Hilary Bradbury (ed.) (2001), *Handbook of Action Research*, London: Sage.

Ree, Hans (2004), 'Architect', *NRC*, 17 February, p. 22.

Rickel, Jeff and W. Lewis Johnson (2000), *Task-oriented Collaboration with Embodied Agents in Virtual Worlds*, Boston, MA: MIT Press.

Rigot-Müller, Patrick (2005), '3-D digital factory and design methods: a case in the automotive industry', in Xavier Fischer and Daniel Coutellier (eds), *Research in Interactive Design*, Paris: Springer.

Rosenau, Milton D. (ed.) (1996), *The PDMA Handbook of New Product Development*, New York: Wiley.

Schön, Donald A. (1983), *The Reflective Practitioner, How Professionals Think in Action*, London: Temple Smith.

Sharles, Frederick F. (ed.) (1923), *Business Building, A Complete Guide to Business for the Wholesaler, Retailer, Manufacturer, Agent, etc.*, vol. I, London: Pitman.

Simon, Herbert A. (1945), *Administrative Behaviour: A Study of Decision-Making Processes in Administrative Organizations*, New York: Free Press.

Sullivan, Louis H. (1896), 'The tall office building artistically considered', *Lippincott's Magazine*, March.

Tufte, Edward R. (1990), *Envisioning Information*, Cheshire, CO: Graphics Press.

Tufte, Edward R. (1997), *Visual Explanations: Images and Quantities, Evidence and Narrative*, Cheshire, CO: Graphics Press.

Ulrich, Werner (1983), *Critical Heuristics of Social Planning*, Bern: Paul Haupt.

Urwick, Lyndall F. (1956), 'The managers' span of control', *Harvard Business Review*, **34** (3), 39–47.

US Department of Health and Human Services (2007), 'Can health care providers engage in confidential conversations with other providers or with patients, even if there is a possibility that they could be overheard?', accessed 14 September 2009, at www.hhs.gov/hipaafaq/administrative/197.html.

Vickers, Geoffrey (1965), *The Art of Judgement: A Study of Policy Making*, London: Harper & Row.

Voordt, Theo J.M. van der and Herman van Wegen (2000), *Architectuur en Gebruikswaarde* [*Architecture and Utility Value*], Bussum, The Netherlands: Toth.

Wolthuis, Alinda (2003), 'Architecten luisteren niet' ['Architects do not listen'], *Zorginstellingen*, **28** (11), 19–21.

Zahniser, Richard A. (1993), 'Design by walking around', *Communications of the ACM*, **36** (10), 115–23.

9. Firms in film: representations of organizational space, gender and power

Alexia Panayiotou and Krini Kafiris

> Space is the everywhere of modern thought.
> (Crang and Thrift 2000, p. 1)

Organizations have long been represented in Hollywood film. From those which focus on the corporation to those focusing on the small business enterprise, films on firms have explored themes such as entrepreneurial success, corruption, competition, the vicissitudes of careers, and the dehumanizing effects of bureaucratic mega-corporations (Hassard and Holliday 1998). These themes have emerged and have been articulated in different ways, both across and within particular historical periods.

Popular culture is a valuable source of knowledge for organizational scholars (Gagliardi and Czarniawska 2006, Bell 2008, Rhodes and Parker 2008). Although there is a tendency to treat representations as something 'less than real' or as 'marginal' and 'inadmissible' objects of research (Rhodes and Westwood 2008, p. 4), researchers should note that organizations are in part understood and experienced by a wide public, including employees and potential employees, through their representations in film (Bordwell 2006), as well as in music (Rhodes 2004), theatre (Rhodes and Westwood 2008) and television (Rhodes 2001); in other words, through narratives and images of organizations in popular culture. Taking the power of popular culture as a given, in this chapter we aim to contribute to emerging work on representations of organizations in popular culture by exploring their representation in six popular Hollywood films. The films are: *Wall Street* (1987), *Big* (1988), *Working Girl* (1988), *The Firm* (1993), *Boiler Room* (2000) and *Erin Brockovich* (2000). In particular, we look at the ways in which these films depict the organizational spaces of firms, using a range of spatial elements to convey ideas about organizations and gender-based power relations within them.

We assert that organizational spaces are shaped both by the built environment of an organization and through its spatial practices. Space is not value-neutral. It expresses meanings, and so is an important part of organizational culture, as well as significant to human meaning-making processes more generally (Yanow 1998, p. 216). We also take the perspective that some forms of organization can be seen as replicating patriarchal structures (Chow and Hsung 2002, p. 83), incorporating masculine ideals as these are defined through the gender binary underpinning Western thought and culture and embedded in gendered, unequal social relations. These gender-based ideals are both reflected in and constituted through the physical spaces of organizations and the spatial practices of their members.

This chapter explores the ways that popular Hollywood films represent these gendered, organizational spaces. In particular, we explore the 'vocabulary of space', the representations of the material environment of organizations, through which meanings about gender and power relations within the organizations depicted in these films are both reflected and produced. We investigate the ways that the gendered and power-oriented experiences of the characters in the six films are represented through the spatial practices of these organizations. In our analysis, we found significant tensions, ambiguities and even contradictions. On the one hand, the built environments of the firms reflected and supported masculine understandings of power – that is, power constructed in terms of dominance, hierarchy, control and discipline – as well as other ideals, such as rationality, order and the impersonal, that the feminist philosophical and theoretical literature has defined as 'masculine' (as discussed below). At the same time, these meanings were challenged, undermined or subverted in the films in many ways, especially through the blurring or outright transgression of gendered spatial boundaries, both physical and metaphorical.

We begin by providing a conceptual framework for the relationships among space, power and gender. In the methods section that follows, we discuss how we selected the films in question and how we analysed them in the context of that conceptual framework. We then engage each film individually, analysing the representations of the built environment and the spatial practices of its main characters. In a subsequent section we connect these findings to a larger discussion on the 'vocabulary of space'. Finally, we look at the implications of these meanings for the films' protagonists in terms of gender and power, as well as the ways these organizations are constructed as sites that enable or hinder opportunities and potentials for individuals.

ORGANIZATIONAL SPACE, POWER AND GENDER

Work on organizational space has mostly focused on the built environment and the ways that it constructs and frames organizational meanings: the organization's culture and identity (Yanow 1995, 1998, van Marrewijk 2009), its members (Berg and Kreiner 1990, p. 41), and their relationships within it (Gagliardi 1990). The built environment is understood as including what surrounds the organization, such as an urban setting, as well as its exterior architectural style, interior design and spatial layout, furniture, soft furnishings, decorative objects, colours – in short, all forms of visual material (Berg and Kreiner 1990).

One important theme in work on organizational space is how the built environment expresses power. For example, as Dale and Burrell (2008) note, buildings in and of themselves are associated with power in the most explicit ways. Long before the collapse of the World Trade Centre twin towers in New York in 2001, corporations 'vied with each other to dominate the New York skyline' (Dale and Burrell 2008, p. 49). Building height in this instance is symbolic of domination in the market, and the Chrysler building, for example, constructed in the 1930s, was seen as signifying this position for the company (Dale and Burrell 2008, p. 49).

In addition, the spatial organization of the built environment – or what Rosen et al. (1990, p. 76) call the 'calculative division of space' – may also be used to understand organizational power and individual power within the organization. The layout of the interior, often defined through physical boundaries such as walls and partitions, is a material cue about who has power and who does not within an organization. It is commonplace in Western cultures to know – and accept – that the president of a company is entitled to so many square feet of private office space, several pieces of artwork, certain foliage, drapes covering the office windows, a specific type of desk chair, a conference table with several padded office chairs, and other furnishings, such as a side table and accompanying lamp (Rosen et al. 1990, p. 76). We also know that square footage and the amount of artwork decreases for vice presidents, and as we go down in rank, we expect a decline in the quantity and quality of furnishings. Yet, our very acceptance of this ordering as 'natural' may be one of the ways in which buildings 'produce power effects: because they are the most invisible as social constructs' (Dale and Burrell 2008, p. 44). Organizational aesthetics, too, do much more than 'beautify the workplace'; they are again 'an issue of politics and power' (Dale and Burrell 2003, p. 44). In many ways, the decor and style of offices and workplaces express much about the power, status and hierarchical positions of those who work within them.

Built form also mediates everyday practices in such a way that it reproduces or solidifies existing power relations (Dovey 1999). Through the use of lines, columns and measured wall intervals, organizations tend to discipline and control members. As Markus (2006) has argued, the articulation of space always embeds relations of power, insofar as it governs interactions between a building's users, prescribes certain routines for them, and allows them to be subjected to particular forms of surveillance and control [as we see in Kenis et al.'s discussion of Prison P in Chapter 3. Eds].

Of course, meanings of organizational spaces are not solely produced by cultural meanings expressed through material form. Influenced by Lefebvre (1991), scholars have also conceptualized space in ways that acknowledge the roles of structure, agency, discourse and practice (Savage and Warde 1993, pp. 129–138) in 'producing' space. The meanings of space include, therefore, not only the built environment, but also our practices and experiences within it. This means that we can act, interact and move about in space in ways that accept, recreate and perpetuate the meanings of the organizational built environment (Hernes 2004). At the same time, spatial practices can also resist, negotiate or subvert the meanings expressed through the built environment, as we see in the films analysed here.

We conceptualize the built environment of organizations and the spatial practices within them as *telling* a story. We argue that this story is about power, understood here as a 'complex, strategical relationship in a particular society' (Foucault 1980, p. 93). Power is not, then, something that some have and others do not; it is a shifting relationship that is reinforced or prescribed by the social context. Part of this context is the built environment, both in practice and in practising, as is described here.

It is also important to note that this story about power is a gendered one; namely, organizations' built environments reflect and constitute what the feminist philosophical and theoretical literature has described as *masculine* constructs of power, that is, power conceptualized in terms of dominance, hierarchy, control and discipline (Weedon 1987), as well as rationality, order and the impersonal (Bordo 1989, Jaggar 1992, Butler 1996). In this sense, 'masculine' power is not just something held by men; it may, in fact, be held by women as well, in the same way that masculinity may be practiced not only by men but by women as well in the context of activities in which they 'do gender' (Butler 1996, Martin 2006).

One way in which organizations' built environments reflect and promote masculine constructions of power is through the construction of boundaries. Boundaries are 'complex structures that establish commonalities between people' (Miranne and Young 2000, p. 1), as well as differences. Whether they are physical, invisible or metaphorical, these boundaries embody ideas that are socially constructed and reflective of unequal social relations. To take a specific example: walls and partitions divide space into different kinds of enclosures, separating those with more power from those with less or no power. While, on the one hand, enclosed spaces enable privacy and authority – since those within them can determine who enters their space and who is kept out – open spaces, such as open-plan office spaces, facilitate surveillance, control and discipline of those who inhabit this space. If those with more power, higher status and higher pay are typically found in enclosed spaces that facilitate privacy and unsurveilled movement, and are usually men; and if those with lesser degrees of power, status and pay are typically found in open-plan offices and are usually women, then the partitions are enacting societal ideas about gender.

It is in this context that organizations' built environments can be seen to underscore the gender binary whose prevalence has been noted in Western thought. Feminist philosophers and theorists (Haraway 1991, Harding 1991, Jaggar 1992) have posited that a gender binary underpins Western, patriarchal thought and culture in terms of a male/female axis, where the first term, and the concepts associated with it in this cultural context, is superior and valued, while the second, and all associated with it, is subordinated and devalued. For example, constructs such as power, rationality and culture are typically gendered male in Western cultures, while disempowerment, emotion and nature, their opposites, are gendered female. As many theorists note, the gender binary also underpins the division between home and office, as it reflects and enacts the private public division (Lakoff and Johnson 1980, Hayden 1985, Andrew 2000). In this sense, the office or the public sphere is typically the arena of men (hence, more 'masculine'), while the home and the private sphere are the arena of women (and more 'feminine').

Masculine power, reflected in and constituted through the built environ-ment of organizations, can also be resisted, negotiated or subverted spatially. Interventions in the rationally ordered built environment may include person-alizing a workspace with photographs and mementoes (Dovey 1999), thereby bringing the domestic, private sphere into the public one; having sex in the photocopy room or a private office (Rosen et al. 1990); or transgressing fixed boundaries, both physical – as in moving into and working from a superior's office — and intangible, such as crying about personal problems in the work-place and thereby undermining the literal or figurative boundary between work and home. Through these processes, boundaries become permeable, blurred or provisional, and, as Miranne and Young (2000) argue, they subvert the hierarchy and control which is otherwise imposed by the orderliness of masculine space.

EXPLORING THE REPRESENTATION OF ORGANIZATIONAL SPACE IN FILM

We adopt a socio-semiotic view (Hofbauer 2000, Yanow 2006) to study how meaning is both constructed and understood through the deliberate and symbolic uses of organizational spaces in films. In this sense, we are interested in the 'language of space' (Lawson 2001) and what it tells us about power and resistance in organizations. We thus see the built environment as a source of discourse which constructs and frames meanings (Yanow 1995, 1998).

Films are a useful vehicle for understanding the semiotics of organizational space not only because the experience is visual and the storyline relatively linear and clear, but also because space is so embedded in a film's storyline that its role and meaning are unquestioned and taken for granted, which may lead to disguising their true power effects (Dovey 1999). To make our selection, we conducted a search using the Internet Movie Database (IMDb; www.imdb.com, last accessed May 2009).[1] We imposed two criteria in this search: for inclusion in our study, a film had to (1) be a popular film released in the last 25 years and (2) feature organizational spaces. We specifically focused on the popularity of a film because of the significant role that popular culture plays in contributing to our understandings of work and organizations (Bell 2008, Dale and Burrell 2008, Rhodes and Westwood 2008), as discussed above. To locate the films we searched IMDb's 'most popular films' list for each year going back to 1987.[2] This list includes both English and non-English language films, released in any country in the world, by both large production studios and independent companies. The database determines popularity on the basis of the total number of votes received from voters all over the world, calculated using a market research tool (MOVIEmeter) developed by IMDb to give industry professionals insight into the popularity of film and television productions.[3]

Looking at the 'most popular films' list for each year, we then used a keyword search involving such terms as firm, business, company, manager, work, office, based on the keywords available in the IMDb database. For the purposes of this chapter we decided to limit our sample to two types of business-oriented firms that emerged from our search: investment firms and law firms. We eliminated organizations such as the army, schools and hospitals, which have different institutional contexts from these two types of firms. *Saving Private Ryan*, for example, is found in the list of popular films for 1998, but its military setting, a vastly different institutional context, would introduce another variable and make our comparative analysis more problematic. We use the term 'corporate culture' broadly to cover the organizational culture of these investment and legal firms, not just the organizational culture of corporations in the legal definition of that term.

We selected six films for our analysis: *Wall Street* (1987), *Big* (1988), *Working Girl* (1988), *The Firm* (1993), *Boiler Room* (2000) and *Erin Brockovich* (2000). The keyword search actually yielded more films, but these were dismissed for various reasons found in their plot summaries. The summary of the film *After Hours* (1985), for example, reads: 'A New York office worker has "a very strange night" when he ventures for a late night date with a woman he just meets [sic] ...' (Anonymous 2006). Although our search keywords matched those for this film, it was clear that neither office nor corporation was central to its storyline. Others, like *Schindler's List*, whose summary included the word 'businessman', were rejected because they were set in an era other than the 25 years we were considering. In addition, we rejected animated films since these are best examined as a separate category.

In most instances, to verify the suitability of the film for our research focus, a research assistant and one of the authors watched the film in question. The details of the six films we selected are summarized in Table 9.1.

To critically view and analyse the films, we used an interpretive approach (Yanow 1998, 2006) which encompassed viewing the films several times and compiling what might be understood as 'thick descriptions' (Geertz 1973) of the organizational spaces and spatial practices of the main characters appearing in each film. These thick descriptions included data on all aspects of the built environment (geographical location, outside appearance of building, materials, walls, floors, colours, furniture, decor, etc.), as guided by previous work in this area (Berg and Kreiner 1990, Rosen et al. 1990, Yanow 2006). As shown below, these data were sorted into four analytical dimensions derived mainly from Yanow's (1995) classification. While our categories resemble those of Yanow (1995) and Van Marrewijk (2009), we have developed an additional category in our analysis – doors and windows – since this emerged as an important dimension in the films examined.

We also recorded information on the spatial practices of the main characters. In particular, we focused on how the characters interacted with the built environment, with an emphasis on their movements across physical and symbolic boundaries, both within the organizations and in the natural and physical environments within which the organizations were visually embedded.

The Films

The six films are presented below in the order of their release, providing a brief summary of the plot of each one and a more detailed description of its physical setting and spatial practices.

Wall Street (1987)

In *Wall Street*, Bud Fox (Charlie Sheen) is an ambitious stock broker, who must choose between two opposing ways of life – that of his father, who worked within a tradition of 'lifetime corporate service', and that of his hero, Gordon Gekko (Michael Douglas), who represents 'the Reaganomics decade of deregulation, greed and profiteering scams' (Boozer 2003, p. 2). Bud becomes Gekko's protégé after providing him with insider information, and he enjoys the wealth and perks of the lifestyle that he acquires. However, when

Table 9.1 Films analysed

Film name	Year released	Genre (according to IMDb)	Director	Production company	Main actors
Wall Street	1987	Drama (crime)	Oliver Stone	Columbia	Michael Douglas, Charlie Sheen
Big	1988	Comedy (family)	Penny Marshall	Twentieth Century Fox	Tom Hanks, Elizabeth Perkins
Working Girl	1988	Drama (romance, comedy)	Mike Nichols	Twentieth Century Fox	Melanie Griffith, Sigourney Weaver, Harrison Ford
The Firm	1993	Drama (thriller)	Sydney Pollack	Paramount Pictures	Tom Cruise, Jeanne Tripplehorn
Boiler Room	2000	Drama (thriller)	Ben Younger	New Line Cinema	Giovanni Ribisi, Ron Rifkin, Tom Everett Scott
Erin Brockovich	2000	Drama (biography)	Steven Soderbergh	Jersey Films	Julia Roberts Albert Finney

Gekko betrays him with a plan which threatens to put hundreds of people out of work, including his own father, Bud engineers a plan to thwart Gekko. Bud is arrested for illegal trading and at the end of the film meets with Gekko while wearing a wiretap, in order to pass information on the latter's activities to the FBI. At the end of the film, we see Bud walking up the steps into the court-house for his trial.

The locations, interiors and spatial practices depicted in the film all work together to create the main organizational space of the brokerage firm in a way that expresses exaggerated masculine power, constructed in terms of domi-nance and control. The firm is located in New York City, the archetypal city of the twentieth century, of unlimited opportunity and transformative potential, which is signified with an emphasis on its dizzying skyscrapers and famous landmarks. The city is also represented through images which recall the clas-sic, modernist city-as-machine metaphor of Le Corbusier (Tzonis 2002): flows of people move into the city and its buildings as inputs into a machine, thus emphasizing the power, rationality and standardization of the city that frames the firm, and thereby of the firm itself. Inside the building, too, people flow steadily towards their destinations along predetermined routes mapped by the firm's built environment. Shots of the city's enormous landmarks are continu-ally used in order to signify the outsized power, ambition, potential and invul-nerability of the firm and of the men who work within it. So, when Bud Fox 'lands' the financial mogul Gordon Gekko as his client, he yells, 'I just bagged the elephant!' The subsequent shot of the Statue of Liberty in close-up signi-fies that the hero/protagonist has in fact managed to fulfil the promise of opportunity that the Statue of Liberty holds, in all its enormity.

Within the firm's building, windows and doors play an important role. Only the powerful have access to private offices along the building's outside walls, while the disempowered, both female and male, work in crowded open-plan office areas in the building's internal core. There, inconspicuous individuals work like busy ants in crammed cubicles or stacked desks. The private offices have windows, which the internal core does not: those in power can look out but cannot be observed; those in less powerful positions are subject to constant surveillance, but cannot form visual links with anything or anyone outside the building. The views from the windows are of skyscrapers seen at relatively close range and from high up, which works to emphasize that the firm is also located in a skyscraper. Transformations in the characters' lives resulting in more status, power and wealth are framed by the office windows through which the New York skyline can be seen. Conversely, Gekko's fall from grace at the end of the film is signified by the foggy Manhattan skyline fading out into the distance – the power and unlimited potentials of the city lost to him, out of reach, remote and unavailable.

The interior design of the building, in both its open spaces and its private offices, is modernist.[4] The entrance to the building has revolving doors, imposing greyish-white concrete columns, and a vast empty space of an entry way which leads to an elevator crammed with people. Gekko's office is constructed in stereotypically masculine terms in a more personal and individualistic way: it is filled with dark wood, leather, and shiny steel furniture and other furnishings with a modern flare. These are predominantly hard surfaces and angular shapes, as is the modernist art hung on the walls, one item of which is reminiscent of a Miró. Gekko's desk is framed by a number of computers, the technology strategically used to further emphasize the masculine power of the firm, as well as of Gekko himself (see also Haraway 1991).

The spatial practices within the company largely reaffirm the masculine power expressed through the organization's spatial dimensions and the relationships that these dimensions support. Bud is continuously portrayed entering Gekko's private office, thereby following the unwritten hierarchical norm where it is usually the subordinate who seeks out those with power and enters into their spaces in order to communicate with them. The main spatial practice which contests the organization's masculine power involves Bud passing on information to Gekko which was produced or obtained in the context of Bud's personal life outside the organization, the traditional domain of women and the feminine. This undermining of the firm's control over the flow of information is ultimately punished: Bud is arrested for illegal trading and, losing his power, status and wealth, is emasculated.

Big (1988)

Big tells the story of Josh (Tom Hanks), a nine-year-old boy who wakes up as a thirty-year-old man after making a wish on a mechanical wizard at the fairgrounds to be 'big' or grown up. He moves from his suburban home outside New York City, where he lives with his family, in order to find a job and live in Manhattan. Josh gets a job at a toy store as the person in charge of testing and assessing new toys, where his understanding of them is deemed more worthy than those of his colleagues with MBAs. Despite his success at work and in love, Josh craves his previous life. At the end of the film, he finds the magical mechanical wizard, is transformed back into a boy, and returns to his suburban family home.

The toy company is based in a skyscraper in Manhattan. In this film, as well as in *Wall Street*, New York City, and in particular its Manhattan borough, is constructed as a site of transformation and empowerment (both of which Josh wished for), but only in the realm of fantasy and magic. The construction of Manhattan as such a site is signified in the opening scene of the film where the magical mechanical wizard is positioned against the lights of what appears to be a bridge leading to Manhattan stretched out on either side behind it. In the toy company located in this cinematic Manhattan, creativity, play and experiential knowledge – the feminine, in the theoretical terms discussed above – are valued over rationality, skill and formal education, thus undermining masculine power and ideals. This is reflected in the built environment in different ways and to different extents, in particular in the three main spaces where work takes place.

The ground level of the toy company, stuffed with bright toys and structures and filled with children, is a space of play and consumption which has nothing in common with any form of traditional organizational space. This play space blurs the boundary between fantasy and reality, as the important 'work' that Josh undertakes can happen here. By contrast, the upper floors of the building are more traditional, masculine organizational spaces. Here, space is hierarchally organized, with executives in private offices and subordinates, mostly women, in corridors and open spaces. The decor is minimalist, with white dominant, a colour that symbolizes purity and innocence, in keeping with the firm's focus on children.

Josh's first office is small, stuffed and untidy, much like his bedroom in his family home, with brightly coloured toys arrayed on the surfaces. Its decor is in soft, ice-cream colours. His desk chair, however, is black leather, a classic element of masculine office style, representing authority and seriousness. The office Josh moves to after he is promoted is larger and less cramped. The decor is minimalist, here, too, using pale colours. It has a window with a view of Manhattan, but Josh keeps the shades down, blocking the view for much of the time, signifying his newly acquired, inward-looking attitude at the expense of creativity, playfulness and fantasy.

Working Girl (1988)

In *Working Girl*, Tess McGill (Melanie Griffith) is a working-class secretary who has studied at night school in order to obtain a university degree, which she receives with honours. Despite her efforts, she is unable to advance in her career and is not taken seriously either at work or in her personal life. After she is betrayed by her boss, Catherine (Sigourney Weaver), who steals an important business idea from her, as well as by her boyfriend, whom she catches in bed with another woman, Tess seizes the opportunity during her boss's absence to impersonate her. She conducts business as 'Catherine' and becomes involved with Catherine's partner, Jack Trainer (Harrison Ford). In the end Tess is exposed, but her business acumen is acknowledged and she gains both career and partner.

The dominant theme of this film is that of crossing boundaries – of both gender and class – and thereby contesting the masculine power which rests on the maintenance of these boundaries. Whereas Tasker (2003, p. 40) has noted that this crossing of boundaries takes place largely through 'cross-dressing', as Tess gradually changes her hair and clothing to impersonate her boss, spatially enacted boundaries of gender and class are also crossed within and around the firm where Tess works.

Working Girl opens with a scene of the Statue of Liberty immediately juxtaposed with a crammed Staten Island ferry carrying the aspiring protagonist and her friends from their working class neighbourhood to work in Manhattan. The image of women in the boat moving across the water towards Manhattan is reminiscent of 1930s immigration documentaries, with boats carrying hordes of hopefuls passing the Statue of Liberty to arrive at Ellis Island in search of the American Dream. This image is emphasized by the song 'New Jerusalem' (sung by Carly Simon), played through the opening scene, which links the American Dream and the women's hard work with the New Jerusalem of redemptive, futuristic opportunity. The music helps to establish New York City as a location of power, transformation and potential.[5] However, unlike the exaggerated masculinity of the transformation and potential in *Wall Street*'s cinematic representations of New York, here the city's transformative potential is to be realized through hard work, as it was for the immigrants arriving in the New World.

The main organizational space in *Working Girl* is segregated between an open floor plan where women work and offices with closed doors reserved for the male executives – and for Catherine, the exception, a female executive with her own office. Catherine's presence in a private office crosses an invisible, gendered and typically classed labour boundary that segregates women and pink- and blue-collar workers from men and white-collar employment, an occupational segregation expressed spatially. But Catherine's transgression of the gender division does not subvert class boundaries, as she is most likely upper class, as seen in her Harvard education, ease with foreign languages, and expensive dress and taste. The interior of Catherine's office both reflects and contests masculine power: it contains furnishings and decor which are classically masculine, such as a black leather office chair, an exercise machine with weights, and a bottle of whisky with glasses, but also some decorative items, such as ceramics and bowls on the shelves, which, as household or even kitchen items, are stereotypically associated with femininity. The artwork in Catherine's office is also interesting: she does not hang an abstract painting, like Gekko, but instead has 'ethnic', batik-style cloth hangings featuring animals and other inanimate objects associated with the earth, which seem to emphasize the feminine, according to the gender binary classifications discussed above. Unlike the executives in *Wall Street*, whose windows provide views of skyscrapers, Catherine's view is of the Hudson River – moving water typically symbolizes transition, flow and the feminine (Lakoff 1987). In addition, although views from the windows in *Wall Street* and *Big* focus on the man-made urban environment, Catherine's view is of nature – another articulation of that gender binary.

Tess's spatial practices within the firm involve a series of contestations of masculine power and ideals expressed in the workplace, enacted through spatial transgressions. Tess has decorated her workstation with many personal items; these are juxtaposed against the impersonal, open-plan workplace in which her desk is located. She gets even with a male co-worker who sets her up with a businessman for a date, rather than for the professional meeting she had requested, by typing funny put-downs into a computer so that they appear unexpectedly along with the rolling stock market information on the screen overlooking the open-plan workplace.

During Catherine's absence, Tess moves into her office, impersonating her and taking on her work and responsibilities, thereby transgressing organizational boundaries of both class and gender which have kept her a secretary despite her intelligence, degree, abilities and desire for advancement. In the film, Tess is ultimately rewarded for these transgressions as they empower her, providing her with access to the people and resources she needs in order to pursue the career and the advancement that she desires.

The Firm (1993)

In *The Firm*, Mitch McDeere (Tom Cruise) is a Harvard Law School graduate who accepts an offer with a law firm in Memphis that has made him the highest offer in terms of salary and perks. When he and his wife (Jeanne Tripplehorn) move to Memphis, they discover that the firm spies on them – wiretapping their home, monitoring their every move, and also interfering in their personal life. Mitch discovers that the firm provides lawyers to the Mafia and has engaged in criminal activity, including murder. After finding a way to expose the firm's criminal activity without jeopardizing his own career, he and his wife leave Memphis and the firm to work and live in Boston.

The location of the law firm is a city, but one much smaller than New York – Memphis, Tennessee. Its much smaller size and non-central location diminish the masculine power inherent in the organization, which instead emphasizes its family culture. The interior design is old-fashioned law-firm decor, with deep-red wallpaper, leather sofas, antique armchairs, Persian rugs, palm plants, old-fashioned light fixtures and sconces. Mitch's office has the same wallpaper, heavy wood furniture and decorative brass items as the rest of the building. The office lighting is low, and the room has two narrow windows and only a barely discernible view of what seems to be a bridge (possibly the Memphis & Arkansas Bridge across the Mississippi River). The overall effect is more that of a stately home or a gentleman's club than a workplace. The organizational spaces of this firm reflect upper-class status, wealth and privilege, and in particular, 'old money'.

Throughout the film, the camera looks through office doors opening into the room's interiors, often with someone standing in the doorway speaking to the person occupying the office. In a world in which doors work as important boundaries, their openings and closings may signify not only the regulation of access to people and information, but also the constant entrée the firm has to its employees, in effect negating the presence and role of the door as a barrier against intrusion. The most significant spatial practices in the film involve the blurring of both physical and metaphorical boundaries between work and home. This is achieved through the wiretapping of Mitch's home and the monitoring of Mitch and his wife through their windows. Through these activities, the firm extends its control and surveillance of corporate space into its employees' homes. The camera invites us in as onlookers, and we become involuntary accomplices in the law firm's surveillance as we peer in on family life through those windows. This reinforces a view of the home, in gendered terms, as porous, vulnerable, subordinate and feminine.

The Firm is, in effect, about an organization which has blurred the boundaries between work and home, between masculine organizational spaces and the home spaces most commonly associated with the feminine. This blurring of the gendered boundaries between work and home results in a situation which is represented as abnormal and pathological for men: it leads to the breakdown of Mitch's marriage, cultivates criminal activity, and puts Mitch and his wife, among other characters, in danger. Order is only restored, potentially, at the end of the film when Mitch leaves the firm and he and his wife drive to Boston to start a new life in a larger, more centrally located northeastern city, where one might expect gendered boundaries to be reinforced, instead of blurred, by the urban setting – thereby securing masculine power.[6]

Boiler Room (2000)

The story of *Boiler Room* centres around Seth Davis (Giovanni Ribisi), a young man who gets a job at a suburban brokerage firm after running an illegal casino from his home in Queens, a borough of New York, in an attempt to work legitimately for large earnings and win approval from his father, a judge (Ron Rifkin). The title of the film is telling, in spatial terms: bringing images of an actual boiler room housing steam boilers or hot water tanks, the term is used metaphorically to denote the 'heat' and 'sweat' produced by the pressure the sales people are under to sell stock.[7] Seth is unaware that the firm is corrupt and engaging in stock fraud, selling fake or worthless stock which is making the brokers rich and their clients poor. Seth gradually realizes how the brokerage firm makes money, but he only makes the decision to help bring the brokerage firm down when forced to do so by the FBI.

Boiler Room is another example of the blurring of spatially gendered boundaries which are associated with danger, criminal activity and disempowerment for the male protagonists and those close to them, as in *The Firm*. The investment firm of *Boiler Room* is located somewhere in the suburbs in a nondescript site off of a main road. This framing of the firm, away from the city and the locus of modern power – in fact, far away from Wall Street – signifies the brokerage's relative lack of power and authenticity and the necessarily anonymous nature of its activities. The ways in which the distant firm imitates a real Wall Street brokerage, adopting its corporate culture, are conveyed through its spatial arrangements.

The interior of the firm's office space is crowded and atmospherically dark, depicted in shades of blue, grey, black and white. These colours and the alternating dark tones and harsh light present the boiler room as 'unnatural' and 'unreal' and the protagonist as pale and sickly. There are no windows in the trading room itself, and the absence of views of the outside world suggests that the activities taking place inside are hidden and unknown.

Organizational space is structured by cubes for employees, with phones and PCs at hand, but the real power lies behind closed doors in the office of Michael Brantley (Tom Everett Scott), the elusive and very successful boss/broker. Seth, the new employee, is disempowered as a man; even his own father considers him 'weak'. His disempowerment is represented in spatial terms. He first opened an illegal casino in his home, thereby blurring the boundaries between work and home and their gender implications, destabilizing and diminishing masculine power and creating danger for the male protagonist, something we have already seen in *The Firm*. His new job is in the 'boiler room', which, through its location and built environment, is constructed as anonymous, hidden and unknown, meanings which link the firm with subordination rather than with empowerment. His spatial practices in the brokerage show how he resists the masculine power and control inherent in the organization, creating some semblance of private space away from surveillance by sitting under his desk to talk on the phone and meeting with a colleague in the stairwell to discuss work issues. The fact that Seth, a man, is disempowered in spatial terms supports our claim that masculine power as spatially constructed is not always related to the sex of those espousing it or resisting it, something we have also seen in *Working Girl* with Catherine, a woman, who both holds *and* resists masculine power.

Erin Brockovich (2000)

This film is based on the real story of Erin Brockovich (played by Julia Roberts), a single mother with three children and financial hardship, who takes a job as a clerk in a small California town law office. She discovers evidence that the town's water supply is being poisoned by the corporate giant Pacific Gas and Electric Company (PG&E) and that many people have fallen sick and died. Convinced that a cover-up is taking place, Erin embarks on a struggle to expose the poisoning and bring PG&E to justice. The film traces her efforts and the tensions they cause, both for her working relationships and for her personal and family life. Her success at the end of the film is rewarded with a higher position in the law firm, high earnings, and her own office.

The organizational space of Erin's very small law firm reflects contradictory, gendered understandings of the organization. It is located in a small town, a placement that works to diminish the organization's power, as understood in the masculine terms seen in *The Firm*'s depiction of law firm decor. Although spatially organized for the rational processes required by legal work, with its private office for the boss and open spaces for the secretaries and clerks, the interior is cluttered, stuffed with things hidden in dark corners, partly unseen and unknown. The law firm exists in a contradictory tension between a masculine ordering of space and elements which feminize the space, such as family photographs, fresh flowers and unused items of clothing reserved for professional meetings (such as an extra tie hanging behind the door).

The spatial practices of the male boss, Ed Masry (Albert Finney), are unproductive and inefficient, and he is presented as disempowered. Erin becomes the productive employee, but in doing so, she challenges masculine power in the firm in several ways. She blurs boundaries between work and home, bringing her children in to work and working with her boss at home while reclining on the sofa with her baby. She undermines the rational organization of the workspace by eating at the table usually reserved for client meetings, and she upends the masculine control of space and time by coming and going as she pleases. In de-masculinizing the firm, Erin blurs gendered boundaries, but she achieves masculine goals: success through competition, financial rewards (for those made sick by the pollution, as well as for herself through her promotion) and legal punishment of the offending corporation. In this respect, her spatial practices hold all of the tensions inherent in producing power effects.

In fact, her success in achieving these goals at the end of the film is rewarded by a new organizational space for the firm, a move to downtown Los Angeles in a building where corporate law firms have offices. Outside this new location, we see the ubiquitous skyscraper, a backdrop to organizational spaces which reflect and represent masculine power. Inside, the premises are well-lit, orderly, clean, uncluttered and 'rationally' ordered. In this new building, Erin is spatially rewarded with her own office, with a door and a window and their underlying symbolisms.

The Vocabulary of Organizational Space in Film

What emerges from the analysis of the six films is that organizational space is itself an actor in each film, although one not acknowledged in the end credits. Without all of these spatial elements, it would be much harder to tell these stories of power and their gender and sometimes class entailments. With different spatial elements, the stories told might be very different. We systematize our analysis of the organizational spaces represented in the six films through four analytical categories: geographic location; size, scale and materials of the building; the presence of doors, and windows; and decor.

Geographic location of the organization

The geographic location of the organizations in the six films analysed signifies much about their power and the kind of power and transformative potentials that are on offer to the individual characters. New York City locations figure in four of the films. In *Wall Street*, New York is represented through images which emphasize its enormous power, in the classically modernist spirit of city-as-machine which is the quintessentially masculine image. The skyline and its famous landmarks are used throughout the film in order to signify the dominance, power and hierarchy the characters already possess or their potential for and aspiration towards (em)power(ment) and status. In both *Big* and *Working Girl,* however, New York is not the city-as-machine represented in *Wall Street*, indicating that the organizations in those two films and the power relations within them cannot be understood in unambiguously masculine terms. As noted, the conflicts and juxtapositions in these two films are numerous, stemming perhaps from the fact that their main characters – a boy and a woman, respectively – are negotiating space in non-masculinist terms.

In *Boiler Room,* the fact that the building is *not* in the middle of Manhattan but close to it (on Long Island) is used to signify the pretense and falsity of the corporation – it is not the 'real thing' but an illegal, shadowy version of a typical, more 'authentic' Wall Street brokerage firm. *The Firm*'s location in Memphis similarly uses opposition to New York City and Boston, another northeast business centre, to exemplify the illegality of the firm, and the plot is resolved through relocation to a 'real' city. For *Erin Brockovich* it is Los Angeles and its suburbs or exurbs that constitute the poles, with a similar resolution to *The Firm* at the end of the film.

Size, scale and materials used for the buildings

The size of the buildings – huge – is significant in three of the six films (*Wall Street*, *Big*, *Working Girl*), connoting the power of the corporation. As Yanow notes (1995, p. 411), in Western cultures, 'to take up space physically is a sign of power and control'. The corporations featured in these three films are located in tall skyscrapers, a view which is shown strategically to emphasize certain important parts of the storyline, such as when Gekko decides to sell Bluestar stock, when Josh is promoted, or when Tess is about to 'land a big deal'. *Wall Street*'s building is an imposing concrete skyscraper which seems to echo Gekko's idea that 'we are invulnerable'. The 'killer instinct' that he not only possesses personally but advocates for others is signified by the 'roughness' of the materials used for both outside and inside construction. The buildings in *Big* and *Working Girl* are similar. All three have revolving doors at their entrances, leading to vast, empty spaces, themselves leading to elevators crammed with people and surrounded by imposing Greek-style columns in a greyish-white colour (made of concrete). In all three films, the walls are grey and the elevators open to reveal open-plan floors. These buildings' austerity is pervasive in exterior appearance, layout, and materials used.

By contrast, the exteriors of the buildings in *The Firm*, *Erin Brockovich*, and *Boiler Room* are not frequently shown. In *The Firm*, for example, the building is not shown in its entirety (in fact, we never see how tall it is), but it is situated next to a guarded multi-level parking garage, giving the impression that this is an important and busy place. The name of the firm is hardly visible on the outside, but the building – to the extent that we can see it – seems to have an air of both authority and cosiness with the juxtaposition of its concrete walls and the large, arched French-style windows and door.

In *Erin Brockovich* the firm's transformation is signified through the move to larger offices once the PG&E case is won. It exchanges a small, two-floor concrete building located in a busy residential area surrounded by trees for office space in a tall building similar to those in the other three films – a stark, concrete exterior, with revolving doors leading to an entry way with columns and multiple elevators.

The building housing the 'boiler room' is interestingly nondescript, almost purposefully generic on the outside. Located in what seems like a residential area, it is a seven-floor, dark glass building with no particular characteristics, surrounded by trees and a parking lot. The fact that it could be 'any' corporate building without any clear markings may again indicate the shadowy, clandestine practices of the firm it houses.

Doors and windows

Doors and windows are used in specific ways in all six films. Doors separate those with power from those without power. They signify power in that those who have them can close them and remove what happens behind them from surveillance: all important decisions are made behind closed doors. The power distinction is usually gendered. Whereas women in the films mostly inhabit open spaces (for example, open floor plans), men are found behind closed doors. In *Wall Street*, Gekko is in his enclosed office while his door separates him from the 'powerless' who are found in a vast office area resembling the floor of the New York Stock Exchange. In *The Firm* there is a constant opening and closing of doors, but we know that much happens behind those closed doors, as evident when 'talk' begins to happen and Mitch is shut out, literally.

In *Working Girl*, Catherine is the only woman behind a closed door, which signifies her power and status. The secretaries, all women, and other administrative staff are found in cubicles in the central core outside the private offices.

When Erin in *Erin Brockovitch* is deemed successful, she is rewarded with a self-enclosed office. In *Boiler Room* all subordinates are found in cubicles that do not have doors. Although here the subordinates are all men, the real power is again behind closed doors, in the boss's office.

Windows are used strategically in all films. All the buildings have windows except for the rather dark *Boiler Room,* where a view of the outside is almost prohibited, suggesting the illegality of the business, the lack of transparency and the dark nature of the people involved in the various transactions. The office building in *The Firm* is equally enclosed and dark, with no view of windows or of the outside. The interior of the law firm is often juxtaposed, however, with the protagonist's colourful, flower-decorated home which we are able to see by looking in through the windows. In *Big*, the view of skyscrapers and a park through the windows in Josh's office serves two purposes: to show the symbolic power of the 'VP of product development', but also to ridicule this power. Josh may be 'at the top of the world' in the sense that Gekko is, but he knows, with the wisdom of a child, that all this is meaningless and elusive: what really matters is the time spent at the park.

Decor and furnishings

Generally speaking, the decor and the furniture in these films, including lamps, ceiling fans, carpets and paintings, have a modern flair. The furniture is consistently modernist, with sharp edges, made from a combination of materials such as steel, leather and dark wood (with the exception of the softer edges in *Big*, as might be expected for a toy company). Technology seems to dominate, with most of the work done via PCs and laptops and information sought and obtained via technology.

The furniture's design and materials are used to frame space in masculine terms. Steel and wood dominate in all the interiors, along with the dark (usually black) leather for most of the furniture. Gekko's office (in *Wall Street*) is dominated by steel structures and dark wood. When Josh (in *Big*) gets his own office, it has a big, dark, wooden desk. This scenario is repeated in *Working Girl* and *Erin Brockovich* – even the women have 'masculine' desks. The boardrooms presented in all the films remind the viewer of a 'gentlemen's club', perhaps indicating that both places are the domain of men only. In *Big*, however, the materials tend to be a bit 'softer' and lighter in colour, signifying the child-like positioning of the toy corporation (and the implicit, but poignant critique of managerial skills necessary for running a corporation).

Discussion

Table 9.2 summarizes and presents the 'vocabulary' of corporate space used in the six films.

Table 9.2 *Spatial elements in the six films*

Film	Type of firm presented	Geographic location	Size, scale and materials of building	Doors and windows	Decor and furnishings
Wall Street	Investment firm	New York City	Skyscraper, concrete	Doors for entering offices of those with organizational power; windows for looking at Manhattan	Modernist decor; black leather, steel structures, and dark wood dominate
Big	Toy company	New York City	Skyscraper, concrete	Doors for entering private spaces, such as offices; windows for gazing down at Manhattan	Ornate interior, pastel colours and decorated columns, except for Josh's dark wood desk
Working Girl	Investment firm	New York City	Skyscraper, concrete	Doors to enter private spaces, such as offices and homes; only window is in Catherine's office over-looking Hudson river	Modernist look; dark wood and steel dominate, except for some feminine touches in Catherine's office
The Firm	Law firm	Boston (Harvard), then Memphis, then back to Boston	Austere building, guarded	Lots of openings and closings; clear that some are left *outside* of doors	'Old money' feel, red walls, classic touches, contrast to homes' flowery interiors
Boiler Room	Investment firm	Long Island, NY (residential area)	Imposing dark glass building, seven floors	Those with power are behind closed doors; no windows to view the outside	Modernist interior in shades of blue, grey, black and white
Erin Brockovitch	Law firm	Los Angeles (busy residential area)	Juxtaposition of initial, small law firm building with big, modern new building after success	In first space not many doors, only in partners' offices, conference room; with move and growth, more offices behind closed doors	Decor remains similar before and after the move: offices have home-like feel, with many mementos, family photographs, awards, etc.

193

The spaces in the films have their own language and tell their own stories of power, and because this plotline is familiar to us, the audience, we do not question it. The meaning of space is experienced and understood through the interplay and tension between spatial structures, representation and experience – a tension which may go unnoticed *because* we take the spatial elements of organizations as 'given'. The meanings and possible symbolisms found in the spatial stories told in and by the popular films discussed in this chapter may shed light on some of the power structures experienced in the built environment of organizations.

For one, we have seen that the way power is manifested through built form takes different shapes. One is in the symbolism of the built form itself; for example, the fact that corporations seen in films are often tall skyscrapers. A second, perhaps more interesting, aspect is the ways that built forms mediate everyday practices, constructing or solidifying existing power relations. We have documented, for example, the ways in which doors and windows give expression to and regulate power and powerlessness.

Apart from the design of the physical spaces, we have also suggested that the ways that organizational actors move through those spaces is important to the construction of organizational meanings, including power relationships. Protagonists' spatial practices signify not only their identity but also the power enacted through this identity. For example, Susan (Elizabeth Perkins), the main female character in *Big,* first runs into Josh as they are both hurrying through the long cubicle-stacked hallways of the toy company. Movie viewers do not expect such chance encounters, which also take place between Gekko, the all-powerful mogul in *Wall Street*, and the aspiring young broker Bud Fox, mainly because we do not expect those with power to be found rushing through hallways, which are accessible to everyone in the company. Instead, we expect to find Gekko in his lavish office overlooking Manhattan; those who wish to meet him must enter this space *if he allows it*: it is 'his' space. In fact, a significant part of *Wall Street* is spent showing Bud Fox's attempts to enter Gekko's space. *Who* enters *which* space is an important construct, showing not only specific roles but also how a daily practice – speaking to a secretary, waiting outside of one's office, controlling the time spent in a meeting – enacts power within the organization and puts it on display for others to see.

The act of moving from one space to another in the corporation carries with it certain meaning: it is read as an equivalence of power. When power is not equal, particular ritual acts – knocking on a door, even when it is open – are called for. In addition, the act of *crossing* into a certain space becomes a discursive practice in the sense of 'naming' or signifying who has power and who does not: it shows who has the power to cross where and under what conditions (who knocks, who barges in). In *The Firm* the protagonist is first allowed into certain spaces (the partners' offices or the conference room), but when he is cast in an unfavourable position, this privilege is taken away. Similarly, Tess, in *Working Girl*, transgresses, literally and figuratively, both her secretarial position and her working class identity when she crosses from her own cubicle to her boss's office and claims her own space in this otherwise forbidden room. Taking another's space, as Tess did, represents the transfer of power. The way that power is connoted through depictions of space and spatial elements takes on a Foucauldian dimension: it is not a matter of some people having power and others lacking it; it is, rather, that anyone at any time can be involved in both exercising power and resisting its effects.

Finally, our analysis indicates that the meanings of organizational spaces are created in ways that are grounded in specific social relations, including asymmetrical relationships of power, that are also built or designed along the lines of the gender binary. Boundaries are crucial in the production of difference as they delineate who belongs and who does not, who can enter a certain space and who must be kept out. The depictions of organizations' spatial practices in these films shows that the gendering of space is achieved through boundaries that are reinforced, negotiated, transitioned or transgressed, which means that boundaries are often blurred, shifting or provisional. Women are often found in cubicles, men inside offices; in most of the films women are invisible or absent from the office; and the construct of space has a masculine feel in a way that denotes the ambiguous 'nature' of women found in these spaces. The spatialized narrative is one of segregation in which the boundaries and codes set up or establish specific hierarchies and gendered social relations.

Interestingly, when male characters in the films used spatial practices to transgress gendered boundaries, they were punished through disempowerment: actions which called masculine power into question resulted in diminishing their *own* power. The blurring of gendered boundaries between two spaces, such as that between work and home, had the worst consequences for male characters: this blurring created conditions of danger and criminality, as well as disempowerment. This is the case for Seth in *Boiler Room*, for example, who repeatedly tries to transgress both physical and metaphorical boundaries. When Seth runs a casino out of his home – thereby blurring the boundary between public and private domains – he is disowned by his father, who urges him to 'find a real job … to be a man'. Yet when female characters transgressed or crossed gender boundaries, they were rewarded. In fact, crossing gender boundaries that support masculine power and structure women as fundamentally subordinate to it was necessary for women to succeed. This is the case for the characters in *Working Girl*, for example, showing again that masculine spaces are not necessarily constructed by males (or feminine ones by females) but rather by persons who are 'performing masculinity' (Martin 2006), irrespective of their gender.

CONCLUSION

Films and other forms of popular culture can be a valuable tool for understanding the ways that organizations and their gendered power relations are imagined within particular historical and cultural contexts. The films we have analysed here show how organizational spaces are shaped both by the designed built environment and through spatial practices. We have also argued that architecture inscribes power, especially of a masculine character, into the heart of organizations' spatial elements. Consequently, organizational spaces can be sites of both contestation and resistance to this power. In this sense, space in organizations is never neutral, a mere backdrop to what is happening. It is a fundamental part of daily interactions, at the forefront of shaping and building organizational power dynamics.

This research opens the discussion for further work on the complexities of how space is produced and experienced in the everyday life of organizations. It points the way towards further understanding of how space, gender and power are intertwined in practice, and especially in spatial practices. Our everyday spatial practices – from such simple acts as where we stand to drink coffee, to choices concerning whom we allow to enter our office and when – inscribe particular power relations that are related with 'doing gender' in the workplace. This dimension needs further attention in organizational studies. In addition, if masculine power is reproduced in the spatial designs of organizations, even by female architects, we might want to explore what a feminist orientation towards design and its power dimensions might bring to organizational spaces.

NOTES

1. IMDb (as the site is abbreviated) is the largest and most comprehensive database of its kind, visited by over 57 million users per month, and the recipient of several user awards. It is considered an industry standard and is widely consulted by producers, film-makers and marketers in the field.
2. We set the limit at the last 25 years, a period marked by the dominance of economic neoliberalism, the rise of the corporation, and significant changes in organizational cultures which have been explored, critiqued and constructed through popular film. A historical comparison between films on organizations of different periods may be the subject of future research.
3. MOVIEmeter[TM] is a market research tool developed by IMDb to give industry professionals insight into the popularity of film and television productions and the people who make them. The rankings represent what people are interested in, based not on small statistical samplings but on the actual behaviour of millions of IMDb users. Unlike the Academy Awards, for example, high rankings on MOVIEmeterTM do not necessarily mean that something is 'good'. They do mean that there is a high level of public awareness of and/or interest in the title. The database uses proprietary algorithms that take into account several measures of popularity. The primary measure is who and what people are looking at on the public IMDb website. Other factors include box office receipts and user quality votes on a scale of one to

ten. The rankings are updated on a weekly basis, but since we worked with older films, their ratings are not expected to change.

4. Modernist architecture emphasizes functionality. Inititally seen as a rebellion against traditional styles, it has little or no ornamentation, is stark, uses human-made materials such as concrete and metal, and may rely on factory-made parts. The Seagram building in New York City, built in 1958, is considered one of the finest examples of the functionalist aesthetic and a masterpiece of corporate modernism. Modernism gained much popularity after World War Two and became the dominant architectural style for institutional and corporate buildings until the 1980s. For a further discussion see Crouch (2000).

5. In Christianity, New Jerusalem is the celestial city in heaven that all good souls go to when they die. The Book of Revelation (3:12 and 21:2) writes that Jesus establishes a 'New Jerusalem' with his Second Coming. Metaphorically, New Jerusalem is used as the ideal city or utopia, an idea also found in William Blake's poem 'And did those feet in ancient time' (1804). In *Working Girl* the parallel is drawn between New York City and New Jerusalem as a place of opportunity and redemption where all desires can be fulfilled and ultimate happiness attained for the worthy, which in this case are those who work hard.

6. In fact, another binary may be seen here, understandable in US cultural terms that render 'the South' (Memphis, in this case) as feminine, whereas the northeast (associated with finance and law in New York and Boston, and steel in Pittsburgh and Michigan with its automobile firms) may be seen as masculine.

7. The *American Heritage Dictionary of the English Language* (2006) notes that 'boiler room' is informally used to denote a room staffed with telemarketers who use illegal or high-pressure sales tactics to sell stock, commodities, or land. The *Random House Dictionary* (1987) also notes its slang usage to mean 'any room or business where salespeople, bill collectors, solicitors for charitable donations, etc. conduct an intensive telephone campaign, especially in a fast-talking or intimidating manner'.

REFERENCES

Andrew, Caroline (2000), 'Resisting boundaries: using safety audits for women', in Kristine Miranne and Alma Young (eds), *Gendering the City: Women, Boundaries, and Visions of Urban Life*, Lanham, MD: Rowman and Littlefield, pp. 157–68.

Anonymous (2006), 'Plot summary for *After Hours*' (1985), accessed 12 May 2009 at www.imbd.com/title/tt0088680/plotsummary.

Bell, Emma (2008), *Reading Management and Organization in Film*, Basingstoke: Palgrave Macmillan.

Berg, Per Olof and Kristian Kreiner (1990), 'Corporate architecture: turning physical settings into symbolic resources', in Pasquale Gagliardi (ed.), *Symbols and Artifacts: Views of the Corporate Landscape,* New York: Aldine de Gruyter, pp. 41–67.

Boozer, Jack (2003), *Career Movies: American Business and the Success Mystique*, Austin, TX: University of Texas Press.

Bordo, Susan (1989), 'The body and the reproduction of femininity: a feminist appropriation of Foucault', in Alison Jaggar and Susan Bordo (eds), *Gender/Body/Knowledge: Feminist Reconstructions of Being and Knowing*, New Brunswick, NJ: Rutgers University Press, pp. 13–33.

Bordwell, David (2006), *The Way Hollywood Tells It: Story and Style in Modern Movies*, Berkeley, CA: University of California Press.

Butler, Judith (1996), 'Gender as performance', in Peter Osborne (ed.), *A Critical Sense: Interviews with Intellectuals*, London: Routledge, pp. 109–25.

Chow, Esther Ngan-ling and Ray-May Hsung (2003), 'Gender organization, embodiment and employment among manufacturing workers in Taiwan', in Esther Ngan-ling Chow (ed.), *Transforming Gender and Development in East Asia*, London: Routledge, pp. 81–104.

Crang, Mike and Nigel Thrift (2000), *Thinking Space*, London: Routledge.

Crouch, Christopher (2000), *Modernism in Art Design and Architecture*, New York: St. Martins Press.

Dale, Karen and Gibson Burrell (2003), 'Aesthetics and anaesthetics' in Philip Hancock and Andrew Carr (eds), *Art and Aesthetics at Work*, Basingstoke: Palgrave Macmillan, pp. 32–47.

Dale, Karen and Gibson Burrell (2008), *The Spaces of Organisation and the Organisation of Space: Power, Identity and Materiality at Work*, Basingstoke: Palgrave Macmillan.

Dovey, Kim (1999), *Framing Places: Mediating Power in Built Form*, London: Routledge.

Foucault, Michel (1980), *Power/Knowledge: Selected Interviews and Other Writings 1972–7*, Brighton: Harvester.

Gagliardi, Pasquale (1990), *Symbols and Artifacts: Views of the Corporate Landscape*, Berlin: de Gruyter.

Gagliardi, Pasquale and Czarniawska, Barbara (2006) (eds), *Management Education and the Humanities*, Cheltenham, UK and Northampton, MA, USA: Edward Elgar Publishing.

Geertz, Clifford (1973), *The Interpretation of Cultures*, New York: Basic Books.

Haraway, Donna (1991), *Simians, Cyborgs, and Women: The Reinvention of Nature*, New York: Routledge.

Harding, Sandra (1991), *Whose Science? Whose Knowledge? Thinking from Women's Lives*, Buckingham: Open University Press.

Hassard, John and Ruth Holliday (1998), 'Introduction', in John Hassard and Ruth Holliday (eds), *Organization-Representation: Work and Organization in Popular Culture*, London: Sage, pp. 1–15.

Hayden, Dolores (1985), *Redesigning the American Dream: Gender, Housing, Work, and Family Life*, London: Norton.

Hernes, Tor (2004), *The Spatial Construction of Organization*, Amsterdam: John Benjamins.

Hofbauer, Johanna (2000), 'Bodies in a landscape: an office design and organization', in John Hassard, Ruth Holliday and Hugh Willmott (eds), *Body and Organization*, London: Sage, pp. 166–91.

The Internet Movie Database, accessed 12 May 2009 at http://imab.com.

Jaggar, Alison (1992), 'Love and knowledge: emotion in feminist epistemology', in Alison Jaggar and Susan Bordo (eds), *Gender/Body/Knowledge: Feminist Reconstructions of Being and Knowing*, New Brunswick, NJ: Rutgers University Press.

Lakoff, George (1987), *Women, Fire and Dangerous Things: What Categories Reveal about the Mind*, Chicago, IL: University of Chicago Press.

Lakoff, George and Mark Johnson (1980), *Metaphors We Live By*, Chicago, IL: University of Chicago Press.

Lawson, Bryan (2001), *The Language of Space*, London: Architectural Press.

Lefebvre, Henri (1991), *The Production of Space*, Malden: Blackwell.

Markus, Thomas (2006), 'Built space and power', in Stewart Clegg and Martin Kornberger (eds), *Space, Organizations and Management Theory*, Oslo and Copenhagen: Liber and Copenhagen Business School Press, pp. 129–42.

Martin, Patricia Yancey (2006), 'Practicing gender at work: further thoughts on reflexivity', *Gender, Work and Organization,* **13** (3), 254–76.

Miranne, Kristine and Alma Young (2000), 'Introduction', in Kristine Miranne and Alma Young (eds), *Gendering the City: Women, Boundaries, and Visions of Urban Life*, Boulder, CO: Rowman & Littlefield, pp. 1–18.

Rhodes, Carl (2001), 'The Simpsons, popular culture, and the organizational carnival', *Journal of Management Inquiry,* **10** (4), 374–83.

Rhodes, Carl (2004), 'Utopia in popular management writing and the music of Bruce Springsteen: do you believe in the Promised Land?', *Consumption, Markets and Culture,* **7** (1), 1–20.

Rhodes, Carl and Martin Parker (2008), 'Images of organizing in popular culture', *Organization,* **15** (5), 627–37.

Rhodes, Carl and Robert Westwood (2008), *Critical Representations of Work and Organization in Popular Culture*, London: Routledge.

Rosen, Michael, Wanda Orlikowski and Kim Schmahmann (1990), 'Building buildings and living lives: a critique of bureaucracy, ideology and concrete artifacts', in Pasquale Gagliardi (ed.), *Symbols and Artifacts: Views of the Corporate Landscape*, Berlin: de Grutyer, pp. 69–82.

Savage, Mike and Alan Warde (1993), *Urban Sociology, Capitalism, and Modernity*, London: Continuum.

Tasker, Yvonne (1998), *Working Girls: Gender and Sexuality in Pop Cinema,* London: Routledge.

The American Heritage Dictionary (2006), 4th edn, New York, NY: Houghton Mifflin Harcourt.

The Random House Dictionary of the English Language (1987), 2nd edn, Austin, TX: Random House.

Tzonis, Alexander (2002), *Le Corbusier: The Poetics of Machine and Metaphor*, London: Thames and Hudson.

Van Marrewijk, Alfons (2009), 'Corporate headquarters as physical embodiments of organisational change,' *Journal of Organizational Change Management,* **22** (3), 290–306.

Weedon, Chris (1987), *Feminist Practice and Poststructuralist Theory,* Cambridge: Basil Blackwell.

Yanow, Dvora (1995), 'Built space as story: the policy stories that buildings tell', *Policy Studies Journal,* **23** (3), 407–22.

Yanow, Dvora (1998), 'Space stories: studying museum buildings as organizational spaces while reflecting on interpretive methods and their narration', *Journal of Management Inquiry,* **7** (3), 215–39.

Yanow, Dvora (2006), 'Studying physical artifacts: an interpretive approach', in Anat Rafaeli and Michael Pratt (eds), *Artifacts and Organizations: Beyond Mere Symbolism*, London: Lawrence Erlbaum, pp. 41–60.

Afterword
Organizational spaces: from 'matters of fact' to 'matters of concern'

Kristian Kreiner

> ... if something is constructed, then it means it is fragile and thus in great need of care and caution.
>
> (Latour 2004, p. 246)

INTRODUCTION

Space matters to organizations; and therefore, space should matter in studies of organizations. In a nutshell, this is the message of *Organizational Spaces: Rematerializing the Workaday World.* It follows in the footsteps of books and articles with comparable messages, for example, Hernes (2004), Kornberger and Clegg (2004), and Dale and Burrell (2008). It is, in Taylor and Spicer's (2007) words, 'time for space' in organizational research. By offering the reader opportunities to see, to live, and to think the material world of organizations more richly in the future, travelling through *Organizational Spaces* is an inspiring experience.

Taylor and Spicer (2007) have suggested that the published studies of space in organizations fall into three categories. *Organizational Spaces* contains examples of all three. Space in organizations is studied as a matter of *distance* (Iedema et al., Chapter 3; Kenis et al., Chapter 4; Weir, Chapter 5); it is studied as a materialization of *power relationships* (Dale and Burrell, Chapter 2); and it is studied as *lived experience* (Gastelaars, Chapter 5; van Marrewijk, Chapter 6). The methodological chapters (Yanow, Chapter 8; Mobach, Chapter 9; Panayiotou and Kafiris, Chapter 10) deal with how we write about, how we imagine, and how we picture organizational spaces. With varying emphases and explicitness, they all cover Lefebvre's three processes of making space: practicing, planning and imagining (cited in Taylor and Spicer 2007).

Such richness is a blessing, but for the writing of an intelligible set of reflections it is also a curse. Probably few of us agree on what organizations are, how space should be conceptualized, and which relations exist between the two. Unless I write in such abstract and general terms that nobody can disagree, how could I possibly make anybody feel reflected in my reflections? To cope with this challenge I will draw on the inspirations I got from reading the book seriously. The following thoughts were inspired by the book's chapters, and thus are not linear extensions of them. Furthermore, they are *my* inspirations, blending my own research and experiences into the text.

This results in three themes. First, I reflect on the paradox that whereas we are concerned about organizational spaces, most data show that organizational members take space for granted. Next, I will reflect on the relationships between organizational spaces and organizational practices, warning against the temptation to engage them in a causal fashion. Finally, I will reflect on the design of organizational spaces, arguing not only that design processes reflect the multiple concerns that relate to space, but also that design premises are poor predictors of the future role of organizational space.

TAKING ORGANIZATIONAL SPACE FOR GRANTED

If we readily agree that space matters, we will soon face a paradox. Empirical data, including most of the illustrations in the present volume, seem to suggest that people in practice are little preoccupied with organizational space. To a large extent, space is a facet of organizational life which is more or less taken for granted. For instance, in the study of the outpatient clinic (Chapter 3), it is not the medical staff who treat the corridor bulge as a problematic and liminal space. They share information and manage the complexities of clinical work as a matter of routine, and part of the routine is to coordinate their interactions in time and space. Therefore, they assemble in the niche and communicate in ways that they find necessary and fit for public display but outside the earshot of patients and others. In other clinics, such interaction would take place backstage (Goffman 1959), that is, out of sight and earshot. But in this particular case, in spite of being visible, there is no indication that either the form or the location of the communication was a matter of concern or attention for anybody. Likewise, while it took some social engineering to bend the bars of the Dutch prison (Chapter 4), once the proper practices were in place, the prison could function routinely as a prison, probably being considered a 'matter of fact', not a 'matter of concern' (Latour 2004, Ripley et al. 2009). Furthermore, while a few disoriented American managers revealed the intricacies of travelling the space of a *diwan* (Chapter 7), the very disturbance of ordinary routines demonstrates the fact that culturally accomplished persons would treat the traffic rules of the *diwan* as given, non-negotiable norms, enabling them to concentrate on conducting their regular business. Finally, the fakeness of the modern hierarchy posing as a community with domestic features (Chapter 2) seemed to raise little concern among employees.

The point I am making is a general one. It seems that in most situations, and most of the time, organizational spaces are taken for granted by organizational members. They have their minds on something else, for example, some piece of work they are trying to accomplish, some decision they are trying to reach, etc. Only for the novice in that setting, and only accidentally for accomplished actors, will space become a matter of focal awareness. In ordinary cases, it will reside in subsidiary awareness (Polanyi and Prosch 1975). It takes practice to learn to accomplish things without attending to space. It takes social and organizational practices to coordinate activities as if space didn't matter. Novices and other peripheral characters (Lave and Wenger 1991) will occasionally remind us of the inherent ambiguities and uncertainties of space, which the organization has managed somehow to treat as if it were a matter of fact.

If we can convince each other that organizational space is a highly interesting and complex phenomenon, we might come to conclude that organizational members *should* make space a matter of concern. That would be all wrong. It is exactly because they take space for granted that they achieve the character of an organization. The *diwan* would not be a *diwan* if the traffic rules were to be negotiated every time. The point of calling attention to organizational spaces is not to deconstruct them but to appreciate the integral role they play in constructing organizations. I will have opportunities below to exemplify this point.

ORGANIZATIONAL SPACE: CAUSE OR CONCERN?

The various chapters in *Organizational Spaces* describe organizations in action. We have no difficulties talking about 'the medical clinic', 'the prison', and 'the *diwan*' as integrated units. These are formal and informal organizations, and our ideas about them are socially constructed, of course. Yet we have no reason to doubt the authors when they claim (in some cases implicitly) that these organizations worked in the capacities they were designed to do. People were cured in the clinic, prisoners were isolated from society, and decisions were being made in the *diwan*. As a matter of fact, they were all functioning *as organizations*. However, the ways in which they achieved this are pictured as sources of surprise. 'Hallway medicine', 'bending the bars', and carefully choreographed 'swirls' seemed to be important supplements to the organizations as these were originally designed. These supplements, all of which involved time-space coordination, seemed to make the organizations viable.

That the clinic, the prison and the *diwan* existed as organizations we can assume from the descriptions of the routine manners in which their practices were coordinated in time and space. The discussions in the corridor bulge represented an uncontroversial and routine practice (Chapter 3). The mobilization of the inmates in the running of the prison was part of the ordinary social fabric of the setting (Chapter 4). The clinic and the prison were real as working collectives. However, such real achievements are temporary and fragile – a process as much as an outcome. They have to be reconfirmed in continuous practices. The disturbances caused by those disoriented American managers in the *diwan* (Chapter 7) indicated its fragility. Even if we often take such organizations for granted, we can easily imagine situations where the clinic could no longer cure patients, where prisons could no longer protect society, and where the *diwan* could no longer make decisions. In a sense, what we need to understand is the ways in which the organizational spaces assisted in making these achievements visible and durable.

The real challenge for organizational scholars in 'bringing space back in' (Kornberger and Clegg 2004) is perhaps to avoid treating space as a separate matter of concern. Space is not an isolated factor, but a part of the totality of aspects folded into an organization. Its role and significance are relative to its actors, clients, and other resources and to the character of the particular situation we observe. There is no way in which we could see the medical practices in the clinic being dependent on the liminal space of a corridor bulge. To enact the complexities of clinical work, the staff needed to transgress professional boundaries and norms. The corridor bulge facilitated such enactment, but had the physical layout of the clinic been different, they would still have needed to enact those complexities for the clinic to function well.

The staff already acted inventively by practicing backstage medicine in the open. Had they also been within earshot of patients and others, they would perhaps have had to carry out the conversations in some keyed form (Goffman 1974) or, alternatively, to practice norms of civic inattention (Goffman 1959). Still, the observation that specific ways of utilizing space, like a corridor bulge, work to maintain the integrity of an organization is interesting and relevant, but to imagine that organization could not work without that specific spatial form is wrong. In other words, the corridor bulge enabled a practice to be carried out in a particular form, but the development of that practice in that form did not rest on spatial design alone. We must insist that also in the world of medicine, the bars can be bent in many ways, and whether or not they are does not hinge only on the physical layout of clinics. Different layouts call upon other elements, including human actors, to be shaped differently. Space is not a separate causal variable, but an integral part of a larger collection of factors, aspects, resources, and so forth. To illustrate the point that space is an integral part of organizing, allow me to use an example from my own ethnographic studies of construction work.

Construction Work

In one case, we observed construction workers building sewers. For that purpose, trenches needed to be dug. It takes careful engineering to ensure a sufficient gradient and a minimum of bends. Professional construction work relies on drawings, fine tools and heavy machinery. However, well-documented and planned construction work turns out to be highly uncertain and unpredictable. For example, the interactional complexities from having multiple gangs working simultaneously on the site, and the exposure to inclement weather conditions, often disturbed the prepared process of work. On one particular day, the driver of the excavator had gone home for the weekend, leaving the drawings in his locked excavator. The trenches were flooded after heavy rain, sending workers out looking for pieces of wood, etc., to secure the position of the pipes. Being unable to reach the sewer because of the flood, the leveller was useless and the work had to be controlled by eye, without having the locked-away drawings at hand. The task was evolving, and drawings, fine tools, and heavy machinery played a very different role than customary and expected.

The accomplishment of what otherwise might have been a routine task turned out to entail a constant negotiation and manipulation of the physical scene of work. But as far as we could tell, the construction work progressed as planned, and the construction project retained its integrity. At least three further aspects of the situation explain the fact that the construction site maintained its organized character:

1. The construction workers were able, and willing, to improvise work methods. They would have had plenty of excuses for giving up producing anything more that afternoon. However, they managed to continue by solving problems in an ad hoc manner.
2. The construction workers were able to 'read' the situation and determine what needed to be produced. They were not paralysed by the unavailability of drawings and specifications because they knew what a finished sewer would look like. They inferred the task from the available physical traces of previous efforts – a human variant of stigmergy (Christensen 2009).
3. The physical scene or 'situation' was sufficiently clear for the skilled workers to read. Under different circumstances, leaving the scripted work process might have meant more problems, not fewer. Less skilled workers in more ambiguous physical scenes might still have engaged in improvisations, but the outcomes would have been destructive, not constructive.

Motivation, skill, the nature of the task, and the transparency of the scene would all have to combine to enable construction work to continue. In this combination, space is given its role and significance. If it has an impact on practice, it will have it in an implicit and indirect manner. Iedema et al. (Chapter 3) should not be read to imply that we can change medical work by designing clinics with corridor bulges. Space will play its role in relation to the roles played by many other aspects and conditions. Insisting on an isolated role for space in organization theory risks turning it into a bulge in the complex of ideas and constructions that we wanted to understand in the first place.

In many ways, these reflections lead me towards the concept of affordance (Gibson 1986, Gaver 1996, Hutchby 2001, Latour 2002). It is a somewhat contested concept, but I think it could be made useful in relation to theorizing organizational spaces.

AFFORDANCES

In Gibson's definition, 'The affordances of the environment are what it offers the animal, what it provides or furnishes, either for good or ill. … It implies the complementarity of the animal and the environment' (Gibson 1986, 127). Translated into spatial terms, Gibson would underscore the point that space matters, but what it offers, provides or furnishes is relative to the actor. Human actors vary in their relationships to space simply because they have different roles in the organization. In general, actors are acting within projects (Schütz 1973), an imagined course of action that directs and informs their individual acts (Ryle 2000). The multiplicity of roles, projects and courses of action will make organizational spaces offer, provide and furnish a multiplicity of things.

Gibson supports the claim that things 'tell us what to do with them' (Koffka, quoted in Gibson 1986, p. 138). This 'demand character' of things is true as it reads but possibly false as it is taken. 'The postbox "invites" the mailing of a letter', says Gibson (p. 138), but only when the mailing of a letter is the project of the actor (Schütz 1973). To youngsters, especially around New Year, the same postbox invites the 'mailing' of firecrackers. Such vandalism makes the authorities seal off mailboxes at certain periods of the time, turning mailboxes into something other than a mailbox – perhaps a piece of art. By implication, occasionally mailboxes tell lies about themselves and what they afford: 'A thing may not look like what it is' (Gibson 1986, p. 143).

Affordance, in my view, is a concept that tries to specify why and how organizational spaces matter. It combines a perspective on what space might *potentially* afford with a notion of how it is actually engaged and used: 'The observer may or may not perceive or attend to the affordance, according to his needs, but the affordance, being invariant, is always there to be perceived' (Gibson 1986, p. 138).

Thus, it leaves room for the continuous exploration of new ways of making space matter to organizations. New ways of pursuing 'projects' in particular settings, and new 'projects' to be pursued, are consistent within a given set of physical layouts of an organization. The affordance of organizational spaces both enables and inspires action:

> 'Affordance', at once permission and promise: thanks to the hammer, I become literally another man, a man who has become 'other', since from that point in time I pass through alterity, the alteration of that folding. ... Far from primarily fulfilling a purpose, they [affordances] start by exploring heterogeneous universes that nothing, up to that point, could have foreseen and behind which trail new functions. (Latour 2002, p. 250)

In other words, affordance as a concept does not restrict the ways in which environment and actor can act complementarily. Affordances exist independently of the actor, but they are only significant as they are being perceived and engaged in action. In this sense, affordances 'are neither physical nor phenomenal' (Gibson 1986, p. 143).

As a tentative conclusion to this section, let me list the ways in which the concept of affordance may portray the relationship between the actor and the environment, including its spatial elements:

- The environment may be a resource, in the sense of providing or furnishing certain actions.
- The environment may be a motivational and cultural factor, stemming from an associational reading of the environment (Rapoport 1982).
- The environment may be an inspiration. The spatial context may inspire actors to explore new 'projects'.

Organizational spaces are similar to the environments discussed by Gibson. But they are also different in the sense that they often will have multiple actors interacting and potentially interfering with each other. There is no reason that the corridor bulge should not continue to inspire actors to explore new projects (Chapter 3). However, what this liminal space will afford in terms of possible projects will be relative not only to the individual project but also to all other concurrent and concomitant projects of the clinic. Even the corridor bulge itself may inspire, but not afford 'projects' because of interactional complexity in relation to other things going on elsewhere and at other times. What emerges as a sustainable practice of non-hierarchical interactions in the corridor bulge will have not to undermine the hierarchical interactions in other parts of the clinic if such interactions are also important. The backstage/

frontstage dichotomy reminds us that incompatible forms of practice are often physically separated in order for both to be sustainable. Iedema et al. demonstrate that such separation can be modified. Exactly how little separation is needed before the clinic falls apart as an organized whole can only be determined by exploration and experimentation. There is probably a limit to the affordance of organizational space, first to be found and then to be observed in ordinary practice. In the long run, the actual use of organizational space will therefore also reflect the balance between the exploitation of already known affordances of space and the exploration of new affordances (March 1999).

LINKING SPACE TO WORK: CAUSALITY AND PREDICTABILITY

Organizational researchers are not alone in making organizational space a matter of concern. For example, for an architect designing an office headquarters for an organization, the future workspace of the organization is in focal awareness. Of course, such design matters to architects as a source of work, but it matters also in a more abstract manner. Their task is, so to speak, to make space matter to the client (or the future users). Architects work with words and drawings to communicate a future physical space and the ways in which it matters to whatever concerns the client may have. From the outset, it is not certain that space matters to the client, or in which way it matters if it does. It is part and parcel of architectural work to specify the ways that would enable the suggested organizational space to make a difference in the eyes of the client and the users.

The hardships inherent in architectural design processes are ideal points of observation for understanding the multiple concerns that are folded into a final workspace design. These hardships are taken care of by being verbalized and drawn. But since there are so many different and conflicting concerns, to arrive at a final design that does the job of integrating such diversity is no simple achievement. The integration is done via communication, not through practice – and through simplification, not compromise. For instance, a parliament building designed these days is called upon both to express the transparency of democracy and to protect against terrorism (Markus and Cameron 2002). The dilemma is real, and it is considerably aggravated by the fact that the technology of managing meaning and regulating affordances is a highly uncertain one. The causal links have to be established in communication and require many words. The many words illuminate, but they also gloss over the multiplicity of affordances and the interactional complexities between space and a host of other factors. It should be clear by now that building trust in simple notions of symbolic and functional affordance will require considerable effort to silence divergent voices and viewpoints. However, it is also clear that both designers and decision-makers need legitimate premises for their choices.

Organizational Spaces provides many illustrations of how people improvise and change organizational practices in non-designed and non-intended ways. This should caution us against taking any set of design premises literally. All office or building designs will combine with emergent practices to produce effects, often quite paradoxical effects! For example, the design premises behind the introduction of open-space office layouts highlight knowledge sharing as a desired and intended effect. Knowledge sharing is no doubt important for organizational performance, but it is an effect of many more things than just the office layout. Effects always are, says Ryle (1949 [2000]). It is not difficult to specify a practice that would reduce knowledge sharing in an open-space office. Information that you would want people to share often proves very sticky, while information that you would want people to keep to themselves often proves to be leaky (Brown and Duguid 2001). Encouraging a freer flow of information may increase the level of noise, without necessarily increasing the level of knowledge sharing. However, that noise, rather than the information sharing, may have desirable functional effects, for example, by keeping people awake and mindful of their tasks (Kreiner 2009).

The point is that all types of effects may be imagined to flow from any designed space. The ascription of specific effects is necessary for clients to make design decisions. The notion of a generative building (Hillier, cited in Kornberger and Clegg 2004) is an example of such ascriptions of specific effects. If the design eventually 'combines order and chaos' (Kornberger and Clegg 2004, p. 1105), this will be due at least as much to the practices that people develop once they occupy the space as it is to the spatial design itself. The generative quality is not a quality of the building or its materials, but of the situation that prevails when the building has been integrated into organizational practices.

Even if we strongly believe that designs and effects are not causally connected, they necessarily become related in design narratives about organizational spaces. Thus, designs are presented and justified with postulated practices that would make desired outcomes thinkable, perhaps even likely. Such narratives need not be true or even nuanced in order to be believed. The cynical explanation for such ready belief is that clients act on naïve conceptions of organizational realities, or on what they want to believe about the future. A more pragmatic explanation would be that in buying into the design premises for organizational spaces, organizational decision-makers commit to a managerial task to be accomplished later in order to realize the intended effects of the spatial design. If open-space offices can result in both more and less knowledge sharing, it might become a managerial task to find ways of ensuring that the eventual practices in those offices will increase, not decrease, knowledge sharing. Probably, such commitments are often made and soon forgotten. But implicitly, by narrating a causal relationship between organizational spaces and desired effects, in terms of community, competitiveness or whatever effects are in focus, designers, but also those of us studying organizational spaces, hide the complicated set of actual organizational practices that need to be in place before we could proclaim the ascribed causality real! The complexities of linking practices to organizational spatial design were discussed above.

How architects and organizations get away with narrating a highly simplistic relationship between organizational space and desirable effects is a completely different issue. Why would organizations expect to address such concerns as knowledge sharing, security, branding, etc. through the design of organizational spaces? I suppose that an explanation might be found in prevailing, institutionalized myths about organizations (Meyer and Rowan 1977). Våland (2010) suggests that organizational design and architectural design have become intertwined. Demanding, and having, open-space offices has become a signal of modern management. We know, of course, that the same design can be part of any number of projects (Ryle 2000). The intention, for instance, might equally as well be cost savings (Chapter 2). Whatever the intentions, the link between design premise and eventual effect is very loose outside the narratives of architects and their clients.

CONCLUSIONS

Does organizational space matter? The answer is yes! Physical spaces are real, even if they are real relative to the individual actor or to specific circumstances. Organizations are real to the extent that we can recognize them as integrated and dependable collectives of actors. Space is woven into the very fabric of organizational life. The challenge is to see and understand how it becomes an integral part of organizations. This is a challenge because, like all other things, space also tends to disappear from view by being taken for granted (Latour 1996). When problems arise and things begin to fall apart in the organization, space reappears as a matter of concern in practice. For organization theory, we need not await the empirical reappearance of space. We may analytically separate space, not to establish it as an isolated causal factor, but in order to study and theorize the ways it becomes woven into the organizational fabric.

The concept of organizational space may make us look for an intersection between organization and space. Such an intersection is often found in design processes, as when new building design becomes a part of an organizational development effort, and vice versa. But such designed effects do not translate into practice. There is no reason to assume that practice is consistent and linear. Space plays a role in organization studies, not because it plays *a* role, but because it plays multiple, dissimilar roles at the same time and across time. Its meaning and significance may be a matter of achievement under particular circumstances, but its affordance will exist across circumstances and actors. As we work to integrate studies of spaces with studies of organizations, let us not forget to include the actors and the actions – the practices – along with the 'things' that we study.

REFERENCES

Brown, John Seely and Paul Duguid (2001), 'Knowledge and organization: a social-practice perspective', *Organization Science*, **12** (2), 198–213.

Christensen, Lars Rune (2009), 'The coordination of the building process: Articulation work and practices of stigmergy', unpublished dissertation, Design of Organizational IT Faculty Group, University of Copenhagen.

Dale, Karen and Gibson Burrell (2008), *The Spaces of Organisation and the Organisation of Space: Power, Identity and Materiality at Work*, Basingtoke, Palgrave Macmillan.

Gaver, William W. (1996), 'Affordances for interaction: the social is material for design', *Ecological Psychology*, **8** (2), 111–29.

Gibson, James J. (1986), *The Ecological Approach to Visual Perception*, Hillsdale, NJ: Lawrence Erlbaum Associates.

Goffman, Erving (1959), *The Presentation of Self in Everyday Life*, New York: Doubleday.

Goffman, Erving (1974), *Frame Analysis: An Essay on the Organization of Experience*, New York: Harper Colophon.

Hernes, Tor (2004), *The Spatial Construction of Organization*, Amsterdam: John Benjamins.

Hutchby, Ian (2001), 'Technologies, texts and affordances', *Sociology*, **35** (2), 441–56.

Kornberger, Martin and Stewart R. Clegg (2004), 'Bringing space back in: organizing the generative building', *Organization Studies*, **25** (7), 1095–1114.

Kreiner, Kristian (2009), 'Disruption furthers productivity!' in Mikala Holme Samsøe and Cathrine Schmidt (eds), *Campus and Study Environment: Physical Framework for Universities of the Future*, Copenhagen: Danish University and Property Agency, pp. 148–52.

Latour, Bruno (1996), *Aramis or the Love of Technology*, Cambridge, MA: Harvard University Press.

Latour, Bruno (2002), 'Morality and technology: the end of the means', *Theory, Culture & Society*, **19** (5/6), 247–60.

Latour, Bruno (2004), 'Why has critique run out of steam? From matters of fact to matters of concern', *Critical Inquiry*, **30** (2), 225–49.

Lave, Jean and Etienne Wenger (1991), *Situated Learning: Legitimate Peripheral Participation*, Cambridge: Cambridge University Press.

March, James G. (1999), 'Exploration and exploitation in organizational learning', in *The Pursuit of Organizational Intelligence*, Oxford: Blackwell, pp. 100–13.

Markus, Thomas A. and Deborah Cameron (2002), *The Words Between the Spaces: Buildings and Language*, London, Routledge.

Meyer, John W. and Brian Rowan (1977), 'Institutionalized organizations: formal structure as myth and ceremony', *American Journal of Sociology*, **83** (2), 340–63.

Polanyi, Michael and Harry Prosch (1975), *Meaning*, Chicago, IL: University of Chicago Press.

Rapoport, Amos (1982), *The Meaning of the Built Environment: A Nonverbal Communication Approach,* Beverly Hills, CA: Sage.

Ripley, Colin, Geoffrey Thün and Kathy Velikov (2009), 'Matters of concern', *Journal of Architectural Education*, **62** (4), 6–14.

Ryle, Gilbert (1949/2000), *The Concept of Mind*, London: Penguin Books.

Ryle, Gilbert (2000), 'Courses of action or the uncatchableness of mental acts', *Philosophy*, **75**, 331–44.

Schütz, Alfred (1973), *Collected Papers I: The Problem of Social Reality*, The Hague: Martinus Nijhoff.

Taylor, Scott and André Spicer (2007), 'Time for space: a narrative review of research on organizational spaces', *International Journal of Management Reviews*, **9** (4), 325–46.

Våland, Marianne Stang (2010), 'What we talk about when we talk about space: End user participation between processes of organizational and architectural design', unpublished PhD dissertation, Department of Organization: Copenhagen Business School.

Index